Marcel Proust

A Study in the Quality of Awareness

Marcel Proust

A Study in the Quality of Awareness

EDWARD J. HUGHES

Cambridge University Press

Cambridge

London   New York   New Rochelle

Melbourne   Sydney

Published by the Press Syndicate of the University of Cambridge
The Pitt Building, Trumpington Street, Cambridge CB2 1RP
32 East 57th Street, New York, NY 10022, USA
296 Beaconsfield Parade, Middle Park, Melbourne 3206, Australia

First published 1983

Printed in Great Britain at the
University Press, Cambridge

Library of Congress catalogue card number: 82-9718

British Library cataloguing in publication data
Hughes, Edward J.
Marcel Proust: a study in the quality of awareness.
1. Proust, Marcel – Criticism and interpretation
I. Title
843'.912   PQ2631.R63Z/
ISBN 0 521 24768 3

CE

To my mother and father

Contents

Contents

Acknowledgements

This book is a modified version of a thesis presented for the degree of Ph.D. at Queen's University, Belfast. In preparing it, I have received help from many people. My first and greatest thanks go to my supervisor, Dr Richard Bales, whose guidance and support have been invaluable. I am also greatly indebted to Professor Henri Godin, whose advice was so generous and wise; to Dr Jo Yoshida and M. Maurice Paz for their help with Proust's manuscripts; to Dr Alison Finch for her many excellent suggestions; and to Mrs Josephine Teeuwen for her great help in preparing the typescript. In addition, I should like to thank Editions Gallimard for their kind permission to quote from Proust's manuscripts and published texts. Finally, it is pleasant to acknowledge a special gratitude to my wife Kathleen.

Birkbeck College
London   November 1981

Abbreviations

I, II and III: Marcel Proust, *A la recherche du temps perdu*, ed. P. Clarac and A. Ferré (3 vols., Paris: NRF (Pléïade), 1954).

BSAMP: *Bulletin de la Société des amis de Marcel Proust et des amis de Combray*.

Cahier [followed by a number]: Bibliothèque Nationale, fonds Proust. Sixty-two manuscript notebooks containing mainly preparatory sketches for *A la recherche*.

Corr.: Marcel Proust, *Correspondance*, ed. P. Kolb (7 vols. to date, Paris: Plon, 1970–81).

CSB: Marcel Proust, *Contre Sainte-Beuve, précédé de Pastiches et mélanges, et suivi de Essais et articles*, ed. P. Clarac and Y. Sandre (Paris: NRF (Pléïade), 1971).

CSB/NM: Marcel Proust, *Contre Sainte-Beuve, suivi de Nouveaux Mélanges*, ed. B. de Fallois (Paris: Gallimard, 1954).

JS: Marcel Proust, *Jean Santeuil, précédé de Les Plaisirs et les jours*, ed. P. Clarac and Y. Sandre (Paris: NRF (Pléïade), 1971).

n.a.fr. 16708:5 [e.g.]: Bibliothèque Nationale, fonds Proust, nouvelles acquisitions françaises: page 5 of volume currently catalogued as 16708.

n.a.fr. 16763:39iii [e.g.]: Bibliothèque Nationale, fonds Proust, nouvelles acquisitions françaises: third page of galley-sheet 39 (8 pages to a galley-sheet) of volume currently catalogued as 16763.

NRF: *Nouvelle Revue Française*.

PMLA: *Publications of the Modern Language Association*.

RHLF: *Revue d'histoire littéraire de la France*.

RLC: *Revue de littérature comparée*.

Winton: Alison Winton, *Proust's Additions* (2 vols., Cambridge University Press, 1977).

Preliminary Notes

Idiosyncracies of spelling and punctuation have been respected in all quotations, especially in the case of Proust's manuscripts. In an effort to avoid manuscript fetishism, however, I do not record all Proust's own deletions and have tried, where possible, to iron out obvious confusions. Throughout this study, the term Narrator is used with a capital *N* when it refers to the central figure of *A la recherche* and by extension to the first-person voice of the sixty-two *Cahiers* and other manuscripts relevant to the main novel. For that reason, I also speak of the Narrator of the *Contre Sainte-Beuve*, as edited by B. de Fallois, since that work is based on the first seven of the sixty-two *Cahiers*. In all other cases, the term is not capitalised.

Introduction

A cursory glance at lists of critical works on Proust shows a considerable number of titles culled in part from the author's work itself. Perhaps the most obvious of these is André Maurois' *A la recherche de Marcel Proust* (Paris: Hachette, 1949). Robert Soupault calls his work *Marcel Proust du côté de la médecine* (Paris: Plon, 1967), while Georges Cattaui adds to his *Proust perdu et retrouvé* (Paris: Plon, 1963) with an article entitled 'Du côté de chez Bloch'.[1] But as well as this perhaps slightly 'gimmicky' borrowing, there are other critics who are indebted to Proust in a much more substantial way. Often in order to support their ideas on Proust, they draw on his own activity as a literary critic. What is to be made of the criteria applied by Proust himself when working in such a capacity? We might begin by examining some of his critical observations, since this will help clarify some of the aims of this book.

Quite early in his career, he speaks reverentially of the role of the novelist:

Nous sommes tous devant le romancier comme les esclaves devant l'empereur: d'un mot, il peut nous affranchir. Par lui, nous perdons notre ancienne condition pour connaître celle du général, du tisseur, de la chanteuse, du gentilhomme campagnard, la vie des champs, le jeu, la chasse, la haine, l'amour, la vie des camps. (*CSB*, pp. 413–14.)[2]

There seems no limit to the variety of roles and situations envisaged by Proust. But perhaps more significant than any of the individual character-types mentioned is the multiplicity of possibilities generally. The writer's strength would seem to lie in his ability to extend our imaginative horizons. Proust sees this as having a liberating effect on the reader. Moreover, the slave analogy gives one a clear impression of just how eagerly desired this new freedom for the mind is. Proust reinforces this idea when, in a rough sketch for the *Recherche*, he comments on how reading helps to 'nous ouvrir de nouvelles perspectives d'existence' (*Cahier 25*, fo 22v).[3]

It is immediately clear that Proust sees any new slant or focus on experience as an exciting prospect. But his enthusiasm for this broadening of consciousness is not just a feature of his literary criticism. When one looks at his main work, one finds him speaking of different experiential possibilities. It is to this question that much of the present study will be devoted.

Looking further into his criticism, one gets a more precise indication of what Proust had in mind. In particular, there is one recurring motif – that of the simplicity of existence – which he singles out for attention in certain authors. Just what I mean by this can be seen in some comments that he makes on George Eliot's *Adam Bede*. What impresses him about this work is the

peinture attentive, minutieuse, respectueuse, poétique et sympathique de la vie la plus laborieuse et la plus humble. Tenir sa cuisine bien propre est un devoir essentiel, presque un devoir religieux et un devoir plein de charme. (*CSB*, p. 656.)

The monotony of domesticity is not something that disconcerts Proust. Indeed he finds this concern with circumstantial pre-occupations reassuring and satisfying. Thus he is singling out in the English novelist what the critic Walter Strauss calls 'the Chardin aspect that Proust liked above all to find in his favourite authors'.[4] It is, then, that atmosphere of humility, of order, of balance in all things that is attractive to Proust. Furthermore, he commends George Eliot for being able to penetrate the mind of a carpenter or a weaver (*CSB*, p. 657). Here too, it is a case of the novelist exploring new temperaments and minds. Unfortunately, Proust does not explain any more fully the merit of her insights. Yet even in this briefest of references, one sees him casting his critical eye in a significant direction.

The same is largely true of some of Proust's notes on Flaubert. In the first of his four *Carnets*,[5] he refers to Flaubert's letters to his niece Caroline. In spite of the great volume of that correspondence, Proust's notes on it are few.[6] But what he does select for mention is significant: 'Je cause avec domestiques [que] je ne trouve pas plus bêtes que des gens bien [...]. Retour à la simplicité après travail comme sueur' (*Le Carnet de 1908*, pp. 75–6). Professor Kolb explains that Proust's notation consists of brief, telling quotes gleaned from Flaubert's text. And even if the cryptic style of the *Carnet* sometimes confuses the reader, Proust's eclectic annotation is again note-worthy. For, as with George Eliot, he chooses to speak of an artist who is involved with intellectually uncomplicated people.

When one reads the correspondence with Caroline, one becomes quickly aware of how serious the task of novel-writing was for

Flaubert. Nevertheless, he finds soothing distraction and consolation in the presence of servants: 'Je répète mon mot: "Oh! je les aurai connues, les affres de la littérature!" Clémence déploie une grande activité et ma petite cuisinière est douce comme un mouton' (*Correspondance*, vol. 5, p. 450). The opposition between Flaubert's complex and anxious reflection and the simple-mindedness of others is characteristic of this correspondence generally. I would suggest that this goes a long way to explaining Proust's inquisitiveness. In this way, he is immediately sensitive to Flaubert's idea that a change of awareness separates himself from others.

In other critical jottings, Proust is less explicit in his reference to these differences in consciousness, and in particular to the question of an uncomplicated being. With Senancour, for example, he makes a few random observations on the simplicity of Nature as seen in the *Rêveries sur la nature primitive de l'homme*. Proust's notes begin with the rather tongue-in-cheek: 'Senancour, c'est moi.'[7] For Senancour, Nature's achievement is something that man should seek to emulate: 'Tout semble commander à l'homme de [...] limiter son être pour le posséder tout entier. Telle était l'indication de la nature.'[8] Moreover, he gives a practical illustration of this, singing the praises of Alpine herdsmen whom he sets up as exemplars of a primordial simplicity. His description is an enthusiastic one: 'C'est à vous que je voudrais être entendu; de vous à qui la félicité naturelle est encore accessible' (Senancour, *Rêveries*, vol. 1, p. 237). Given Proust's well-documented references to Senancour (*CSB*, pp. 567–9), he must surely have been familiar with this particular aspect of the *Rêveries*.

If one combines this with the nature of his interest in George Eliot and Flaubert, the result is an intriguing one. For in his remarks on all three writers, Proust's critical attention comes to focus on the portrayal of an idyllic monotony of existence. This in many ways ties in with his own conception of novel-reading: that it should spur us on to enjoy new perspectives of existence, even if such perspectives are on occasions paradoxically confining in their scope (*Cahier* 25, fo 22*v*). So much for this orientation in Proust's literary criticism. What is equally striking is that in *Jean Santeuil* and *A la recherche*, similar leanings are discernible. In both works, Proust presents and explores widely ranging modes of existence and consciousness. One has the varying but in themselves constant life-styles of different characters such as Françoise or the 'jeunes filles'. As well as these 'existence-types', so to speak, there are the immensely entangled personalities of Jean Santeuil or the Narrator of the *Recherche*. They are so prominent and so complex that one is able to see in them a wide range of emotional and intellectual responses. In the case of these characters, then, we find important shifts in consciousness. This inner movement is complemented by the more obvious outer contrasts that separate them from others.

But whether the contrasts rest within the individual or are interpersonal, the over-riding principle in this work is to delve into the nature of perception and feeling. This is because Proust himself throws the net as wide as possible, to take in not only the extreme self-awareness of the Narrator but also the faint glimpses of consciousness, as is the case with Françoise.

Irrelevant though it may at first seem, there is an essay on pornography by an American critic that has a bearing on this work. In it, Susan Sontag is trying to dispel much of the taboo surrounding her subject and she makes an interesting general observation: 'The question is not *whether* consciousness or *whether* knowledge, but the quality of the consciousness and of the knowledge. And that invites consideration of the quality or fineness of the human subject – the most problematic standard of all.'[9] Proust himself has very developed ideas on this same question, and a large part of the present study pays especial attention to this notion of quality.

In keeping with what Miss Sontag advocates, one would do well to take as open a view as possible of consciousness. Proust speaks over and over again about the limitless variety of situations in which the human psyche finds itself. This can range from a hyperawareness of being and feeling to a sense of almost inanimate existence. A case of the latter would be the Narrator's sensation that he is no more conscious than the objects in his room. His sleep is occasionally broken by brief moments of a vague awareness that is enough for him to 'goûter grâce à une lueur momentanée de conscience le sommeil où étaient plongés les meubles, la chambre, le tout dont je n'étais qu'une petite partie' (I, 4).[10] The effect of such experience is to make human consciousness almost infinitely elastic. It is this same much wider interpretation of feeling that one finds in the *Carnet de 1908*:

Ainsi ne pouvons-nous pas nous intéresser quand on nous parle d'un art plus humain, moins humain. Cela n'a pas de sens pour nous. Les boutons dans une chaise de cuir, un point dans une étoffe [...] valent autant qu'un art humain. (pp. 102–3.)

It is not hard to appreciate how, in defining what is human, Proust is anxious to sweep away oversimplification and excessive demarcation. The range of experience becomes almost limitless as a result. Again, Susan Sontag's comments are germane to Proust's own thinking on the question:

It is facile, virtually meaningless, to demand that literature stick with the 'human'. For the matter at stake is not 'human' versus 'inhuman' (in which choosing the 'human' guarantees instant moral self-congratulation for both author and reader) but an infinitely varied register of forms and tonalities for transposing *the human voice* into prose narrative. (*Styles of Radical Will*, p. 41; author's italics.)

These introductory remarks will be developed in Chapter 2, where the concept of dehumanisation is to be dealt with. The term is used in such a way as to have none of the crisis overtones attributed to it by those thinkers who argue that the material world is now cold, overpowering and menacingly outside man's control. Writing in 1925, Ortega y Gasset speaks of the modern artist as 'brazenly set on deforming reality [...]. He leaves us locked up in an abstruse universe, surrounded by objects with which human dealings are inconceivable.'[11] Not so with Proust. Indeed there can be no mistaking the reassurance that the Narrator of the *Recherche* experiences in the very 'thingness' of objects. Perhaps the point Proust is trying to make, when he ridicules the idea of 'un art plus humain, moins humain', is that the sheer breadth of experience outstrips language itself. In this way we may have the verbal paradox of *humans* being able to know a *dehumanised* feel of the world.

This book, then, takes as its mandate Proust's own view that multiple ways of feeling and reflection form a source of artistic potential. Structurally, it tries to follow the stages in Proust's writing. So Chapter 1 is mainly devoted to *Les Plaisirs et les jours* and *Jean Santeuil*, Chapter 2 to the period between *Jean Santeuil* and the earliest drafts for the *Recherche*, and so on. With the *Recherche*, however, the ordering of later chapters is less straightforward. For there is on the one hand the chronology of the story, and on the other the chronology of Proust's composition. Still, my sections follow the course of the Narrator's development. In that sense, their order is self-imposed, beginning with his childhood and moving on from there into his adolescent relationship with the 'jeunes filles', the protracted affair with Albertine, and finally the denouement of *Le Temps retrouvé*.

On a thematic level, I shall begin by trying to show how Proust's thinking on the notion of human awareness is generally taking shape in *Jean Santeuil*. Chapter 1 is more extensive than intensive in approach, and aims at highlighting many of the issues that are to gain prominence in the later *Recherche*. One finds, for example, enthusiastic evocations of a peasant existence, life in the animal world or a simple communion with Nature. Their importance is that they seem measured to contrast with much of Jean's more troubled reflection.

The problems of artistic self-expression, for example, or a difficult love relationship may leave the hero quite scarred. It is soon clear that there is an organic link between these pleasurable and problematical areas of experience. Proust touches on this when he suggests that 'la pensée et la vie nous sont comme administrées par Dieu comme antidotes l'une de l'autre'.[12] It will be interesting to see if this counterbalancing movement is as readily discernible in Proust's novel. In his work immediately prior to the *Recherche*, one sees how the notion of multiple forms of consciousness develops in this important gestation period, a period that shows intriguing experimentation with possible moods and feeling, and most notably speculation about the world of things inanimate. With the mature novel itself, it is clear that much of Proust's theorising on the quality of human awareness is being channelled into the mind of the Narrator. The latter examines the distance separating him from many of those who people his childhood and adolescent worlds. Among them are Françoise and the Narrator's grandmother, who throw into relief the Narrator's character, and in particular his intellectual and emotional agitation. Even more startling is the contrast that he sees between himself and the band of girls in Balbec. Here, it would seem that Proust is very consciously engineering a clash of temperaments.

Indeed at times, his characterisation may take on an almost dialectic quality. On one occasion, for example, referring to his meeting with the Balbec girls, he detects

l'éternel malentendu d'un 'intellectuel' (représenté en l'espèce par moi) et des gens du monde (représentés par la petite bande) au sujet d'une personne mondaine (le jeune joueur de golf). (III, 607.)

Proust is obviously satirising the Narrator's confident assertion of his own position and quality as an 'intellectuel', to say nothing of the ridiculously rigid caste system into which different individuals are thrown! The same tendency to schematise can, however, have an important and serious bearing on the inner workings of character portrayal, and I shall be looking at this in Chapters 3 and 4.

In the first-person narrative of the *Recherche*, it is not surprising that many of the character contrasts revolve around the Narrator. *Pari passu* with this, the Narrator's own inner conflict unfolds. This involves his experience of mental crisis, which is occasionally interrupted by a sense of liberation from intellectual doubt. In many ways, the range of feeling that he finds within himself can be as great as that which sets him apart from others.

The social and personal worlds come together, for him, in his relationship with Albertine. Chapter 5 deals with this. Quite clearly, the troubled consciousness of his adolescence is not to be sedated in that perplexing love match. This explains the note of caution that he utters after Albertine has fled: 'Laissons les jolies femmes aux hommes sans imagination' (III, 440). Once more, the Narrator is exploiting the notion of differing human perceptions; the more conscious one is, the more susceptible one becomes to an anguished experience of love. And for the Narrator, there is always someone less imaginative, less sensitive, in short less troubled than himself. Yet even faced with love's precariousness, he struggles to restrict the girl's perceptions. To him, consciousness for Albertine is synonymous with her individuality and represents a will contrary to his own. For a period, it is as if the Narrator can transfer the inanimacy of the material world onto Albertine.

The final chapter looks at the denouement of *Le Temps retrouvé* in the light of the whole question of awareness and its shifting quality. This involves assessing the Narrator's self-realisation as an artist, to see how it is related to the registers of feeling that are present in Proust's work.

In all this, it should be said that many of the individual areas of study that I have mentioned have been at least partially covered by others. Much has been written, for example, on the Narrator's love for Albertine. A particularly valuable contribution is that of Claudine Quémar, and some of the detail of her own article reappears in Chapter 5.[13] Or again, there is the critical work sparked off by Proust's own pronouncements on the respective merits of human instinct and intelligence. Commentators, however, have often gone only as far as Proust's own theorising will take them.[14] They tend to stop at such oracular statements as 'Chaque jour j'attache moins de prix à l'intelligence.'[15] Yet if one pushes beyond this and looks beneath the surface of his work, one finds the same issues being turned over, but this time in much richer contrasts of character, of place and of mood.

To that extent, there does seem to be room for a study attempting a more general synthesis of Proust's thinking on the quality of individual consciousness. His enthusiasm for George Eliot and Flaubert can be correlated with the Narrator's predilections in the *Recherche* – his fascination with the primitive Françoise, the obsession with the 'jeunes filles' or his enjoyment of Albertine in his home. The common denominator linking all these experiences would appear to be a simplicity of life-style, a positive monotony of feeling and outlook. In addition, the Balbec girls are outrageous in a way that is keenly appreciated by the Narrator. All this speaks volumes for his hyperconsciousness, with which it contrasts markedly.

Before I end this introduction, some brief comments are required on methodology. Undoubtedly one of the most tantalising aspects of Proust's work is the great volume of unpublished manuscripts, and any publication that draws from the corpus of these writings awakens great critical interest. The appearance of *Le Carnet de 1908* (1976) is an obvious example of this. The work in question has made a significant impact, confirming many accepted opinions on Proust's work as well as showing the inaccuracy of others.

While most of the other manuscripts remain unpublished, they do nevertheless contain references as enlightening as those of the *Carnet*. This is especially true of the sixty-two *Cahiers*, which contain valuable preparatory sketches for the *Recherche*. Bearing in mind that half of the novel was published posthumously, without the author's customary reworking, the emphases and directives in the *Cahiers* acquire fresh rellevance. Henri Bonnet offers a balanced view of the merit of these insights when he remarks: 'On peut donc dire que grâce aux Cahiers l'oeuvre de Proust s'enrichit de versions, frustes sans doute, mais précieuses pour celui qui s'intéresse au processus de la création.'[16] Certainly, references to the manuscripts in this study are made not in any spirit of unhealthy idolatry. Proust's published work is what is most important, his imprimatur being in itself, one might say, a guarantee of meticulous preparation and selection. But in considering such selection, it is obviously helpful to make reference to the general body of manuscript material from which Proust is working. Just why certain passages 'survive' and others get no further than the *brouillon* stage is often an interesting question. The bald manuscript development may present feelings and ideas in a primitive or crude manner; or again it may distort them. In the course of reflecting on Albertine, the Narrator comments in an original base text:

On aime une femme comme on aime le poulet à qui on est heureux de tordre le cou pour en manger à dîner, seulement pour les femmes on veut les tuer non pour en avoir du plaisir, mais pour qu'elles n'en prennent pas avec d'autres. (n.a.fr.16712:1.)

The violence of the language is as arresting as that of the sentiments expressed. But the aphorism does not appear in the *Recherche* itself, where the inescapable complexity of the hero's relationship with Albertine excludes such an inflexible reaction. More generally, what is clear-cut and controllable in the sketches may become something much more diffuse and many-sided. That process of 'densification' characterises much of the creative process in *A la recherche*, and has an obvious bearing on the quality of individual awareness in the novel.

Maurice Bardèche reminds us of Proust's fear that his manuscripts might be ruthlessly dissected by critics. But this, Bardèche argues, should not obscure the positive value of manuscript study: 'Une bonne "lecture" d'un écrivain est une meilleure présentation de son oeuvre qu'un dossier de fiches et de variantes. Malheureusement, l'oeil du critique n'est pas toujours assez pénétrant pour se passer des repères que les manuscrits lui offrent.'[17] In view of this interest in the manuscripts, it has been necessary to quote frequently and sometimes extensively from what are largely unpublished documents.

A final general observation might be made concerning both the manuscript and printed texts. I have attempted to respect the separation of the Narrator's own fortunes from those of Proust. The author himself is conscious of such a distanciation and indeed is anxious to maintain it. Writing to Jacques Rivière in 1914, he impresses upon him that in the case of the first-person Narrator of the *Recherche*, 'cette évolution d'une pensée, je n'ai pas voulu l'analyser abstraitement mais la recréer, la faire vivre'.[18] The divorce could not be more clear; the Narrator is clearly allowed to develop and create himself. At the same time, nevertheless, it would be wrong to see Proust himself as stagnant, having reached some artistic terminus. Just as the hero of the *Recherche* will change, so Proust's own thinking will continue to develop in the years after 1914. While not confusing them, I shall be attempting to bring out the evolution of awareness in both.

1

Proust's Early Work

A l'âge que vous avez et dans un esprit comme le vôtre, il y a chaque jour du nouveau. Vous souvenez-vous de l'époque où vous mesuriez les feuilles naissantes et me disiez de combien de lignes elles avaient grandi sous l'action d'une nuit de rosée ou d'une journée de fort soleil? Il en est de même pour les instincts d'un garçon de votre âge. Ne vous étonnez pas de cet épanouissement rapide, qui, si je vous connais bien, doit vous surprendre et peut-être vous effrayer. Laissez agir des forces qui n'auront chez vous rien de dangereux: parlez-moi seulement pour que je vous connaisse [. . .]. Surtout soyez naïf dans vos sensations. Qu'avez-vous besoin de les étudier? N'est-ce point assez d'en être ému? La sensibilité est un don admirable; dans l'ordre des créations que vous devez produire, elle peut devenir une rare puissance, mais à une condition, c'est que vous ne la retournerez pas contre vous-même.

Eugène Fromentin, *Dominique* (Paris: Garnier-Flammarion, 1967), pp. 118–19.

(a) Simple-mindedness providing a backdrop to creative thought

The principal character in the preface to *Jean Santeuil* is the creative writer, denoted as B. or C.[1] This is hardly surprising when one considers how prominent the theme of artistic creativity is in Proust's work generally. Moreover, the reverential way in which the first-person narrator describes C.'s literary pursuits confirms the privileged position enjoyed by the artist in Proust. In moments of inspiration, C. can be seen making his way up to a physically elevated and secluded place, where he practises an almost sacred ritual:

Et là, dans ce lieu véritablement sublime il examinait le vol des oiseaux qui passaient sur la mer, écoutant le vent, regardant le ciel, à la façon des anciens augures. (*JS*, p. 186.)

Every movement of his body appears to reflect and to be in harmony with the inner spiritual exhilaration that he experiences. At the moment of supreme insight, he enters the lighthouse, a humble dwelling and yet now become a sanctuary for the inspired creative writer: 'Puis tout d'un coup il paraissait joyeux, prêt à écrire. Alors il entrait dans la petite maison du gardien du phare' (*ibid.*). And if the keeper and his wife clearly experience nothing of the artist's elation, C. still feels drawn to the calm that seems synonymous with their existence. This is evident from the idyllic description of their home:

La lumière du fourneau et d'une bougie n'éclairait pas toute la pièce, mais la clarté qu'elle y concentrait sur le mur était si paisible et si empreinte du calme de la vie dont elle éclairait chaque soir les scènes les plus tranquilles à l'heure où les travaux sont finis. (*JS*, p. 188.)

Blending in with this Millet-like impression of a day's tasks done are multiple images of a simplicity that so enchants the artist. While obviously content with his writing, he seems no less happy to savour something of the lighthouse keeper's joys. Accordingly, as he moves further away from their home, the now faint concentration of light is still visible as a reassuring symbol of 'le calme de ces occupations, la simplicité de ces coeurs, le confort de ce réduit, la douceur de cette vie' (*JS*, p. 189).

The even-paced ordinariness of that life-style contrasts with the impression one has of C.'s literary activity, his moments of inspiration involving great excitability and physical exhilaration (*JS*, p. 186). They also suggest an element of mental complexity: '[C.] semblait regarder quelque chose qu'il ne comprenait pas bien' (*ibid.*). Nevertheless, the 'simplicité de ces coeurs' (*JS*, p. 189) seems a not unimportant source of sustenance for the writer. But for the present, the exact nature of this sustenance remains elusive, the narrator committing himself no more than to speak in terms of the vague support that comes with this contact. As early as the preface of *Jean Santeuil*, then, one sees how two seemingly unconnected modes of existence – that of the creative artist and that of the uninvolved life of the peasant – reveal a measure of interaction, however ill-defined this may be.

A broadly similar process can be seen in that part of the preface where B. is the main protagonist. Here again, the writer's work necessitates solitude and uninterrupted silence. Still, his total inner absorption is occasionally replaced by a desire to communicate freely with those around him. Thus he enthusiastically questions the servant woman on the day-to-day activities of the local community,

demandant des nouvelles du procès du boulanger, de la santé de la vache, de la pêche de la veille, étendant avec plaisir sa vie de toutes ces vies placées à côté de la sienne. (*JS*, p. 192.)

It is interesting that B. does not dismiss these events as being banal and irrelevant, nor is there any suggestion of false glamorisation as he rejoices in his own existence being exposed to the very different quality of living exemplified by these humble folk. And to reinforce how desirable this opening out of the self is, the author uses an extended metaphor based on the morning sun's joyous communication with Nature. The sun radiates boundless light and affection,

appuy[ant] légèrement son regard sympathique sur le matelot parti dès l'aube sur sa barque jusqu'à l'enivrer de chaleur, de bien-être, de gaieté, jusqu'à lui tirer du front une goutte de sueur. (*JS*, p. 192.)

In painting a picture of well-being, Proust again uses the device of a neat cluster of images; the weight of the accumulation guarantees pleasurable emotion. Earlier, the concentration of 'calme', 'simplicité', 'confort' and 'douceur' (*JS*, p. 188) served a similar function.

B. also experiences a sense of happy inebriation in his dealings with those at the inn, for they provide the necessary 'écho à sa gaieté et un retour à sa sympathie' (*JS*, pp. 192–3). The reciprocal movement that this implies is significant; it enables one to see that what appeared in the first part of the preface as a vague sympathy between C. and the lighthouse inhabitants now assumes the character of an easily identifiable relationship. In this way, one can see a very real interchange between the artist figure and the simple-minded peasants. By providing this 'echo', they assist the artist in a positive way, albeit unknown to themselves.

One might add that the first-person narrator of the preface confesses to sharing a joy like B.'s when he sees a fisherman

dans la simplicité de son respect et la sûreté de son instinct [. . .] se retirer sur la pointe des pieds ou rester à causer avec B. quand il le fallait et aider ainsi inconsciemment à l'éclosion si délicate d'une oeuvre qu'il devait ignorer toujours. (*JS*, p. 193.)

The impression of solidity given in 'la sûreté de son instinct' complements the intangible, weightless qualities associated with artistic composition. What is happening essentially is that B. and the narrator concur in their enthusiasm for the limited mental horizons of the fisherman and the servant woman. Their predominantly instinctual being imparts a feeling of calm simplicity to the writer.

At this point in the manuscript of *Jean Santeuil*, there is a series of apparently unconnected references to animals etc. (*JS*, p. 988). These are jotted down in what seems a quite arbitrary fashion: 'Insectes – Mouvements de la femme qui accouche – le poumon, le coeur et la pensée – le requin et le pilote – un petit oiseau' (*JS*, p. 988). If one bears in mind what has been said about the simplicity of the peasants, it may be possible to read some pattern and significance into these notes. Clearly, any interpretation is, in the final analysis, conjectural, but the prominence of various animal forms of life is striking. Insects, birds and fish all display an instinctual response to living, so that some comparison may have been envisaged with the fisherman and the 'sûreté de son instinct'. Possibly Proust saw the pilot fish, renowned for its navigational skills, as proving a very apposite image for conveying this instinctualism. But I shall be considering how Proust sings the praises of animal existence later in the chapter. As for the allusion to woman in labour, he may have been interested in the instinctual act of childbirth as one excluding any cerebral considerations.

Such conjecture appears the more plausible when correlated with Proust's essay on Chardin and Rembrandt written round about the same period.[2] In it, he discusses the mysterious character of the artistic experience in terms that may help explain the bald reference to a woman giving birth:

Ainsi le gynécologiste pourrait étonner une femme qui vient d'accoucher en lui expliquant ce qui s'est passé dans son corps, en lui décrivant le processus physiologique de l'acte qu'elle a eu la force mystérieuse d'accomplir, mais dont elle ignore la nature; les actes créateurs procèdent en effet non de la connaissance de leurs lois, mais d'une puissance incompréhensible et obscure, et qu'on ne fortifie pas en l'éclairant. (*CSB*, p. 382.)

In the light of this, it is likely that Proust envisaged an analogy between the creation of art and that of a child when jotting down the telegram-like memo in the manuscript of *Jean Santeuil*.

With that in mind, one can return to the preface of the novel. B. is aware of the positive value deriving from the intuitive simplicity of those around him. The mysterious subterranean course of his inspiration appears, in a still vague sense, to be better captured in the atmosphere of the peasants' deep primitivism. One cannot go as far as to say that these forces are identical. But the 'puissance incompréhensible et obscure' that the young Proust attributes to the creative experience somehow harmonises with the felt level of awareness of the simple folk.

The preface assumes a mildly polemical character when B. rejects Balzac's view of life in the provinces leading to an impoverishment and stagnation of the intellect. B. is forthright and articulate as he attacks his predecessor's claim that accepted cultural activities and Parisian life enrich the mind, and he advocates in its place a life lived in close contact with the intimate self:

Je sais bien que [le théâtre, la société] me font du mal: je vois les choses moins à fond, cette manière superficielle qu'on a d'y sentir s'étend sur le reste de mon temps, avec une excitation stérile qui me gêne pour travailler. Non vraiment, je ne peux pas dire du mal de la vie que je mène ici. (*JS*, pp. 198–9.)

Balzac of course was not alone among nineteenth-century artists in decrying the drudgery of small-town life and in yearning for intellectual stimulation and sophistication. Significantly, Proust's response to provincial life is different. Indeed, with B.'s very positive assessment of the country, he goes some way to rescuing it from the opprobrium in which it had been held. It will be interesting, too, to see how in the *Recherche*, the Narrator enjoys the company of peasant people who are manifestly unintellectual. Returning to B., one cannot fail to notice the confidence with which he harmonises intellectual activity and light-hearted socialising:

J'aurais été, comme cela eût été très bien pour moi, professeur de philosophie dans une petite ville de province, que tous les soirs j'aurais été jouer aux cartes et boire des bocks au café. (*JS*, p. 198.)

But in spite of B.'s enthusiasm, one is again forced to say that the benefits deriving from this broadly based social contact are not specified here. Proust has yet to articulate the quality of the inter-relationship.

At another point in *Jean Santeuil*, one finds the same loose alliance with less complicated minds as that forged by B. in the preface.[3] At Beg-Meil, it is Jean himself who is helped in his creative task by an attentive shipmate remaining silent as Jean writes (*JS*, p. 383). So too, images of Nature's calm proliferate at this point in the narrative, helping to intensify Jean's state of exaltation and enchantment.

We might move on from this to noting how Jean responds to the 'Bonsoir, bonne pêche' addressed to him by a passing fisherman. His eager reception of these banal words can be explained by the fact that he is 'heureux d'avoir reçu comme un pêcheur ce bonsoir dit avec simplicité' (*JS*, p. 384). Not that Jean's own reaction is in any sense an uncomplicated one, for the stranger's greeting sparks off an intense emotional response within him. Yet he reflects with some joy on the contrasting nature of the feeling in himself and the fisherman.

[Jean] répondait 'Bonsoir, bonne pêche', en tâchant de mettre dans les mêmes mots le même accent, y cachant l'immense tendresse qu'avaient soulevée ces mots dans ces moments portés ainsi par le silence, où l'âme est si calme et si pleine que la moindre sensation inattendue suffit à y remuer [tant] de choses, mais malgré lui plus tendre qu'eux, moins simple aussi, et ayant dans son coeur un tiers qui l'écoutait leur dire bonsoir. (*JS*, p. 384.)

It is clear from the 'immense tendresse' that swells his inner being that Jean's consciousness of the experience is extended and far-seeing. But this does not diminish his sense of delectation in the pleasurable simplicity of the fisherman's words. His joy is that of hovering between two different levels of awareness – his own fuller awareness of language and the fisherman's unreflecting use of it. For a brief moment, he even succeeds in pulling on the latter's psychological mask with a mechanical, automatic use of language: 'Quelquefois Jean était devenu si vrai pêcheur qu'il répondait: "Bonsoir, bonne pêche", sans y penser, en regardant ses filets' (*JS*, p. 384). But of course the pleasure in the experience is all Jean's. The fisherman himself is not manifestly moved by the encounter; only in the eyes of Jean do his intellectual limitations assume a beauty. The conclusion to be drawn here is analogous to that relating to the writers in the preface to *Jean Santeuil*. Perhaps unusually, a creative mind detects some value in a well regulated and pleasantly mechanical existence. B. and C., and Jean himself all quickly see this. Their superiority over others lies in their very ability to recognise a quality of feeling that is different from their own. They are then simultaneously aware of their own situation and that of others.

(b) Characters as foils to Jean's own temperament

Up until now, I have been dealing largely with early references to artistic writing in *Jean Santeuil*, and the images of idyllic simplicity frequently invoked in the same context. Still, the full significance of this interconnection seems far from clear. We might extend our field of reference, therefore, by considering the general complexity of Jean's consciousness and how other characters appear in the light of this.

In the fisherman's greeting, one has an illustration of how everyday spoken language may exert a singular fascination on Jean. By the same token, what might otherwise be viewed as inconsequential comments on the state of the weather can excite great joy in him. A measure of this happiness is that it may equal the delights he finds in agreeable sense-impressions:

Ce n'était pas un moins vif plaisir pour Jean, sentant contre sa peau la double chaleur de son sang excité par une belle promenade et de son paletot doublé, de dire: 'Il ne fait pas chaud, madame, quel drôle de temps!' (*JS*, p. 302.)

Perhaps it is the limited unambiguous character of Jean's words that is appealing to him. Certainly this is the inference in other, comparable situations. Going to speak to the servant, on his return from the village of Réveillon, he delights in his uncomplicated words, 'heureux de dire ces choses si simples qu'il sentait pour les domestiques tout un événement, une surprise, une joie' (*JS*, p. 501). On another occasion, as he savours the 'camaraderie' so characteristic of the military life, his totally spontaneous use of the familiar 'mon vieux' reassures him, in that he now feels immersed in this untroubled atmosphere (*JS*, p. 569).

Looking more closely at the context of the words 'Il ne fait pas chaud, madame', one senses Proust's interest in the psychological significance of this light familiar chat. In requiring little mental effort, these words may become as automatic as the solidly physical sensations that abound in the same section, '[Journée froide de printemps]' (*JS*, pp. 302–4).[4] Certainly this is implied in the image of the man who is happy

après une laborieuse journée, de distraire son esprit sainement fatigué et de réveiller sa langue depuis longtemps immobile, en attendant qu'elle ne se délecte plus directement au contact d'un poulet verni de jus, [en disant]: 'Ça ne fait rien. Nous vivons sous un drôle de régime!' (*JS*, p. 302.)

Verbal expression may thus function largely independently of the intellect. What is more, in being likened to the gustatory pleasures enjoyed by the tongue, the words acquire something of the mindless, passive character of the latter sensation. Jean then expresses his satisfaction with this pre-intellectual zone of experience. For him, it is as though the speakers owe the happiness of their satisfaction to a freedom from unnecessary intellectualising and reflection.

Another experience producing an analogous effect relates to Jean's enjoyment of the domestic's company in his Éteuilles home. Significantly enough, it is when he has tired of the imaginative and intellectual work of reading that he comes to listen to the simple kitchen maid. Immediately, he describes the sweet calm of the setting, and enthuses about the joy that this arguably restricted existence can hold:

C'était un de ces moments paisibles où les choses sont comme environnées de la beauté qu'il y a à être, où le charme est dans l'ombre qui emplit le fond de cette pièce où est le lit des petits enfants, dans la douce lumière qui blanchit le pied du lit, dans le tic-tac de la pendule, dans la figure, bien éclairée par la lampe, de la cuisinière qui bavarde, dans le fond mystérieux de la cuisine éclairée des rouges reflets de l'invisible brasier où se consomment les opérations délicieuses. (*JS*, p. 320.)

Jean's happiness lies in his being sensitive to every play of light and colour and shadow. His perception of humble insignificant effects is sufficient for him. The mere fact of their existence assumes the proportions of 'la beauté qu'il y a à être'; this imparts to Jean a feeling of unchallengeable philosophical certainty. The maid herself plays an equally prominent part in this depiction of joyous being. Her vitality is endowed with the timeless, permanent qualities of elemental fire:

On a si peu à songer à ce qu'on dit à la cuisinière, et dans la gaieté de son regard brille quelque chose qui n'est pas moins vif et pas moins affectueux que la flamme du feu. (*JS*, p. 320.)

In this case too, verbal expression has become effortless, reinforcing the atmosphere of instinctual ease that pervades this tranquil kitchen scene.

The reader of Proust will be familiar with Jean's complexity of being and perhaps more so with the Narrator's hypersensitivity in the *Recherche*. In view of this leaning towards tortured self-analysis, the uncomplicated character that existence takes on in the kitchen scene can only come as a surprise. This is so, however oracular the conclusion to the passage might appear: 'Les choses sont si belles d'être ce qu'elles sont, et l'existence est une si calme beauté répandue autour d'elles!' (*ibid.*).

When one compares this unqualified assertion of life's felicity with Jean's greedy enjoyment of the warmth of his bed, one soon finds a note of equivocation in the latter. The faith in a pleasurable sensationalism is now undermined by what follows immediately afterwards. Jean speaks of our shielding ourselves from the elements,

nous pelotonnant, nous retournant, nous enfermant, nous disant: la vie est bonne, et [nous sommes] trop gais pour trouver même de la mélancolie dans la constatation du bonheur et de la médiocrité [dans] son essence. (*JS*, p. 519.)

So Proust introduces a tinge of ambiguity just sufficient to tarnish the categorical ring of 'La vie est bonne.' The happiness of existence then appears veneer-like in its fragility. But I shall be returning to the wider implications of this later.

In projecting himself imaginatively into the mind and situation of the maid or of the anonymous fisherman, Jean is betraying a more general propensity to explore ways of feeling that are not his own. This may imply mild dissatisfaction with one's own being and a resultant flirtation with other possible responses to living. More importantly, however, it may point to a more radical need to escape from one's own self. There is a faint suggestion of this in Jean's meeting with the shopowner in the village.

The happiness of the experience is anticipated in the 'vive satisfaction' with which Jean turns the handle of the shop door. And when the shopkeeper arrives with the writing-paper for him, this becomes an immense pleasure for Jean. The quire itself is described as 'une belle main si vaste, si unie, si douce, si brillante' (*JS*, p. 529). But of course the endearing beauty of material objects is here a reflection of the reverence that he feels for the shopkeeper. Indeed, Jean is so filled with emotion that he speaks collectively of what he sees as the noble-minded race of small traders:

[Ils] donnent l'impression du bien-être et vous laissent, au moment où vous tirez la porte qui tinte en se fermant, l'impression d'une vie plus heureuse dont la matière est exquise et qui n'est assujettie à aucune loi triste. De sorte qu'on sort le coeur plein de sympathie et de gaieté. (*JS*, pp. 529–30.)

The euphoria so evident in the evocation of the kitchen maid returns to the description of the shopkeeper. Again one is prompted to speculate that Jean's rush of emotion is due to the fact that his own existence is more generally clouded by uncertainty and melancholy. The connotations of inevitability and permanence in the 'loi triste' tend to confirm this view. By the same token, escape from any such damning principle guarantees Jean's attraction to the experience. For a brief period, he can live the well-being that he senses in others. These people, then, offer a contrast to, and at the same time complement and expand, his own awareness.

Away from the world of casual encounters with peasants and others, the process is taken a significant step further in the development of Jean's love for Marie Kossichef. There is at once a sharp contrast between Jean, seen as a withdrawn introvert on these occasions, and the vivacious, outward-going girl. Yet no less remarkable is his fascination with her, 'avec de grands cheveux noirs, des yeux clairs et moqueurs, des joues roses, et qui brillait de cette santé, de cette vie, de cette joie qui manquaient à Jean' (*JS*, p. 216). By virtue of this admittedly vicarious process, Jean attempts to experience something of life's vigours and joys. The precise nature of the 'santé', 'vie' and 'joie' is not however defined here. In this sense, although they are doubtless of an instinctual kind, they have yet to reveal the explicitly unintellectual character that they assume in the portrayal of the 'jeunes filles en fleurs' in *A la recherche*. That however will be dealt with more fully in Chapter 4.

In the case of his relationship with Marie, the contrast moves forward on a somatic, as well as an affective level. Her carefree and even indifferent manner throws Jean's 'surexcitation constante' (*JS*, p. 220) into relief. But her vitality is also set against images of his helpless physical debility:

Son petit corps [i.e., celui de Jean] qui depuis si longtemps portait des fers trop lourds pour un vigoureux corps d'homme, n'avait pu sans souffrance en être délivré tout d'un coup. (*JS*, p. 220.)

One can appreciate the complex dialectic of physical weakness and *vigueur*, so close is the link between them that the relieving of the love burden becomes almost as onerous as the burden itself. Seen in this way, the relationship highlights significant contrasts between Jean and Marie, but also reveals a strong movement of interpenetration.

This same search for a vigour of mind and body, the author surmises, may account for the self-conceit that emerges in Jean at school. The suggestion is that his vulnerable body and soul have,

dans la nécessité de lutter contre [la vie] trouvé un peu de cette force de résistance, de cette dureté, de cette écorce qui a souvent comme toutes les rudes choses ses écailles et ses verrues et qui avait poussé autour de lui parce qu'il en avait besoin, comme les pieds des oiseaux qui doivent aller sur l'eau se palment. (*JS*, p. 230.)

Possibly this is the spontaneous growth of a defense mechanism to dull the impact of life's violence on the otherwise unprotected Jean. In particular, one senses reassurance in the multiple evocations of resilience and solidity. For Jean, then, existence may on occasions narrow down, becoming synonymous with the protection of 'son corps et son âme trop tendres' (*JS*, p. 230). But it is important to see where this will to survive springs from. The answer lies in the image of the bird developing its anatomy in such a way as to adapt itself to travel on water. Effectively, what motivates Jean is a similar self-preservation. For him, awareness becomes limited, temporarily at least, to the primitive life-principle of the animal world, and giving undivided attention to this instinctual self is immensely calming for him.[5]

(c) Jean's attraction to animal living

Fuller references to animal existence are very common in *Jean Santeuil* and merit attention. One such instance occurs in Jean's description of the *dolce far niente* associated with digestion:

Nous envions le boa pour qui digérer est l'occupation d'une semaine et qui peut alors dormir plusieurs jours de suite. Nous envions le lézard qui reste des journées sur une pierre chaude à se laisser pénétrer de soleil. Nous envions la baleine qui fait de beaux voyages dans le Pacifique, les phoques qui jouent dans la mer au soleil, les mouettes qui jouent dans les orages et se laissent porter par le vent. (*JS*, pp. 368–9.)

The recurring 'Nous envions' engenders the rhythm of a litany addressed to an enchanting animal world. Moreover, it is notable that the generalising 'nous' should reappear in what is the normally third-person narrative of *Jean Santeuil*. This tends to unite human kind in its attraction to an acutely different existence. For Jean himself, the covetousness associated with 'envier' might recall his yearning for the kitchen maid or the shopkeeper (see above, section *b*). But clearly the implications are much more radical and striking here. By promoting the exclusively instinctual world of the animal kingdom, Jean introduces a register of awareness that is even further removed from his own hypersensitivity.

From his eager delight in the oblivion of the boa's prolonged sleep, one can see how the absence of conscious being becomes a source of joyous reverie for him. Likewise, the passivity implied in 'se laisser pénétrer de soleil . . . se laissent porter par le vent' adds to the sense of pleasurable escape from active, responsive being. That sense of inertia is reinforced by the dulling weight of time in these gradual, drawn-out animal processes. The pace of change is as imperceptible as the boa's rate of digestion. Interestingly enough, one sees something of that slackness and lack of energy, this time in the human world, in the portrayal of sleepy Combray in *A la recherche*. The imperfect continuous tense in much of the *Combray* section suffuses the whole depiction of village life with an impression of remissness and stasis, a monotony for which the Narrator's aunt feels genuine attraction: 'Ainsi passait la vie pour ma tante Léonie, toujours identique, dans la douce uniformité de ce qu'elle appelait, avec un dédain affecté et une tendresse profonde, son "petit traintrain"' (I, 109). The Narrator's reaction may not be that different. Certainly he himself, when commenting on the ritual early Saturday lunch, takes delight in

ces petits événements intérieurs, locaux, presque civiques qui, dans les vies tranquilles et les sociétés fermées, créent une sorte de lien national et deviennent le thème favori des conversations, des plaisanteries, des récits exagérés à plaisir. (I, 110.)

But the Narrator's experience is a relaxed and effortless enjoyment of what he terms solidarity and patriotic fervour (*ibid.*); the desire for evasion underlying the *Jean Santeuil* evocation of animal life springs from a real anxiety with the reflective mind. So it is that Jean's enthusiasm for animal life increases when he considers how it can eschew the problems of the mind: 'Et ce n'est que dans la vie des animaux que nous pouvons envisager [le sommeil, la nourriture, la mer, le vent] tout purs, remplissant la vie tout entière' (*JS*, p. 369). Jean is thus calmed by this sentient plenitude, and he nurtures this vision of an existence without fragmentation, a world without mental doubt. We might also see this as faintly anticipating the joy experienced by the Narrator of *A la recherche*, where a woman's presence is often described as having similar replenishing powers. This is especially true of his relationship with Albertine. Yet in the earlier novel, Jean Santeuil appears unabashedly fascinated by the instinctual character of animal life. Proust actually ventures to suggest that our enjoyment of pleasurable digestion and *far niente* may be greater than that of the animals, given that the human self is capable of intellectual as well as sentient experience. And if one views mental activity as being often perplexing, then any escape into a totally bodily feel of living has its consolation. Hence Proust's concluding remark in which the thinker is singled out as one of two favoured types: 'Ce n'est que pour le penseur et pour le malade que la vie animale a tous ces enivrements' (*JS*, p. 369). Interestingly, the reflecting man and the sick person appear as abstract personifications. This helps reinforce my earlier point that a concern with problems of both mind and body is central to *Jean Santeuil* (see above, section *b*). The relieving of either is a consolation for Jean.

The final paragraph of this development has thematic implications relevant to those already mentioned above. But a slight change in emphasis now gives the elements of the natural world an equal place alongside the animal one. More significantly, it now becomes clear that the limitless vitality of the elements and the non-reflection of animals are not the attainable gains that they had briefly appeared to be. Yet the writer's sense of ecstasy helps sustain and prolong the evocation:

Illusion qui enchaîne tant de malades dans les lieux sauvages où la nature est pleine de force, tant de penseurs épuisés là où il n'y a que des forces sans pensée, la mer aveugle, le vent sourd, les animaux qui ne pensent à rien, le boa qui digère pendant dix jours, la marmotte qui dort un hiver, la baleine qui vit trois cents ans, la mouette qui vole un mois sans se fatiguer et en dix jours va au Pacifique, au milieu desquels êtres inaltérablement calmes, ou desquelles forces éternellement vivantes la mort ou la folie qui les guettait les prend. Nous avons beau nous pencher au-dessus du réservoir de toutes les forces. (*JS*, pp. 369–70.)

It is curious that while asserting how illusory the aspirations of the sick man or the intellectual are, Jean still experiences a strong nostalgia for this idealised view. Evidence lies in the very energetic description of the life that he finally concedes to be inaccessible to man. The burden of mental reflection is made light in the mindless-ness of the 'forces sans pensée' of the natural world or 'les animaux qui ne pensent à rien'. But Jean does not only escape from the thinking mind. In the presence of 'la mer aveugle, le vent sourd', he may be implicitly willing the absence of even more fundamental perceptions. Indeed, it would seem reasonable to suppose that he looks to a dissolution of the problematic individual self in the greater natural and animal worlds.

The final comment I have to make on this extract relates to the accumulation of different examples of instinctual prowess in ani-mals. In the note of trance and reverie that such a rush of evocations engenders, one senses something of the fascination with the exotic that fanned Baudelaire's imagination. The latter's hymns of praise are often addressed to an elusive female beauty, a source of inspiration markedly different from the present one. Nevertheless, the gentle, soothing presence of '[ces] êtres inaltérablement calmes' is reminiscent of the mood of inviolable tranquillity that the poet tries to evoke. As for Jean's yearning for distant lands and a seemingly endless vitality, one can detect something of Baudelaire's celebrated nostalgia for a delectable paradise.[6]

In the context of Proust's own work, this overt interest in animal living is significant, even if it is only in *Jean Santeuil* that it receives the writer's total attention. There are traces of it in the *Recherche* as well however. At the beginning of that work, for example, we find the Narrator experiencing something of that primitive existence as he awakens: 'J'avais seulement dans sa simplicité première le sentiment de l'existence comme il peut frémir au fond d'un animal' (1, 5). But we shall be returning to the opening of the *Recherche* later.

It is clear that the eulogistic treatment of animal living has an interesting bearing on the question of levels of consciousness in Proust's work. For in the young novelist's eager depiction of these instinctual forces, one can detect more than a flirtation with mindlessness and pure sensation.

(d) Communion with Nature: its non-human dimension

I now want to pursue the nature of Jean's identification with natural phenomena, and in particular the sea, which soon becomes a frequent source of stimulus and exhilaration for him. There is an illustration of this in a description of Jean's feeling of intoxication following upon a period of prolonged reading:

Il descendait l'escalier dans un mouvement fou, et faisait deux ou trois fois en courant de toutes ses forces le tour du jardin, secouant la tête, fendant l'air les bras tendus, se figurant qu'il était cheval dans une prairie, mouette au ras des flots, fou de joie. (*JS*, p. 312.)

The division between the mental pastime of reading and the undiluted bodily frenzy of what follows this is very forcibly drawn. The use of animal imagery serves a useful function in this way. But here, the attempt to identify with Nature is not shown up as something illusory. Far from seeing it as being inaccessible, Jean has abandoned the confines of his own individual self to sense the rapturous flight of the bird in close communion with the primordial sea. For a brief moment, he may feel that he can take on the instinctive form of the horse or the gull. It is as if he were stepping outside of himself and 'son esprit lassé', to taste the exhilaration of bodily movement enjoyed by these creatures.

The sound of wind announcing a storm triggers off a similar reaction. For Jean, the storm is the great laying-open of the mysterious elements. He sees this epiphany as having a transforming effect on his own self:

[Le premier bruit du vent] lui avait fait battre le coeur, l'avait rempli de joie, avait gonflé ses ailes, comme s'il était de la race des mouettes et se [sentait] appelé vers les tempêtes. (*JS*, p. 396.)

Jean's sense of individuality, then, becomes increasingly remote. The unlimited vitality within him is subsumed into a very different order, one based on the primitive natural rhythm of the elements. This points to what J.-P. Richard defines as being the significance of the storm motif in Proust: 'Il renvoie au désir, au désir-effroi, d'une sorte d'inhumanité absolue, d'une pureté de la nature.'[7] This 'inhumanité absolue' is the obvious corollary to Jean's belonging to the 'race des mouettes'. The ability to empathise and to lay oneself open has a very positive value for Jean. To this end, one should avoid interpreting Richard's 'inhumanité' in any morally condemnatory sense. He himself sees the term as having its neutral, etymological meaning of 'in-humanus'.

Nevertheless, Richard's conclusions are not totally justifiable. In Proust he sees

[le] désir-effroi d'une sorte d'inhumanité absolue, d'une pureté de la nature. D'où la puissance moralement roborative de l'éventé (il arrache à toutes les complaisances narcissiques), la foncière tonicité de l'aéré. (Richard, *Proust et le monde sensible*, p. 46.)

Granted, the idea of a salutary escape from Narcissus-fixation may be applied to the Narrator's experience at a storm-swept Balbec, in the *Recherche*:

Je n'étais curieux, je n'étais avide de connaître que ce que je croyais plus vrai que moi-même, ce qui avait pour moi le prix de me montrer un peu de la pensée d'un grand génie, ou de la force ou de la grâce de la nature telle qu'elle se manifeste livrée à elle-même, sans l'intervention des hommes. (I, 384.)

But against this, the impact of the storm on Jean Santeuil is quite different. It is in fleeing the prison of 'son esprit fatigué de lire [...] son esprit lassé' that he longs to be the seagull. Such taxing reflection has little in common with any 'complaisances narcissiques'.

The impact of another seascape on Jean is interesting; what strikes one is the prominence of sun and wind:

A ces moments-là il n'avait plus de doute, plus d'inquiétudes, plus de tristesse. Et son calme profond semblait, comme le ciel bleu au-dessus de sa tête et les verdures bruissantes à ses pieds, cacher une sérénité, une joie silencieuse. (*JS*, p. 392.)

Again one finds the pattern of Jean burying reflective and emotional scruples, stealing in as it were on Nature's limpidity, and in this way escaping the three-pronged attack of 'doute', 'inquiétudes' and 'tristesse'.

Clearly, Jean's contact with Nature may serve a vital palliative function. He welcomes the raging storm, which purges him of his involved individuality. His search for communion with Nature may even grow into a longing for absorption into the world about him. Seeing him 'avide de sympathiser avec toute la nature qui était en lui comme autour de lui' (*JS*, p. 532), one can appreciate how the gap between individual selfhood and the external world is declining.

R. C. Zaehner's work, *Mysticism, Sacred and Profane*, is of relevance here. In his study of mystic thought, Zaehner looks at the composition of self in such experience. Curiously enough, he devotes a full chapter to a discussion of Proust and Rimbaud.[8] I am quoting, however, from his illuminating section on Nature mysticism in Tennyson and Forrest Reid: 'In this experience, the subject is not only swallowed up in the greater whole; the greater whole, by an inconceivable paradox, actually seems to be part of oneself.'[9]

But this fascination with the non-human dimension of natural forces can assume different forms of significance in *Jean Santeuil*. The wind, for example, is described as being ubiquitous at the time of the storm. Its provenance is unknown, while it is so all-pervading as to seem without beginning and end. He stops to deliberate on ce bruit que n'accompagnait l'idée d'aucune cause, qui ne marchait pas à terre, qui ne venait pas du toit, qui était partout à la fois, qui battait le pays, qui enveloppait tout le château! (*JS*, p. 532.)

The total absence of causation characterising this sound endows it with a primal necessity in the eyes of Jean. It is self-existent, unconditional, beyond the grasp of any human mind. This sense of the non-human is established even more firmly in further enthusing:

Ainsi Jean écoutait le vent, s'exaltant de sa force, et enchanté de sa douceur si poétique en effet, car elle est toute pure d'éléments étrangers, elle semble sans cause, elle ne peut faire penser à rien d'humain, à aucune action. (*JS*, p. 532.)

A poetic element thus comes to enhance Jean's intimate contact with Nature. Its beauty grows as concern for causation declines. In fact any causal probing is interpreted as a sign of deficient, human intellect, set on restricting and categorising experience. On the other hand, Jean sees the elements as existing *ab initio* and enjoys the presence of these absolutes from which the human is excluded.

This brings to mind an analogous observation made in the brief study, 'La Mer', in *Les Plaisirs et les jours*. There too, Proust sees our contemplation of the sea's movement as generating great inspirational energy:

[La mer] rafraîchit notre imagination parce qu'elle ne fait pas penser à la vie des hommes, mais elle réjouit notre âme [...]. Elle nous enchante ainsi comme la musique, qui ne porte pas comme le langage la trace des choses, qui imite les mouvements de notre âme. (*JS*, pp. 143–4.)

There is an obvious resemblance here to the spell of the wind '[qui] ne peut faire penser à rien d'humain' (*JS*, p. 532). Later in the text, however, the broader implications of this become evident too. In this connection, the musical analogy is especially informative – a pointer, perhaps, to the importance that it is to assume in *Le Temps retrouvé* (see below, Chapter 6). As music is to verbal language, so is the inner soul to the outer surface self. Proust's point is that the elemental rhythm of the sea leads us into the realm of the irrational and the non-conceptual. From the musical allusion here, one can see how this deep communion with Nature may even foster an artistic creativity.

Assuming this to be true, the identification with the sea then takes on a new dimension. We have seen how Jean's frantic exhilaration in the storm tends to destroy any awareness of individual consciousness. This is linked to the 'inhumanité absolue' of which Richard speaks (*Proust et le monde sensible*, p. 46). Yet in the passage quoted from 'La Mer', emphasis shifts to an awakening of artistic emotion in the individual. What previously extinguished the self now acts as a fan to the highest form of individual human activity – the search for an artistic goal.

From this examination of some references to Nature in *Jean Santeuil*, one does not then see only a joyful immersion of the self in seascapes and landscapes. In another, quite different sense, contact with Nature may awaken a creative potential in man. I mention this last idea as a corrective to any assumption that the young Proust's primary concern was for a mental nothingness. Even so, one can see that, as early as *Jean Santeuil*, there is a developed awareness of the difficulties with which intellectual and artistic reflection may be fraught. Often Jean's most effective means of escape is to throw off individual consciousness and abandon the self to all-embracing Nature.

(e) Vicarious living for Jean: his friendship with Henri de Réveillon

My first observation on the preface to *Jean Santeuil* was that the writer figure was assisted, in some indirect way, by the natural manner of the peasants around him. Jean, too, was conscious of a vague inspiration when in conversation with the kitchen maid (*JS*, p. 320). When one relates this to his enthusiasm for Nature, some interesting points of comparison appear. For example, the fellow-feeling that characterises B.'s dialogue with the servant woman (*JS*, p. 192) is echoed in Jean's being 'avide de sympathiser avec toute la nature' (*JS*, p. 531). The interpenetration of the self and Nature is an exhilarating experience for Jean, and is not unlike B's empathising with those about him: 'B. étendait avec plaisir sa vie de toutes ces vies placées à côté de la sienne' (*JS*, p. 192: see above, section *a*). Common to both sensations is an agreeable dependence on a vitality outside the self. The instinctual character of the one and the elemental nature of the other are in this respect contiguous.

One finds additional evidence of this in Jean's efforts to check what he sees as his own physical and emotional inadequacy. Inclement weather can serve as an invigorating stimulus to him:

Dans cette pluie son âme s'était retrempée, le vent lui avait soufflé son courage et il avait repris les dispositions hérissées du froid. Mais il aimait cette heure dramatique, cette nature batailleuse contre laquelle il luttait. (*JS*, p. 530.)

In an indirect way Jean's savouring the aggression and daring of Nature speaks volumes for his debility, huddled behind this new rush of vitality. The vicarious way in which he lives this resilience is reminiscent of his delight on seeing Bertrand de Réveillon leaping over the restaurant furniture to join his friend:

> [Jean] sentait que toute la libre, vigoureuse, alerte vie de ton enfance [i.e., celle de Bertrand] était tout entière présente en ce moment à ton service, et que tu la mettais au sien comme un hôte généreux qui donne tout ce qu'il possède. (*JS*, p. 453.)

The instinctual grace of Réveillon's body movement has something of the vigour instilled in Jean by '[la] nature batailleuse'. In both experiences, one is made aware of his eager desire for 'toute cette force si éloignée de notre faiblesse' (*JS*, p. 453). Such a sharp juxtaposition heightens Jean's will to transcend the limitations of his feeling and situation.

We might go further and say that a general feature of Proust's early fiction has been this interest in a quality of experience and awareness unrelated to one's own: the artist B.'s contentment in the presence of the intellectually inferior peasantry; Jean's enthusiasm for the simplicity of diction of the fisherman; the vivacity that he finds in the person of Marie; his fascination with animal living; his efforts to transcend the limits of his own self in intimate communion with Nature – each of these reflects a different aspect of the generally primitive quality of being that Jean or B. long to graft onto their own selves. The process even extends to artistic activity, and, indeed, Jean's fertile imaginative being is active in evoking this primitivism. Invariably, it is with a strong nostalgia that he looks on this largely pre-intellectual awareness. The presence/absence conflict that this yearning implies begins to generate a tension that is to become all the more prevalent in Proust's later work.

There is some illustration of this in references to Jean's artistic vocation. For him, the problems coming in the wake of literary activity are frequently as prominent as any elation it may bring. Often, he finds his thought-processes and emotional responses alike increasingly burdensome. But Jean's attempts to alleviate this are of interest in the present study:

> Toute main agitée qui devra écrire en tremblant des vers [...] recherchera toujours une plume qui n'ait, elle, aucune incertitude, qui ne tombe pas du manche au moment où le mot imaginé l'attend immédiatement pour le tracer, qui ne tremble pas d'une manière énervante, qui reçoive l'encre sans paresse et tout entière également d'un seul coup, qui n'ait pas comme la pensée qui la guide ses caprices. (*JS*, p. 409.)

Thus the inanimate pen at the writer's disposition is endowed with a regularity and predictability. In forging this association with the pen, the poet seems to long for his thought to acquire some of its positive instrumental qualities. He thereby combats the 'incertitude', the 'manière énervante', the 'caprices' that are all features of the creative process. On a comparative level, the constancy attributed to the pen recalls the sameness that B. finds in the unchanging peasants of the preface. But in the more immediate context of this section, '[Pourquoi Jean préfère la compagnie d'Henri à celle de Mlle des Coulombes]', the enthusiasm for the pen foreshadows the praise heaped upon Henri de Réveillon by the intellectually troubled writer.

Henri is eagerly described as being one of the 'natures positives', who, although oblivious to artistic questions, comes to assume a great value for the poet. In the imaginative upheaval confronting the writer,

combien il goûte ces natures positives et avisées dont la vie a l'harmonie paisible d'une chose à sa place, d'un mouvement parfait, la monotone douceur des heures qui sonnent régulièrement! (*JS*, p. 409.)

The delightful sense of symmetry and equilibrium that he admires in Henri throws into relief the problematic imbalance of his own being. Immediately, the monotonous takes on a singular beauty. As the description of Henri unfolds, further interesting comparisons are made with Jean. Even the simplest of observations can throw much light on their respective temperaments. The succinctness of the following opposition is a good case in point: '[Henri] tenait beaucoup à la vie mais il ne pensait jamais à la mort' (*JS*, p. 410). This embraces not only Henri's total commitment to the immediacy of living but also Jean's excessive metaphysical speculation. The third-person narrator later points out that, in the same way, Henri's human relationships do not reveal the intense character, the 'impuissante exaltation' of Jean's social intercourse (*JS*, p. 410). More generally, the former's consciousness lacks the hypersensitivity of Jean's mind. Equally, he is less exposed to scruples – another string to his bow in the opinion of an admiring Jean: 'Aussi, les habitudes, douces aveugles qui prennent soin de nos actions si elles suivent toujours le même chemin, lui [i.e., à Henri] épargnaient de la peine' (*JS*, p. 410). Habit then acts like the 'forces sans pensée [de la nature], la mer aveugle', in holding Jean's attention (see above, section *c*). In the case of both, the lessening of perceptions effectively consoles Jean.

Henri may even take on the passivity of 'un outil fidèle que la main aime à retrouver' (*JS*, p. 411), clearly echoing the reliability of the pen. As before, this derives from Jean's attraction to the harmonious, the regular, the pleasantly predictable – calming qualities that Henri epitomises. He is further likened to the steady, unflickering light of a lamp 'qui répand avec une insouciance affectueuse une chaleur égale et brillante' (*JS*, p. 411);[10] or, again, he shares the sense of proportion and balance of an Italian church. The soothing impact of both appeals to Jean.[11]

The lines of contrast are firmly drawn, then. If Henri lacks Jean's creative side, the order of his life-style guards him against intellectual agitation. The greatest disparity, however, is glimpsed in the concluding sentence to the extract, where Henri's ability to live within present experience seems a great boon: 'Il avait cette poésie de la journée bien emplie plutôt qu'écoulée, qui n'est ni la poésie triste d'hier ni la poésie obscure de demain' (*JS*, p. 411). Past and present, reflection and anticipation, represent spiritual enigmas for Jean and as such distract him from what is the substantiality of immediate perception and experience. He suffers from his sensitivity and exposure to what was and what is to be. The present moment all too often evades him. Not so with Henri. The total sufficiency of the present for him recalls how Jean, speaking with the maid, experienced something of 'la beauté qu'il y a à être' (*JS*, p. 320). On that occasion as well, he saw how existence may be reduced to the simple, assimilable proportions of the here and now. Sadly for Jean, the reassurance of this uncomplicated view of living is as passing as it is immediately satisfying. Only in Henri does it gain a greater permanence.

The idea of finding happiness in restricting the self is clearly a commonplace in literature, popular as well as learned. I should like, however, to single out two authors for very brief mention. One is Senancour, already referred to in the Introduction, and the other is Schopenhauer. In Chapter 4, I shall be looking at the latter's 'Counsels and Maxims' (Chapter 5 of *Aphorisms on the Wisdom of Life*) specifically commented on by Proust. But one of his counsels in particular merits a mention here as finding a possible exemplar in Henri: 'We should not cast a gloom over the present by looking peevish over the vain hopes of the past or over our anxiety for the future.'[12] In Senancour's *Rêveries*, from which Proust took fairly precise notes (see *CSB*, pp. 568–9), the greatest pleasures are similarly described as being

étrangers à l'avenir, indifférents à ce qui ne sera peut-être pas comme à ce qui n'est plus, ils s'alimentent du présent; et le présent les ramène toujours, tandis que ces jouissances indirectes et composées, enfants de l'imagination, finissent avec son délire. (*Rêveries*, vol. 1, p. 158.)

Senancour's distinction follows broadly the course taken by Proust in separating Henri and Jean. Indeed, the denomination of '[les] enfants de l'imagination' seems especially applicable to Jean. To that extent, the young Proust appears to share Senancour's caution.

We have seen in an earlier quotation from *Jean Santeuil* how the Narrator views the poet's situation (*JS*, p. 409). Another development further exploits these contrasting temperaments. Henri remains discreetly behind as Jean contemplates a solitary flower, and when Jean's spiritual reflection comes to an end, 'fatigué d'être fortement concentré en lui-même, sa pensée se porta joyeusement vers son ami' (*JS*, p. 472). so the intensity of the artistic experience is quickly relieved in amicable conversation with Henri. Moreover, although Jean's 'épanchement' is beyond Henri's comprehension, the latter still holds out what is seen as the very positive support of his friendship. In the same way, the plainness of Henri's exhortation, 'Maintenant que tu ne réfléchis plus, marchons plus vite', is immensely comforting for Jean:

Ce n'était nullement pour blâmer implicitement l'élan de Jean, mais par le prosaïsme de sa nature qui, tout en le trouvant doux, était incapable de lui répondre par des élans semblables, mais par une amitié égale qui offrait à la sienne, moins comme des présents d'égale valeur que comme des remèdes souverains et introuvables, en échange de son génie, sa sympathie intelligente, contre sa nervosité son calme, et pour sa personne, sa personne à lui, avec ce qui en dépendait, toute sa vie. (*JS*, p. 472.)

It is easy to see the network of by now familiar contrasts on which the passage is based, contrasts asserting Jean's hypersensitive character. Furthermore, by referring specifically to Henri's 'remèdes', Jean is stressing the palliative function that this friendship serves.

This is not unlike another situation where Jean is alone in a hotel room. On that occasion, a sense of physical claustration induces a pleasurable impression of security and limitation in Jean. In its effect, it is like the 'remèdes souverains' offered by Henri:

[Jean était] reconnaissant aux lieux qui, d'un coup, par un mystère peut-être des proportions où un être malheureux et souffrant d'angoisse trouve l'équation de ses exigences nerveuses, lui avaient ôté le poids de ces soucis et communiqué cette ivresse. (*JS*, p. 555.)

Here, Proust goes as far as to suggest an equation, a cancelling-out of forces. In the case of Henri's role vis-à-vis Jean, the contrasts are scarcely less explicit. The narrator's description of their relationship as Jean studies the flower throws important light on the artistic experience itself. For it appears both uplifting and perplexing, now engaging Jean totally, now leaving him happy to enjoy Henri's prosaic companionship. The degree of tension that this implies adds to the conflict of temperaments. Henri's existence is one of clockwork regularity. While his horizons are restricted to the present, Jean is open to reflection on past and future (*JS*, p. 409). So his concern lies with imponderable absences, Henri's with an unchanging, solid presence.

Generally, by insisting on these contrasts and simultaneously confessing to a strong attraction to the limitation of self that he sees in Henri, Jean is voicing an intermittent need for a similar restriction. The emphasis is different from that of the preface to *Jean Santeuil*, where C. enjoys the uncomplicated company of the peasants without singling out his dependence on them. In the case of Henri, he counterbalances the more extreme self-searching in artistic experience. Nor is the harmonious existence that he represents to be equated with the instinctual primitivism of animal living that excites Jean's curiosity. We see evidence of this in his measure of sensitivity as he allows Jean to study the flower (*JS*, p. 472). Yet even then, he epitomises a more unthinking mode of being. For that very reason, it is notable that as Jean develops his own artistic sensitivity, he should feel nostalgia for an order in which excessive intellectual preoccupation does not occur. Perhaps it is only to be expected that in the exploratory world of *Jean Santeuil*, there should be this toying with differing levels of awareness. The flux of Jean's mind might fairly be said to reflect something of Proust's own developing ideas.

(f) Jean's hesitant steps towards intellectual formation

Flux is also a key word in the adolescent Jean's taste in poetry. His fundamental belief is that it is the conceptual that is of primary importance in one's appreciation of such writing. To this end, he has developed a rigorous system of 'principes du Devoir' to which he adheres religiously (*JS*, p. 237). For Jean, the guiding spirit of that code is 'que le mal [est] de lire de beaux vers et le bien d'en expliquer de mauvais' (*ibid.*).

One finds a sharp departure from this in the aesthetics promoted by his teacher, Rustinlor. When the latter, echoing Gautier, insists that the verse 'La fille de Minos et de Pasiphaé' is Racine's most beautiful, Jean experiences what can only be described as profound mental crisis. He ponders how poetry could be founded on anything other than the 'grandes réalités en présence de qui il vivait' (*JS*,

p. 240). But quite suddenly, Jean waives these pre-conditions. His feeling of intellectual confusion gives way to a more favourable view of the complexity involved, and indeed to 'cette surprise joyeuse que nous éprouvons chaque fois qu'une parole neuve vient changer pour nous la face du monde ou les termes du problème de la pensée' (*JS*, p. 240). Thus, a shift in mental perspective is enough to arouse Jean's excitement. Nonetheless, reference to the 'problème de la pensée' tends to cast a perplexing shadow over the workings of the mind. This confirms the point made earlier that Jean feels inevitably non-plussed by certain experiences.

Part of Jean's joyous surprise is his wonderment that he should be seduced by the non-conceptual beauty of the Racine verse. But one can afford to be less cautious in judging a later evaluation of the same line from Racine. In an early version of *Du côté de chez Swann*, the Narrator is torn between what he feels, subliminally as it were, and what rational analysis reveals:

Que ce vers de Racine, que certains vers de Leconte de Lisle fussent plus beaux que des vers philosophiques de Sully Prudhomme, cela me troublait d'autant plus profondément que cette beauté que je ne pouvais légitimer je la ressentais.[13]

It is as though the Narrator senses this beauty in spite of his own logical self.

Essentially, Jean's response to this newly-found poetic beauty can be linked up with the contrasts between Henri and Jean. As the former's disposition excludes mental complexity, so Racine's line opens up a whole area of non-intellectual significance in poetry. It may seem arbitrary selecting these two separate experiences. But taken together they assume significance, for Jean gains relief from self-doubt in both the effortless world of Henri and the irrational appreciation of Racine's poetry.

With Racine, Jean's escape is away from the confines of narrowly intellectual evaluation and towards a more nebulous aesthetic insight. Yet he sees his views as coming under fire from Beulier, his philosophy teacher. The latter's positivist ideas clash head-on with Jean's vague romantic aestheticism:

[Jean] ne trouva dans toute la leçon aucune de ces images splendides et parfumées, auxquelles il aurait pu pendant cette rude course intellectuelle faire halte comme auprès de reposoirs de fleurs. (*JS*, p. 261.)

In particular, Jean laments that Beulier should make no reference to 'les doux mots de "vanité de la vie", de "nirvâna"' (*ibid.*). These allusions are relatively meaningless until correlated with that section of the novel in which the influence of Rustinlor's poetic credo is dealt with. There, Jean appears deeply interested in the Buddhist-inspired verse of Leconte de Lisle with its decrial of the vanity of everyday existence. Rustinlor also recommends, with much laughter, that Jean might 'goûter horizontalement sur un banc le nirvâna divin' (*JS*, p. 237). The references to Buddhism are best understood when set against Beulier's views. These have a rational, quasi-scientific character, so that Jean comes to see Nirvana as representing mystic escape from 'cette rude course intellectuelle'. The upshot of all this is that Jean is near to jettisoning the categorical assertion of certain phenomena,

lui qui savait qu'il n'y a ni bien ni vrai, il fut stupéfait d'entendre cet homme dont on lui avait vanté le génie, parler du bien, de la vérité, de la certitude. (*JS*, p. 261.)

It is clear that what Jean sees as being a vague, dream-like relativism lies outside the logical confines of Beulier's system. As for Beulier's concern for recent technological innovation, Jean dismisses this as being solely for 'cette race disciplinée mais barbare, ennemie des muses et des dieux' (*JS*, p. 261).

The atmosphere of mysticism that these brief but informed references to Buddhism introduce points to Jean's interest in an inspiration and transcendence forgoing all arid conceptualisation. His hopes that this would accommodate Beulier's teaching are initially disappointed.[14] Again, of course, all this can be related to the enigmatic line from *Phèdre*. In both cases, getting beyond a strict rationalism allows Jean to experience the enchantment of intuitive beauty. While the degree of transcendence is not identical in both cases – Jean's anxious anticipation of references to Buddhism in Beulier's class indicates a much stronger interest in the mystical – they confirm a tendency to exclude intellectual analysis from the perception of beauty.

Confirmation of that tendency comes with Jean's involuntary recall of childhood, prompted as it is by a reflection of sunlight onto a table. Significantly, the non-rational quality of the experience becomes almost a prerequisite to any awareness of the beautiful:

Aussi la couleur que nous pouvons dire vraiment belle, c'est-à-dire qui sans avoir besoin de raisonner nous remplisse d'une sorte de rêve heureux, ce n'est pas celle de l'or [...]. Non c'est celle de toute chose a l'ombre, fût-ce au fond d'une pauvre chambre, sur laquelle le soleil donne. (*JS*, p. 299.)

What follows the explicative 'c'est-à-dire', in particular, confirms the intuitive character of Jean's aesthetic awareness.

Another recollection of a past moment produces an analogous response in the beholder, who is this time identified as the first-person 'moi':

Ce lac qui est devant moi n'est plus un spectacle dont j'aie à chercher la beauté, c'est l'image d'une vie longtemps vécue et dont la beauté et le charme [retentissent] trop vivement dans mon coeur pour que j'aie besoin de chercher en quoi elle consiste. (*JS*, p. 399.)

The spontaneous, 'unprovoked' character of memory in both these instances foreshadows the celebrated moments of recollection in the *Recherche*. Yet so intense is the lake's beauty for the 'moi' of *Jean Santeuil* that any need to give further expression to its spiritual significance becomes irrelevant. In this, *Jean Santeuil* differs from the later novel, where the Narrator feels compelled to find the source of his felicity:

Arrivera-t-il jusqu'à la surface de ma claire conscience, ce souvenir, l'instant ancien que l'attraction d'un instant identique est venue de si loin solliciter, émouvoir, soulever tout au fond de moi? (I, 46.)

Far from achieving the lucidity of 'ma claire conscience', the experience described in *Jean Santeuil* seems to thrive on the immediate beauty of colour (*JS*, p. 299) and of the lake (*ibid.* p. 399).

This follows the pattern of the Racine verse in not looking to any intellectual stimulus for pleasurable experience. But there is another important dimension to Jean's sensing a non-analytical charm. On occasions, he speaks with pessimism of how our joys may be carved up by the intelligence. For a person who has just finished reading a book, for example,

Une fois le livre fermé on n'ose pas avouer sa satisfaction complète, soit honte, soit désir d'être toujours plaint, de ne pas paraître trop heureux, soit que le bonheur dès qu'il est examiné, mis en question, s'évanouisse. (*JS*, p. 368.)

A questioning self-analysis may therefore undermine one's sense of elation. This has far-reaching implications in the novel generally. Clearly, if happiness is to be enjoyed in this unthought state, so to speak, Jean will try to live experience in an intensely immediate, unreflecting way. The probing mind thus assumes a menacing character in so far as it jeopardises that felicity; happiness becomes the great imperative, under siege from the mind.

An interesting off-shoot of this is that the strong pleasure principle that activates Jean is similarly threatened. One might consider the young Proust's confidently forthright observation on Jean's awareness of experience – and indeed on our own perception, for we are swept along by the generalising 'nous':

D'ailleurs, à partir d'un certain âge, dès que nos idées philosophiques se sont assises, nous jouissons mieux des choses, car nous n'en cherchons plus le bien-fondé métaphysique. Nous savons que les sensations qui se présentent à nous d'une manière vive et particulière et éveillent en nous un retentisse-ment poétique sont réelles en cela, et nous ne cherchons pas à les discuter, ce qui nous donne une sorte de repos pour en jouir. (*JS*, p. 747.)

Such an explicit statement is particularly valuable for our purposes. For it affirms that one's enjoyment of life's experience is pro-portionate to the dulling of the inquiring philosophical mind. That enjoyment is marked by a largely undefined, yet no less real, poetic dimension. The impressions that automatically impinge themselves on us recall the vague beauty of the lake, which 'retentit trop vivement dans mon coeur pour que j'aie besoin de chercher en quoi elle consiste' (*JS*, p. 399).

So the light in which metaphysical reflection is cast also reveals the mental complexity that may come with it. The constant inner excavation that it entails leads one further and further away from the centre of lived experience itself.

Jean's liking for instantaneous living has been a dominant feature, of course, in this study of *Jean Santeuil*. This is shared by the peasant folk who succeed in endearing the writer B. to their limited existence. The same also holds for Henri, while the freedom from a taxing reflection finds its most radical expression in depictions of 'la vie animale'. For Jean, the choice would seem to lie between involved self-questioning and a tranquil indulgence. The dominant movement in this passage is to by-pass the 'bien-fondé méta-physique'.

Another of the advantages in this extended maxim is that it homes in on the nature of Jean's desire for an automatic living. It emerges that it is not an undiluted hedonism that motivates him. Rather, he senses a need as well as a desire to cushion the blow of philosophical preoccupation. This element of psychological necessity is of great moment, and I shall be examining some of its other ramifications, especially in the chapter on Albertine (see below, Chapter 5).

In this same section of *Jean Santeuil*, Proust goes on to give some practical illustrations of these 'principles'. He mentions, in particu-lar, one's enjoyment of the theatre:

Quand on aime [le théâtre] et qu'on y cherche l'absolu, qu'on dévore chaque intonation pour tâcher de saisir en quoi elle peut avoir de l'importance pour notre esprit et de la valeur, on ne connaît aucun plaisir. (*JS*, p. 747.)

The young Proust is stressing the irrelevance of any spurious intellectual justification. He even ventures to say that intuitive beauty may become effectively crowded out by this dry dissection of the theatrical art. And just as Jean sees the 'bien-fondé métaphysique' in terms of an obstruction, so any insistence on finding some aesthetic absolute at once condemns the artistic experience to failure. By constantly looking behind and beyond it, Jean finds himself face to face with a disconcerting void. The same is true of his first love. The hyperactive mind that scrutinises that relationship aborts any instinctive happiness (*ibid.*).

The question of intellectual doubting is just as prominent in the *Recherche* itself. More particularly, the perplexing experience of the theatre reappears, with Berma's enigmatic beauty engaging the Narrator's attention (see below, Chapter 3*b*). In addition to this, we shall be seeing in Chapter 5 how love itself is to assume more alarming proportions in the later novel. For the present, however, it is enough to note how with the calming of 'nos idées philosophiques' (*JS*, p. 747), pleasurable living can go on unhindered in *Jean Santeuil*. That remedy may not be as efficacious in the *Recherche*, where the Narrator lives a denser, more entangled reality, but Proust's earlier fiction reveals a greater contentment with sensation itself than with any lucid analysis of such experience. The drive towards mental *approfondissement* that emerges so forcefully in the *Recherche* has yet to acquire the same intensity in the earlier novel. Perhaps this spiritual excavation is too daunting a task for Jean, who seems ever mindful of the precariousness of happiness.

(g) Similarities in the artistic and love experiences

It would, however, be naive to say that Proust's first novel is concerned solely with the evocation of one pleasurable sensation after another. We have seen how Jean admires in others a freedom from mental complexity and often sets his own sights in that direction. Yet this in itself betrays his own troubled inner self. Likewise, although the simplicity of language spoken by others enchants him, he is conscious that his own response to such utterances must be looked for on several levels. When he exchanges greetings with the fisherman, for example, the simplicity of their words cannot conceal Jean's underlying emotion. There, and indeed elsewhere in Proust's early work, there exists a very real awareness of verbal expression and its problems.

One instance of this involves Honoré, a young socialite whose society evening is described in a section of *Les Plaisirs et les jours* entitled 'Un Dîner en ville'. Leaving the *soirée* in a state of intoxication, Honoré feels a sense of exhilaration, as pleasurable associations and ideas well up within him. But he is at the same time irritated at being unable to 'atteindre immédiatement tous les sites qui étaient disposés çà et là dans l'infini de sa perspective' (*JS*, p. 103). Even more depressing for him is his inadequacy of language in conveying this state of mind. The third-person narrator comments on how Honoré's limp expression, 'La vie est triste, c'est idiot', is but 'une bien banale traduction de pareilles visions qui, pensa-t-il, n'étaient peut-être pas exprimables' (*JS*, p. 103). Honoré's primary concern is to relay faithfully his intricaate feeling, but he is hindered by what seems to be either the ineffability of the experience or possibly the opacity of his own unresourceful language. The latter is more probable when one recalls how the passage develops with the narrator allowing Honoré to give voice to his intellectual frustration:

'Hélas! sans doute l'intensité de mon plaisir ou de mon regret est seule centuplée, mais le contenu intellectuel en reste le même. Mon bonheur est nerveux, personnel, intraduisible à d'autres, et si j'écrivais en ce moment, mon style aurait les mêmes qualités, les mêmes défauts, hélas! la même médiocrité que d'habitude.' (*JS*, p. 103.)

These words undermine Honoré's very real preoccupation with self-expression, and by extension with creative writing. So it is that he equates his inability to find a transparent medium for experience with artistic failure.

Nevertheless, the burden of disappointment is quickly alleviated for Honoré. Significantly, the source of relief is not unfamiliar in the light of what we have seen in *Jean Santeuil*: 'Mais le bien-être physique qu'il éprouvait le garda d'y penser plus longtemps et lui donna immédiatement la consolation suprême, l'oubli' (*JS*, p. 103). Again, a bodily, instinctual well-being mitigates the problems of the mind. Yet what is most notable about the references to joyous mental oblivion is its being in apposition to the unequivocal 'consolation *suprême*' (italics mine). At a first glance, this parallelism might imply the advocating of total mindlessness. The balance is restored when one realises its essentially consolatory function. Still, we now have an alternative to the earnestness of Henri's creative aspirations in a pleasurable atrophy of the intellect. We might now move on from the question of sensation and its verbal expression, to problems that are related to it, and arise from the experience of love. In particular, Jean Santeuil's love for Marie Kossichef has something of the intense emotion attributed to Honoré.

Before Marie's arrival, Jean is conscious of the ambiguous nature of his emotional state. A combination of enthusiasm and apprehension leaves him greatly confused:

Une immense agitation faisait trembler le coeur de Jean. Car ses espérances, mais mêlées aux craintes, étaient rentrées dans son coeur et l'agitaient en tous sens. L'une disait: 'Cela va recommencer', l'autre: 'Non, c'est fini.' Mme Santeuil avait dit: 'Il n'y aura personne aux Champs-Elysées.' La bonne: 'On ne sait pas.' (*JS*, p. 251.)

The succession of sharp, conflicting forecasts is especially effective in relaying Jean's turbulent emotional and mental state. The rapid convergence of these views captures that chaos. His anguish gains in intensity until finally the realisation that night is soon to fall overwhelms him. But as with Honoré's experience of 'l'oubli', a bodily form of release presents itself:

'La nuit.' Jean devint pâle à ces mots. Le jour allait donc finir sans qu'il l'ait vue [i.e., Marie]. Tout en regardant du côté d'où venaient les Kossichef, il se mit à jouer avec les autres et courait de toutes ses forces pour s'étourdir. (*JS*, p. 251.)

Vigorous physical exertion can thus dispel much of the mind's obsession. In particular, the use of 's'étourdir' connotes a numbing and deadening of preoccupation, and seems especially apposite. In its effect, it is analogous to Honoré's 'consolation suprême, l'oubli' (*JS*, p. 103).

The tie-up between Honoré and Jean has its importance. Granted, the former speaks of his difficulties as a creative writer, and specifically of the step from impression to lucid verbal expression. Jean's concerns, on the other hand, grow out of his love for Marie. But the almost philosophical doubting of the one and the amatory preoccupation of the other reveal a common hypersensitive character. What is more, the cares of both are dissipated in a bodily kind of ecstasy.

This link between the complexity of art and that of love is forged by Proust himself in a character portrait in *Les Plaisirs et les jours*. Nicole is the subject of this vignette, a delectable woman whose great beauty lies in the way in which she harmonises Nordic and Italian grace:

Aussi la plus petite fleur prend entre ses seins ou dans sa main, le compliment le plus banal prend dans sa bouche, l'acte le plus vulgaire, comme l'offre de son bras pour aller à table, prend, quand c'est elle qui l'accomplit, une grâce qui trouble à l'égal d'une émotion artistique. (*JS*, p. 166.)

It is revealing that a woman's enigmatic beauty should provoke such a response. The lack of transparency suggested by the use of *troubler*, is as reminiscent of the opacity of Honoré's diction (*JS*, p. 103) as it is of Jean's confused emotions as he awaits Marie (*JS*, p. 251). Accordingly, artistic intention and the pursuit of love are seen to prompt a similar kind of self-doubting. The most obvious illustration of love's onslaught in Proust's work concerns the Narrator's relationship with Albertine in the *Recherche*. But we get a foretaste of this in 'La Fin de la jalousie', where Honoré is torn by doubt and suspicion. His attempts to remedy this show some consistency with other means of escapism that I have already mentioned:

En vain le jour il avait marché, s'était fatigué à cheval, à bicyclette, aux armes, en vain il avait rencontré Françoise, l'avait ramenée chez elle, et, le soir, avait recueilli dans ses mains, à son front, sur ses yeux, la confiance, la paix, une douceur de miel, pour revenir chez lui encore calmé et riche de l'odorante provision. (*JS*, p. 153.)

One detects a measure of similarity with the language of the much later *La Prisonnière*. The images of nutritional sufficiency, for example, point forward to the mature work where Albertine's presence

remplissait ma demeure, jadis vide, d'une permanente provision de douceur domestique, presque familiale, rayonnant jusque dans les couloirs, et de laquelle tous mes sens, tantôt effectivement, tantôt, dans les moments où j'étais seul, en imagination et par l'attente du retour, se nourrissaient paisiblement. (III, 59.)

Other parallels are discernible. Being aware of the ephemeral nature of his happiness, Honoré is anxious to gain the world of sleep,

avant que fût altéré son bonheur qui, couché avec précaution dans tout le baume de cette tendresse récente et fraîche encore d'à peine une heure, parviendrait à travers la nuit, jusqu'au lendemain. (*JS*, p. 153.)

The idea of freezing and hence preserving this joy is close to the Narrator's desire for 'le silence sensitif où, comme grâce à quelque pédale, aurait pu survivre longtemps en moi la tonalité du bonheur' (II, 835).

In Honoré's attempts to insulate his reflective self against suspicion, one detects a preference for experience with a reassuring sense of plenitude. So, when he is desperately keen to banish from his mind the image that so graphically confirms his jealousy,

[il] lisait, s'efforçait, avec le sens des phrases qu'il lisait, d'emplir sans trêve et sans y laisser de vide son cerveau pour que l'affreuse image n'ait pas un moment ou un rien de place pour s'y glisser. (*JS*, p. 153.)

This ploy of crowding out all doubt is one especially common in *La Prisonnière*. We shall be seeing its varied use in Chapter 5.

For the present, however, it is useful to note these parallels in the treatment of the love experience. Clearly, the massive scale on which Proust was to present the Albertine/Narrator liaison is nowhere as great in *Les Plaisirs et les jours*. As to when the prisoner motif originated, Bonnet considers that it can be related directly to the death of Agostinelli in 1915. Professor Kolb, while prepared to go further back, still sees it as being no earlier than the first drafts of the *Recherche*.[15] Nonetheless, it is worth remembering that the language of emotional war and peace evident in *La Prisonnière* is already present in embryonic form in *Les Plaisirs et les jours*. And it is difficult not to think of the Narrator's happier days in *La Prisonnière* when reading evocations such as that of *dolce far niente* in *Jean Santeuil*.

That experience of undiluted sensual delight comes with the slow, lazy period of digestion enjoyed by the unhurried diner. This is the time when all preoccupations fade into oblivion, 'une sorte de temps d'arrêt, plein de douceur, de l'intelligence et de l'énergie, où rester sans rien faire nous donne le sentiment de la plénitude de la vie' (*JS*, p. 286). In a way that recalls the description of animal living (see above, section *c*), the reflective self is anaesthetised and existence assumes more pleasant, instinctual proportions. The narrator goes on to point out that all sadness and remorse are dispelled in this atmosphere of inviolable calm. The image of the pipe-smoker is particularly effective in reflecting an instinctual bliss. As he inhales the smoke of his pipe, 'il soulève doucement sa poitrine qui retombe et fait vibrer, en passant lentement d'une position à l'autre, les cordes les plus douces du bien-être' (*JS*, p. 287). Proust does not stop at evoking a vague harmony, but also strives to introduce a specifically musical frame of reference. As part of this, the soothing notes of the piano blend in with and enhance the listener's quietude:

Si le piano est trop loin, il l'écoute de sa place. Mais celui-là, c'est la mélodie qu'il charge de son bien-être et de lui donner le mouvement délicieux dont il est susceptible sans sortir de son repos. (*JS*, p. 288.)

It is particularly these musical analogies, of which there are several in '[Farniente après le repas]' that announce something of the more untroubled days of Albertine's captivity. Admittedly, the images in *Jean Santeuil* are somewhat precious and vague. A case in point is the mention of 'les cordes les plus douces du bien-être' (*JS*, p. 287), which lacks the precision and solidity of the more carefully forged images in *La Prisonnière*.[16] Nevertheless, the later metaphors have

their chrysalis stage in this early evocation of *dolce far niente*.
Moreover, the periods of Albertine's sleep, when all is motionless,
are not unlike the still of the room in this period of total indolence:

L'intermittent tambourinage [des mouches] fait sentir plus profondément
l'immobilité complète de la chambre où elles seulement bougent encore, le
silence qu'elles troublent seules et qui, dès qu'elles se taisent, est si uni qu'on
y descend pour ainsi dire jusqu'au fond. (*JS*, p. 1006: n. 3 to p. 294.)

Evidently, the fact that common images and themes can be found in
both works does not mean that Proust expressly sought to compare
dolce far niente with the Narrator's experience of Albertine's presence.
Such a claim would be excessive and dangerous. But what is
apparent is that the absence of reflective doubt in the 'temps d'arrêt
[...] de l'intelligence' (*JS*, p. 286) is like the ending of the Narrator's
anguish in tranquillity with Albertine. This confirms the observation made earlier that the primitive security of instinctual living may
be invoked to alleviate both intellectual and emotional burdens.

(h) *Les Plaisirs et les jours*: a check on instinctualism

Jean-Pierre Richard sees in *dolce far niente* 'le signe d'une conscience
devenue pur écho charnel' (*Proust et le monde sensible*, p. 18). But while
pointing to its presence in both *Jean Santeuil* and *A la recherche* he
contrasts the general tone of the respective works: 'Ce simple mais
profond plaisir de digérer s'indique discrètement dans la *Recherche*,
plus naïvement et presque impudiquement dans maint passage de
Jean Santeuil, livre plus archaïque, situé plus près du vécu d'enfance'
(*Ibid.*). His distinction is a largely valid one. Certainly, one can see in
much of the earlier work the unrepentant pleasure-seeking that the
critic is asserting. As we have seen, this is particularly true of the
enthusiasm for animal living.

One obvious factor in the lack of subtlety spoken of by Richard is
of course the form of *Jean Santeuil* itself. What we now treat as a
novel was little more than an experimental study for Proust.[17] It
should however be said that the unmitigated hedonism in much of
Jean Santeuil is not present in the early *Les Plaisirs et les jours*. This
runs contrary to Richard's thesis that the reliance on instinctualism in
Jean Santeuil is attributable to the artist's youth. For in *Les Plaisirs et
les jours*, already published in 1896, the tenor of many of the
epigraphs seems to counter the sensationalism of youth: from
Mallarmé, Proust cites 'La chair est triste, hélas' (*JS*, p. 15); from
Mme de Sévigné, 'Sa jeunesse lui fait du bruit, il n'entend pas' (*JS*,

30p. 17); from *Macbeth*, 'La vie n'est qu'une ombre errante [...] qui ne signifie rien' (*JS*, p. 22); and from Thomas à Kempis, he quotes an admonition that has itself been drawn from the Bible (1 Peter 1:24; cf. Isaiah 40: 6-7): 'Toute chair est comme l'herbe et sa gloire passe comme la fleur des champs' (*JS*, p. 30). These cells of didacticism seem designed to undermine any joyful experience being described in the main body of the text.

The case of Alexis, in 'La Mort de Baldassare Silvande', serves as a useful illustration of this. Having been preyed upon by his own hyperanxiety, he now finds himself escaping this in his pursuit of robust physical pastimes:

Les courses incessantes sur le cheval que son oncle lui avait donné, en développant ses forces, avaient lassé tout son énervement, et avivaient en lui ce sentiment continu de la bonne santé, qui s'ajoute alors à la jeunesse, comme la conscience obscure de la profondeur de ses ressources et de la puissance de son allégresse. (*JS*, p. 17.)

Alexis' situation is clearly very reminiscent of Jean's. Yet what Proust chooses to single out in Alexis is how his physical well-being leaves him insensitive to the suffering of his uncle Baldassare. By introducing a faint suggestion of moral condemnation, the author thus imbues the episode with a tonality quite foreign to the emphasis of self-gratification in *Jean Santeuil*.

Alexis était entré dans cette période ardente où le corps travaille si robustement à élever ses palais entre lui et l'âme qu'elle semble bientôt avoir disparu jusqu'au jour où la maladie ou le chagrin ont lentement miné la douloureuse fissure au bout de laquelle *elle* réapparaît. (*JS*, p. 17; Proust's italics.)

Here it is an omniscient author who sees not only the sensual concerns of vigorous, unthinking youth, but also the later, spiritual crisis that is to cloud these untroubled horizons. In the case of Jean, the intensity of present living excludes any such considerations. But the most striking aspect of the passage is the quite rigid demarcation between body and spirit – an unhesitating separation that even becomes a material, substantial partitioning.

Interestingly, the moral overtones in *Les Plaisirs et les jours* were what attracted Gide to it. He speaks of this aspect of the work most enthusiastically, lamenting its absence in Proust's later writings.[18] Before concluding his article, however, he expresses the hope that what is yet to be published of Proust's novel will fill this void. Looking back now, we might say that if the unduly heavy note of moralising in *Les Plaisirs et les jours* does not recur in the *Recherche*, the idea of life's passing returns forcefully towards the close of the novel.

Proust's writings before 1900 are not to be seen solely as preparation for the *magnum opus* of his mature years. Undoubtedly, early versions of episodes in the *Recherche* do exist. But there is other material that does not filter through. Gide's remark about the qualms of conscience so central to *Les Plaisirs et les jours* later 'disappearing' is largely true. Likewise, the open hymn of praise to animal existence sung by Jean is not heard in *A la recherche*. Where there is overlapping between the pre-1900 writing and the *Recherche*, the former may express quite directly its author's aims, given its less polished form. The more developed and subtle Proust's artistic intentions and outlook become, however, the less likely one is to find a blunt or oversimplified presentation of that growing intricacy. Still, the unfinished character of the early work seems particularly valuable to the present study, in so far as it affords useful insights into the young Proust's developing vision. The Jean/Henri de Réveillon antithesis, for example, is a much more forthright opposition than that between the Narrator and Saint-Loup in the *Recherche*. Equally, the early maxims reveal emphases that are not always so readily apparent in the *Recherche*. The following is a *locus classicus* of that naive frankness and clarity: 'Dès que nos idées philosophiques se sont assises, nous jouissons mieux des choses, car nous n'en cherchons plus le bien-fondé métaphysique' (*JS*, p. 747). The advantage of such a bold assertion is that it is not only lucid but also strikingly representative of the young Proust's thought.

This first chapter is not designed to challenge in any way the centrality of the *Recherche*. Its aim, on the contrary, is to capture the mood of the young Proust. As an eager though not always subtle writer, he is anxious to offer insights into the quality of Jean's experience. Often, he shows himself to be capable of controlling his narrative; the device of using the imaginary writers B. and C. in the preface is an illustration of this. Yet occasionally, Proust allows the third-person narrative to slip, and rushes into generalisations on human experience itself. There, it is as though the process of self-discovery is so novel and exhilarating that it must be conveyed in a more immediate way. Hence, I think, the occasional breakdown into first-person narrative in *Jean Santeuil*. And in such breakdown, one sees a recurrent notion, that of the problematic mind. Thus, characters become unwitting exponents of a sentient life – an idea perhaps to be striven after, and always offering solace to Proust's hypersensitive protagonists. We shall find that the preoccupations of the *Recherche* are of a similar complexion, although more developed and provoking more elaborate solutions.

2

Between *Jean Santeuil* and *A la recherche*

It would be extremely arbitrary to insist on a clearly definable gap existing between *Jean Santeuil* and the years of the *Recherche*. In the first instance, *Jean Santeuil* never had the rounded, completed character that publication would have conferred on it. The truth of the matter is that the creative drive for this early work simply petered out. The same indefiniteness can be applied to the beginning of *A la recherche*, which is impossible to date with any precision. One might best describe the genesis of the mature novel in terms of a slow fruition of ideas rather than a lightning flash of inspiration. And even when Proust's thinking on what is now the *Recherche* was well underway, he was perhaps still uncertain as to the form his work was to take (see below, Chapter 3*b*).

Once it has been realised that the ending of *Jean Santeuil* and the start of the *Recherche* are not sharply definable landmarks in Proust's writing career, we are in a better position to assess his other work round about the turn of the century. Rather than consciously abandoning *Jean Santeuil*, Proust is turning his attention at this point to other subjects, where the interests and concerns voiced in his novel still come to the surface. There is, however, the common fallacy that the period around 1900 was one of intellectual stagnation for Proust. Yet one has only to look at the number of reviews, articles and other publications in these years to see just how erroneous this is. Apart from his much publicised work on Ruskin, we have, for example, his several pastiches (written between 1900 and 1908), descriptions of society life in Paris, reviews of works by such writers as Anna de Noailles, Robert de Montesquiou and Henri de Régnier, and contributions on subjects of public debate at the time (see *CSB*, pp. 436–552). As well as that, there are the sketches for what Proust had envisaged as a study refuting Sainte-Beuve's literary criticism. He planned to counter his predecessor's methods by giving a practical illustration of what artistic writing should be.[1]

The aim of this short second chapter is to take those emphases which we have seen in *Jean Santeuil* and trace how they come to prominence in the writings of this transition period. Far from being unproductive, it is for Proust the novelist the time of fallow necessary for the later flowering of the *Recherche*.

(a)   The prominence of the material world in some early critical sketches

In the last chapter, we saw something of the diversity of being present in *Jean Santeuil*. In particular, it emerged that Jean was frequently captivated by a quality of living foreign to his own. Nor is it extravagant to say that Proust is already thinking in terms of different experiential possibilities. He himself defines the novelist's role as one of promoting this variety of feeling and situation. In a brief note dating from the *Jean Santeuil* years, the young Proust explains what he believes the novelist to be capable of:

Par lui, nous sommes Napoléon, Savonarole, un paysan, bien plus – existence que nous aurions pu ne jamais connaître – nous sommes nous-même. Il prête une voix à la foule, à la solitude, au vieil ecclésiastique, au sculpteur, à l'enfant, au cheval, à notre âme. Par lui nous sommes le véritable Protée. ('[Le Pouvoir du romancier]', *CSB*, p. 414.)

In this way, the writer opens up an endless versatility. Interestingly, it is a versatility that allows access to more than the situation of other people. 'La solitude' and 'le cheval' clearly transcend that category.

There is a faint suggestion here of the radical change in perspective brought about by dreams in the *Recherche*. The novel opens with the Narrator marvelling at how his own consciousness is transformed in the topsy-turvy world of sleep: 'Il me semblait que j'étais moi-même ce dont parlait l'ouvrage: une église, un quatuor, la rivalité de Francois Ier et de Charles-Quint' (I, 3). Admittedly, these surreal reversals bear little resemblance to the discursive, ordered manner in which Proust describes his Protean novelist. Yet in both, the direct identification of the self with an atmosphere or a building, for instance, is an indication of the imaginative potential in such a non-human field.

But for Proust, it is not only the novelist who is able to extend the horizons of the perceiving mind. Writing an appraisal of the painter Chardin in 1895, he refers to how one is reborn to the world, the freshness and life of which have been recaptured by the artist. Proust outlines his plans for this study in a letter to Pierre Mainguet:

J'essaye de montrer comment les grands peintres nous initient à la connaissance et à l'amour du monde extérieur, comment ils sont ceux 'par qui nos yeux sont déclos' et ouverts en effet sur le monde. (*Corr.*, vol. i, p. 446.)

In the case of Chardin, it is in his studies of still life that he effects this *déclôture* of one's own vision. At the beginning of his essay, Proust introduces a fictional character who is weary of the seemingly mediocre objects around him. The drab unexciting contents of the sideboard are an example of what is for him the 'banalité traditionnelle de ce spectacle inesthétique' (*CSB*, p. 372). Proust insists, however, that it is precisely this narrow limited view of aesthetics that Chardin's art seeks to dispel. For the latter, the terms commonplace and inanimate are without meaning. So the world of objects takes on prominence, and becomes increasingly alive in his work.

Les métaux et le grès s'animeront et les fruits parleront [. . .], la nature morte deviendra surtout la nature vivante. Comme la vie, elle aura toujours quelque chose de nouveau à vous dire, quelque prestige à faire luire, quelque mystère à révéler. (*CSB*, p. 374.)

Language itself, Proust sees, has enshrined the accepted view of the inert, unchanging aspect of the material world: hence his need to recast these words, endowing 'la nature vivante' with a vigour and animation that 'nature morte' inevitably stifles. Curiously enough, the English equivalent, 'still life', does manage to convey something of the vital qualities that Proust sees in Chardin's art. In fact, when published posthumously, the article was given the more apposite title: 'Chardin, ou le Coeur des choses'.[2] This captures the drift of Proust's interpretation, reflecting as it does the move away from an anthropocentric view of the world. For in Chardin, there exists an effacement of the lines of demarcation between subject and object. Replacing this is what Proust sees as a delightful interpenetration of people and things. His enthusiasm is unmistakable:

Comme entre êtres et choses qui vivent depuis longtemps ensemble avec simplicité, ayant besoin les uns des autres, goûtant aussi des plaisirs obscurs à se trouver les uns avec les autres, tout ici est amitié. (*CSB*, p. 379.)

The sense of uncomplicated interdependence that Proust evokes is especially significant. It announces a reassuring world, where a real, all-engaging friendship seems possible. Perhaps, indeed, this is the only 'amitié' that can be totally satisfying in the context of Proust's work overall.[3] Reinforcing this is the description of the warmth that this fusion generates in terms of 'des plaisirs obscurs'. It is as though 'êtres' and 'choses' communicate in some subterranean recess, not reached by the light of full human consciousness. Significantly, the image of darkness recurs in another reference to Chardin:

Chardin entre comme la lumière, donnant à chaque chose sa couleur, évoquant de la nuit éternelle où ils étaient ensevelis tous les êtres de la nature morte ou animée, avec la signification de sa forme si brillante pour le regard, si obscure pour l'esprit. (*CSB*, p. 374.)

However strong the visual impact of the still life is, it does, nevertheless, provoke the same 'dark' response in the mind. For in this twilight zone, replacing the day/night separation of conscious being and inanimacy, the thinking mind ceases to have an unchallenged awareness of itself. Rather it becomes largely subsumed into the homogenising world of 'la nature morte ou animée'. I shall be commenting again on this imagery of darkness in just a moment.

One of Proust's final remarks on Chardin recalls the 'amitié' that binds these seemingly different worlds together. Indeed, so inseparable are the animate and the inanimate that Proust announces, without equivocation, the 'mariage [. . .] entre les êtres et les choses, – entre le passé et la vie, – entre le clair et l'obscur' (*CSB*, p. 380). For him, the artist's achievement is to have awakened a greater sensitivity to the world of objects, which now acquire strangely vital qualities.

As for its relevance to Proust's main work, such an interest in the still life illustrates a fascination with the almost conscious existence that objects may assume. In fact, in the *Recherche* itself, the inanimate can come playfully and even magically to life, as the Narrator's creative imagination effects transformations in the material world that are no less radical than those introduced into the child's room by the magic lantern (see I, 9–10).[4] It is perhaps superfluous to say that in bringing about that metamorphosis, the Narrator of the *Recherche* is intellectually active. But there is some tension between this and Proust's response to Chardin, which invites us to envisage the thinking self as being scarcely more cognisant than the material world. What the essay suggests in other words is a diminishing consciousness of self, an emphasis that emerges largely unchanged in some preparatory sketches for the artist Elstir, in *A la recherche*. Speaking of the painter's uniqueness of vision, the Narrator sees as a distinguishing characteristic,

une sorte de répartition presque égale de la vie et de la pensée entre la nature qui devait [*sic*:=devenait] presque consciente et l'homme dont la conscience s'affaiblissait jusqu'à faire de lui quelque chose d'à peu près aussi passif que la nature. (*Cahier 28*, fo 3r.)[5]

It is obvious that Chardin's style of painting differs in some respects from Elstir's late or post-impressionism. Nevertheless, Proust's response to Chardin, and his Narrator's observations on Elstir reveal a strong similarity. For the concern with the 'conscient'/'inconscient' interplay in Elstir echoes the merging of traditional opposites in Chardin. Equally well, both appraisals reflect a fascination with the material world. The central position that these artists reserve for objects provokes no anguished cries of dehumanisation. On the contrary, such art serves the very positive function of reawakening our sensitivity to 'ce qu'il y a de plus profond dans les choses' (*CSB*, p. 381).

It is a fair sign of Proust's interest in this question that it should encroach on his preface to the translation of Ruskin's *Sesame and Lilies*. This appeared in 1906, although the preface had already been published, with some variations, in *La Renaissance latine* of 15 June 1905.[6] Even more so than the notes that he intercalated in Ruskin's text, the preface is really a statement of Proust's own emerging ideas, and references to the English author become almost incidental. Indeed, with its recall of childhood and the favourite occupation of reading, the preface may be seen as an early draft for some of the later *Recherche*.[7]

At one point in the preface, Proust discusses the intrinsic value of the objects in his room. In doing so, he singles out the theories of William Morris as running contrary to this view. To oversimplify, as indeed Proust himself does on this occasion, the latter's aesthetics is based on a utilitarian conception of the material world. Decoration becomes totally functional, and beauty is dependent on this principle of use. Proust's response to Morris' credo is interesting, especially when seen in conjunction with his earlier attraction to Chardin:

A la juger d'après les principes de cette esthétique, ma chambre n'était nullement belle, car elle était pleine de choses qui ne pouvaient servir à rien et qui dissimulaient pudiquement, jusqu'à en rendre l'usage extrêmement difficile, celles qui servaient à quelque chose. (*CSB*, p. 164.)

This represents a shift away from the notion that objects have a purely implemental role to play. In addition, Proust's use of 'pudiquement' even suggests a horror that objects should cease to exist in themselves and become prostituted to function. For him, they are not to be seen as mere extensions to man. Rather, they are to enjoy an independent and, to the human eye, mysterious existence of their own. And it is precisely their power to fascinate that may heighten one's aesthetic enjoyment, Proust speculates: 'Mais c'est justement de ces choses qui n'étaient pas là pour ma commodité, mais semblaient y être venues pour leur plaisir, que ma chambre tirait pour moi sa beauté' (*CSB*, p. 164). In Proust's assessment of the world of objects, there is an implied rejection of the subservience that Morris might impose on them; in a new independence, the material world becomes as alive and self-asserting as humans themselves.

Occasionally for Proust, however, it is not just a question of levelling out the conscious and the unconscious, as was the case with Elstir. One senses, for example, that the growing prominence of objects in his room may be challenging the position of his own conscious self. This overshadowing movement is implicit when he ventures to say that these things had the effect of filling his room 'd'un mystère où ma personne se trouvait à la fois perdue et charmée' (*CSB*, p. 166). The move away from an anthropocentric world brings with it a confusion of otherwise clearly defined roles. The position of the 'moi', for example, is ambiguous here, a fact which is visible in the somewhat paradoxical combination of 'perdue' and 'charmée'. For these epithets imply both a presence and an absence of the person. The self is, as it were, remote, eclipsed, and yet at the same time pleasurably aware of its immersion in the 'vie silencieuse et diverse'. This tension in language itself helps reflect the writer's own sense of being delicately balanced between the spiritual and material worlds.

The experience of the inanimate may have an additional value here, namely that of stimulating imaginative creativity. To some extent, this is reminiscent of Jean Santeuil's almost vested interest in studying forms of consciousness unlike his own (see above, Chapter 1). But whereas that involved an inter-relationship with people – and occasionally a consideration of animal awareness – the imaginative leap in the preface to Ruskin is somewhat more spectacular:

Pour moi, je ne me sens vivre et penser que dans une chambre où tout est la création et le langage de vies profondément différentes de la mienne, d'un goût opposé au mien, où je ne retrouve rien de ma pensée consciente, où mon imagination s'exalte en se sentant plongée au sein du non-moi. (*CSB*, p. 167.)

Proust energetically bridges the gap between his own thinking self and the intriguing quality of existence that he sees the room as enjoying. What seems particularly striking is that the desire to escape individual thought is stated quite as explicitly as it is.

Nevertheless, this retreat from consciousness is not an isolated instance in Proust's work, and an examination of some *brouillons* for the *Recherche* in the following section will reveal a parallel tendency. On a broadly similar note, it should be said that the effacement of the individual self in 'le non-moi' is an extension of the ideas voiced in the Chardin study. The centrality of the material world in the still-life paintings, together with the increasingly obscure role of the thinking mind, are precursors of the notions contained in the preface to Ruskin. And while both suggest a movement away from selfhood, it is not towards a different quality of being as seen in others. Rather, they involve the, in some ways, more exhilarating adventure into the world of matter made animate.

(b)   Sleep as a partial escape from selfhood

We have seen that Proust's criticism and translation of Ruskin are accompanied by budding ideas for his novel. In fact, one might see this work on the English art critic as a stone on which Proust may grind his own axe; not long after this, in about 1908, we find him making his first tentative drafts for what was to become his mature novel. These again reveal an author intent on exploring the world of objects.

This time, it is in studying the subliminal zone between sleep and consciousness that he develops his ideas on the inanimate. The frequent reworkings of the sleep motif in his manuscripts indicate how Proust considered its implications with some care. The seven preparatory *Cahiers*, now classified as containing the *Contre Sainte-Beuve* material proper, have multiple developments on 'le sommeil'.[8] Some of these have been published in Bernard de Fallois' *Contre Sainte-Beuve* (*CSB/NM*), but not however in the corresponding Pléïade edition. To that extent, the former volume shows how Proust was shaping important developments for the *Recherche* in 1908–9.

Admittedly, many of these descriptions are virtually indistinguishable from the first pages of the novel. But in other respects, there are some intriguing modifications. One view of sleep expressed in an early *Cahier* recalls the warmth of 'le non-moi' in the preface to *Sésame et les lys*. 'Mon sommeil', the Narrator reflects, 'n'était qu'une sorte de communion avec l'obscurité de ma chambre et à la vie inconsciente de s[es] murs et de ses meubles' (*Cahier 5*, fo 113*v*).

The darkness referred to is a twofold one, for not only is the room without physical light, but the Narrator also senses the psychic night engulfing the lucid conscious self. This second dimension is confirmed in another version, which varies slightly from that just quoted: 'Le plus souvent, je dormais à peu près aussi obscurément que pouvaient faire le lit, les fauteuils, toute la chambre' (*CSB/NM*, p. 68). The close identification with the room's furnishings points to a doubly unreflecting Narrator, without mind, without light.

Generally, one detects in the opening pages of the *Recherche* an almost identical fascination with the world of sleep. For the Narrator, it is the liberation from full consciousness that excites him, an idea that Proust again conveys by exploiting this dual register of the darkness motif:

J'étais bien étonné de trouver autour de moi une obscurité, douce et reposante pour mes yeux, mais peut-être plus encore pour mon esprit, à qui elle apparaissait comme une chose sans cause, incompréhensible, comme une chose vraiment obscure. (I, 3.)

The gentle anaesthetisation of the mind becomes an immeasurable boon for the Narrator. Ceasing to feel reality and the world comes to represent some ideal experience or, perhaps more accurately, a non-experience. He is oblivious to the origin and nature of the 'obscurité'. For him, it is somehow self-evident, beyond the confines of causation and intellectual justification. In so far as this is the case, it is remarkably similar to the language used to describe Jean Santeuil's rapturous contact with the ubiquitous wind: '[la] douceur [du vent], elle semble sans cause [. . .], ce bruit que n'accompagnait l'idée d'aucune cause' (*JS*, p. 532).

In the case of both Jean and the Narrator, the beauty of such experience seems enhanced precisely because it pre-empts any deliberation of the questioning self. Now, we have already seen how Jean reacts to a steady intellectual dissection of lived experience (Chapter 1). His anguish at excessive analysis of feeling foreshadows the troubled mental world of the Narrator, to which I shall be turning presently. It is equally true of both characters that a primitive awareness of existence is a pleasant alternative to intellectual crisis.

But for Proust himself, to convey verbally the virtual absence of consciousness in sleep will make great demands on language itself. The writer will often stretch its resources to the limit in an effort to capture a state that, by its very nature, outgrows the normal constraints of any linguistic system. A good illustration of this occurs in Fallois' chapter '[Chambres]', where the Narrator awakens to imagine himself as being no more aware than objects in the kitchen:

Je n'étais dans ces courts réveils-là que ce que seraient une pomme ou un pot de confiture, qui, sur la planche où ils sont placés, seraient appelés un instant à une vague conscience, et qui, ayant constaté qu'il fait noir dans le buffet et que le bois joue, n'auraient rien de plus pressé que de retourner à la délicieuse insensibilité des autres pommes et des autres pots de confiture. (*CSB/NM*, p. 68.)

His almost complete merging with an apple or a jam-pot is immensely appealing to the Narrator. Yet the equivalence of Narrator and humble kitchen objects is never quite total, something reflected in the use of 'la délicieuse insensibilité'. Were he in a state of complete unfeeling, the Narrator would be incapable of the strong sensual enjoyment that the choice of 'délicieuse' implies. In this way, a verbal tension reflects the ambivalence of his own feelings. He does not achieve, nor indeed does he appear to desire, a full abdication of his individual self. Rather, he hovers in this twilight zone of 'vague conscience', an area of transition allowing him to sense the primal, remote experience. It is mildly paradoxical that his being is both present and absent, preserved and yet transcended in this partial absorption of the self into 'thingness'. To that extent, the reference in *Sésame et les lys* to 'ma personne se trouvait à la fois perdue et charmée' (*CSB*, p. 166) is analogous to the two-way pull of 'la délicieuse insensibilité'. It is as though awareness is thrown into a chiaroscuro world of faint consciousness.

Although most of the sleep passages in *Cahiers* 1–7 find their way into the *Recherche*, the images of the pantry and its contents form a notable exception. When in the novel the Narrator expresses a longing for the insensitivity of the material world, it is worth noting that Proust does not repeat the 'délicieuse insensibilité'. This is so even though the Narrator still speaks of 'le tout dont je n'étais qu'une petite partie et à l'insensibilité duquel je retournais vite m'unir' (I, 4). The omission is perhaps all the more interesting when one considers that Proust uses the same wording on at least three occasions in the early *Cahiers*.[9] Proust himself, therefore, may have been aware of what on one level could be seen as a contradiction in terms. Against this, however, it might well be argued that, on the threshold of the world of sleep, the total distortion of normal conscious perspective cannot be conveyed without a degree of linguistic improvisation.

In the light of this, it is perhaps informative to point to a parallel phenomenon in D. H. Lawrence, particularly in his *Women in Love*. In some respects, the frame of reference is quite different from Proust's. More specifically, while Proust explores the individual self's descent into the unconsciousness of sleep, Lawrence uses a comparable vocabulary, this time in an attempt to capture something of the mysterious union between man and woman. For Ursula, her intercourse with Birkin opens up for her, 'the reality of that which can never be known, vital, sensual reality that can never be transmuted into mind content, but remains outside, living body of darkness and silence and subtlety'.[10] The superfluous role of the reflecting mind clearly recalls Proust's Narrator searching for 'la vie inconsciente' about him (*Cahier 5*, fo 113v). As well as this, the image of obscurity, designed to harmonise with the idea of a plunge into some mysterious realm, is familiar to the reader of Proust. It recurs slightly later in the text, when the lovers attempt to escape their knowing, conscious selves: 'It was so magnificent, such an inheritance of a universe of dark reality, that they were afraid to seem to remember. They hid away the remembrance and the knowledge' (*Women in Love*, p. 361). But Lawrence, too, is aware of the restrictions of language in his evocation of such experience. Like Proust, he does not hesitate to introduce seemingly paradoxical verbal forms, in an effort to convey the sloughing of the individual, reflective self. Yet in Lawrence, the challenge of this paradox is perhaps more blatant, in what becomes a kind of linguistic somersaulting: 'She must lightly, mindlessly connect with him, have the knowledge which is death of knowledge, the reality of surety in not knowing' (*Women in Love*, p. 359).

Nevertheless, close scrutiny of Proust's diction, and in particular the case of the 'délicieuse insensibilité' reference, tends to suggest a similar awareness of language's rigidity, and a need for a more malleable, plastic form. We might for a moment consider what a contemporary critic sees as Lawrence's difficulty in getting beyond the dualism of traditional Western thought. Her comments would seem equally relevant to Proust: 'Lawrence's attempts to depart from a dualistic view of man's nature meet resistance from the conservatism inherent in language itself.'[11] The critic's observation on language is most perceptive. In judging it to be conservative, she is showing how linguistic structures may lag behind intimate feeling and perception. Although this inefficiency does not preclude experience, it makes its verbal communication a frustrating exercise. This is an impotence that Proust's own characters do not escape. One has only to look at the celebrated 'Zut, zut, zut, zut' cries of *Du côté de chez Swann* to see this crisis of language (I, 155). But that particular episode falls more within the scope of my next chapter.

As for Elizabeth Tenenbaum's allusion to dualism as a kind of exile for Lawrence, it is clear from what we have seen of Proust's own writing in this chapter that he too is anxious to get beyond a matter/spirit dichotomy. There is the deliberation on Chardin's 'mariage entre les êtres et les choses'; the writer's desire to penetrate 'au sein du non-moi' in the *Sésame* preface; and the Narrator's will to coalesce with the inanimate objects that surround him as he sleeps. Each of these particular emphases confirms the move towards a more monistic view of life, whereby individual consciousness tends to merge with the material world. The old dualities of the 'moi' and the universe, internal and external, animate and inanimate, are broken down.

There remains the question of the Narrator's eagerness to escape from full consciousness. Evidently, there is an element of keen sensual delight in his enjoyment of the slumbering jam-pots. Yet one sees an interesting dimension to the experience of sleep in what is a revealing manuscript passage:

Suivant le conseil que m'avait donné le médecin souvent j'essayais de dormir un peu dans la journée et aussi parce que j'aimais à me plonger dans cette fontaine translucide, profonde du sommeil, d'où l'on ne sort qu'enveloppé d'une sorte de lustre, de vernis imperméable pour quelques instants encore aux impressions douloureuses dehors. (*Cahier 50*, fo 58.)[12]

Thus, sleep may act as a very real palliative for the Narrator. To that extent, images of its durable, resplendent qualities may not only captivate him, but simultaneously form a buffer to the harsh reality of conscious being. The same is true of the Narrator's relationship with Albertine. Nowhere is existence more problematical for him and yet there too, sleep affords gentle release. Marvelling at how the aspect of things is transformed in his dreams, he remembers

les matins où cette fortune [i.e., le rêve] m'était advenue, où le coup d'éponge du sommeil avait effacé de mon cerveau les signes des occupations quotidiennes qui y sont tracés comme sur un tableau noir. (III, 121.)

The purging of doubt follows on, then, from sleep's destruction of the world.[13]

In his important first *Carnet*, Proust is aware of the potential existing in a state of insensitivity. The editor of that document, Professor Kolb, explains the use Proust made of it: 'A cette espèce de grimoire qu'est le *Carnet de 1908*, il n'a confié que ses pensées les plus intimes' (p. 29). Certainly, the reference that I am to quote has all the appearances of an obscure, not easily decipherable image:

Mais dans les moments où on a besoin de se verser dans l'âme du potage chaud, visite Parent – Montargis qu'on ne savait pas à Paris comme gaie lampe. (*Le Carnet de 1908*, p. 99.)

The editor's note explains that the arrival of Montargis (later to be known as Saint-Loup) comes as a great uplift to the Narrator, who is despondent that Mme de Stermaria should decline his invitation to dinner (II, 395). But what requires further elucidation is the allusion to the 'besoin de se verser dans l'âme du potage chaud'. When interpreted in the light of other references in this chapter, it becomes meaningful and of direct relevance to this study. I have already considered the idea of an immersion in something outside the self. Even more revealing, perhaps, is the need and urgency of this movement. For the Narrator, the great imperative again is to elude his individual consciousness. Moreover, the plurality of 'les moments' confirms the recurrence of the emotion.

But it is surely the expression 'l'âme du potage chaud' that is most enigmatic. The very fact of endowing food with a soul would seem incongruous. One possible interpretation might be to take the phrase on the level of synecdoche. This would imply that what the Narrator longs for is the untroubled atmosphere of meals in the company of friends. After all, he had anticipated that his evening at the restaurant with Mme de Stermaria would be idyllically carefree (II, 382–6). And on the same occasion, he recalls 'le flamboiement de Rivebelle', nights of pleasurable dining with Saint-Loup and his colleagues in that garrison town (II, 390).

Perhaps, however, this is another case of language proving inadequate in the conveying of intense emotion. Seen in this light, 'l'âme du potage chaud' comes into the same category as the reference to 'la délicieuse insensibilité des autres pommes et des autres pots de confiture' (*CSB/NM*, p. 68). Clearly, the degree of animism in 'l'âme du potage chaud' is absent from the latter reference. But this can be explained by their separate contexts. The second of the two images is geared to capturing the sense of unfeeling in sleep. The greater fluidity and movement of the 'potage', on the other hand, conveys the Narrator's search for a warmth and vitality outside of himself. Yet in spite of their different applications, these images are, in one fundamental respect, very similar. Their sameness is that each suggests a diminishing consciousness of self in the Narrator.

Yet it would be misleading to say that the world of sleep offers pleasurable associations unfailingly to the Narrator. Occasionally one finds a less emotive description of the state, in place of the language of eager immersion. An example of this almost factual tone occurs at the beginning of the *Recherche*: 'J'avais seulement dans sa simplicité première le sentiment de l'existence comme il peut frémir au fond d'un animal' (I, 5). So the experience of awakening is given this elemental character, yet with no visible reference being made to its desirability or necessity. The same is true of the way in which the Narrator records the effect of oversleeping, this time in *La*

Prisonnière. Nevertheless, the atrophy of human consciousness is still unmistakable:

On a trop dormi, on n'est plus. Le réveil est à peine senti mécaniquement, et sans conscience, comme peut l'être dans un tuyau la fermeture d'un robinet. Une vie plus inanimée que celle de la méduse succède, où l'on croirait aussi bien qu'on est tiré du fond des mers ou revenu du bagne, si seulement l'on pouvait penser quelque chose. (III, 123.)

We have here different gradations of the inanimate, with the images of the water pipe and the jellyfish bringing interesting nuances of unconsciousness into the evocation. But again, the description is more neutral and unemotive than others we have seen. Even then, incidentally, Proust continues to be scrupulous about language, insisting how, in this unthinking state, *croire* is a frank intruder.

To conclude briefly, one might say that sleep is always a pleasant non-activity for the Narrator. Often it seems to him a delectable haven from the mind. But to imply from this that he relentlessly strives after a state of mindlessness would be overstating the point, clearly; the mood would appear a much more intermittent one. Besides, he realises that escape from individual consciousness into sleep is never quite total. Vestiges of the self linger on – and, paradoxically, it is this very residue of selfhood that enables the Narrator to savour the experience. Indeed, this intermediate zone of faint cognisance frequently engages Proust's imagination to the full. We might now move on to see how, for the hypersensitive Narrator of *A la recherche*, there exist alternatives to the overshadowing of the conscious mind.

3

The Narrator's Childhood and Adolescence: Formative Influences

(a)   Early seriousness and adult irony

In Proust's work, one senses occasionally that the mind's activity can be menacing. But it would be a distortion to suggest that the menace is constant and unrelenting, and gross misrepresentation to say that in the *Recherche* intellectual life is intrinsically problematical. Behind so many descriptions of the young Narrator's sometimes muddled experience, one finds a teasing and often confident mature Narrator. Expressions of naive adolescent doubt are often tempered, however subtly, by adult perspicacity. In the overlapping of narrative voices, therefore, questions of tone become all important.

With the young Narrator's first trip to Balbec, the reader becomes immediately conscious of his appetite for novelty and adventure. Symptomatic of this is the attention he heaps upon an anonymous milkmaid who makes a brief appearance at one of the railway stations. For him, the encounter offers an exciting release from sterile abstraction and theorising, and prompts agreeable speculation:

La vie m'aurait paru délicieuse si seulement j'avais pu, heure par heure, la passer avec elle, l'accompagner jusqu'au torrent, jusqu'à la vache, jusqu'au train, être toujours à ses côtés, me sentir connu d'elle, ayant ma place dans sa pensée. Elle m'aurait initié aux charmes de la vie rustique et des premières heures du jour. (I, 656–7.)

His response to this host of different activities is unequivocal. Their worth would seem to be guaranteed. But for the mature Narrator, now distanced from the experience of a former self, the evocation of life with the milkmaid is suffused with irony and humour. This is clear from the unusually dizzying activity that the neophyte sees as coming with initiation. The original manuscript description is, intentionally or otherwise, even more cruel in its irony, for in addition to going with the peasant to milk the animals, the Narrator even imagines the possibility of 'peut-être courir avec elle dans les bois au–dessus desquels j'avais vu le ciel rouge'.[1] In view of his more normal sedentary existence, the prospect of the Narrator engaging in such vigorous physical activity can only produce a bizarre and comic effect. The humour of this easy and instant solution to life's problems intensifies when one remembers the web of doubt and procrastination that entangles so many of the Narrator's activities.

But if his athleticism never becomes actual, the loss is hardly a sore one for an older and wiser Narrator who on one particular occasion treats so mockingly the sporting potential of Mme de Surgis' son, Arnulphe. The range of the latter's outdoor activities is not enough to fend off the Narrator's ruthless irony:

Arnulphe, avec une voix zézayante qui semblait indiquer que son développement, au moins mental, n'était pas complet répondait à M. de Charlus avec une précision complaisante et naïve: 'Oh! moi, c'est plutôt le golf, le tennis, le ballon, la course à pied, surtout le polo.' Telle Minerve, s'étant subdivisée, avait cessé, dans certaine cité, d'être la déesse de la Sagesse et avait incarné une part d'elle-même en une divinité purement sportive, hippique, 'Athénè Hippia'. Et il allait aussi à Saint-Moritz faire du ski, car Pallas Tritogeneia fréquente les hauts sommets et rattrape les cavaliers. 'Ah!' répondit M. de Charlus, avec le sourire transcendant de l'intellectuel. (II, 703–4.)

If the Narrator himself is not directly involved in the conversation, it seems fair to say that Charlus, with his own tendency to intellectualise, helps accentuate Arnulphe's empty-headedness. Clearly, the discrepancy between the cerebral Charlus and the idiotic sportsman is so essential to the humour. The burlesque mythologising, with the young man being elevated to the position of 'une divinité purement sportive, hippique', crowns his ridiculousness. Indeed, the whole elaborate depiction, with fanciful speculation about Minerva's metamorphosis, deflates Arnulphe all the more. In him, the total absence of reflective being provides a rich source of irony.

There can be no doubting the hilarious tone of the character portrait. In the extravagant idea that Minerva and mind itself might be subverted, one sees an intellectually playful Narrator in full flight. He reveals the same self-indulgence in lampooning the academic Brichot, who is not the light years removed from the clown-like Arnulphe one might expect. The don's invective against the Symbolists is predictable and unsubtle:

'Nous en avons trop vu de ces intellectuels adorant l'Art, avec un grand A, et qui, quand il ne leur suffit plus de salcooliser avec du Zola, se font des piqûres de Verlaine. Devenus éthéromanes par dévotion baudelairienne, ils ne seraient plus capables de l'effort viril que la patrie peut un jour ou l'autre leur demander, anesthésiés qu'ils sont par la grande névrose littéraire, dans l'atmosphère chaude, énervante, lourde de relents malsains, d'un symbolisme de fumerie d'opium.' (II, 956.)

A strong element of caricature is readily visible here. In this and in the Narrator's dismissal of Brichot's 'couplet inepte et bigarré' (*ibid.*) one has clear confirmation of the hero's own literary taste. What linked the self-parodic evocation of life with the milkmaid to the Arnulphe portrayal was a common reliance on an intellectual/sentient split. Now with Brichot, the terms of reference do shift somewhat, although again a movement away from complex imaginative activity is essentially what he is advocating. In all three cases, the Narrator's treatment is ironical and playfully irreverent.

In the *Recherche*, nevertheless, the treatment of such themes does reveal crucial variations in tone. Irony may give way to a more serious, even solemn note in the narrative. In the case of Brichot, the Narrator shows scant respect for his opposition between 'l'effort viril' of patriots and 'la grande névrose littéraire'. Later in this chapter, however, I shall be examining the role of the Narrator's grandmother. In so many of her recommendations to her grandson, the language is ostensibly similar to that in Brichot's tirade. But the Narrator conveys her comments on art and artists in a sympathetic and at times reverential manner. She too wants to outlaw Baudelaire and Verlaine. But lying behind her censure is the hope – laudable to the Narrator – that his exacting sensitivity might be calmed. As such, her aspirations are demonstrably different from those of the witch-hunting Brichot, whose condemnation of Symbolism is exposed for the bigotry in art that it is. The Narrator can then exercise a conscious seriousness as well as merciless irony in his character portrayals. Similarly, Arnulphe is ludicrous but the sporting life does not invariably provoke the Narrator's scorn. Looking at the 'jeunes filles' of Balbec in Chapter 4, I shall consider his fascination with a quality of life that is tantalisingly different from his own. The awe that these girls inspire leaves much less room for the kind of waggish treatment shown Arnulphe.

In discussing the *Recherche*, one has to bear in mind both the ironical and the serious treatments that Proust gives to a central theme – the meeting of the tortured, imaginative sensibility with a simpler, more primitive one. Certainly that tonal variation will emerge in what follows. But before concluding this section, we might look at some perceptive comments that Proust makes on the question of 'le sérieux':

Un ouvrage même qui ne s'applique qu'à des sujets qui ne sont pas intellectuels est encore une oeuvre de l'intelligence et pour donner dans un livre ou dans une causerie qui en diffère peu, l'impression achevée de la frivolité, il faut encore une dose de sérieux dont une personne purement frivole eût été incapable. (*Cahier 44*, fo 4.)[2]

What this manuscript extract highlights is that the writer should be familiar with both sides of the 'frivole'/'sérieux' coin. His then becomes an essentially dual perspective, affording him contact with the non-intellectual and yet allowing him ultimately to transcend it. Yet as the following section will show, the adolescent Narrator does not enjoy that discernment and clearness of understanding.

(b)   The philosophical preoccupation of the adolescent Narrator

Proust's reticence about theorising on his novel is evident from the relatively small amount of material available outside of the *Recherche* itself. Perhaps the best example is the Elie-Joseph Bois 'interview' in 1913.[3] This was followed by the publication of a dialogue with André Arnyvelde in *Le Miroir* (21 December 1913). Critics' frequent reference to these publications is evidence of the precious little material made available to the public.

Given this paucity of information, Proust's first *Carnet* assumes a very real importance. The beauty of *Le Carnet de 1908* is that it allows the critic to penetrate the intimate world of Proust's creative process. Not surprisingly, one finds glimpses of the writer's hesitation and doubt, as well as ideas on his work's evolution and structure. One particularly revealing moment of uncertainty occurs when Proust poses some fundamental questions on the nature of his writing: 'La paresse ou le doute ou l'impuissance se réfugiant dans l'incertitude sur la forme d'art. Faut-il en faire un roman, une étude philosophique, suis-je romancier?' (*Le Carnet de 1908*, p. 61). The significance of this is that it opens up the perspective of Proust embarking on a project, the outcome of which he is not sure of at the inception. His uncertainty concerns the very form the work of art is to take. Allowing for the extremely condensed references of the *Carnet*, one wonders just what is to be understood by the allusion to 'une étude philosophique'. Clearly if the work is to remain artistic in form, this will exclude any rigid philosophical system. But in an attempt to elucidate the philosophical study that he mentions somewhat elusively, it would be profitable to correlate the text of the *Carnet* with that of the *Recherche* itself.

The self-questioning of the young Narrator is a notable feature of Proust's novel. Indeed the different expressions that this self-doubt takes can sometimes go to make up the stuff of the work itself. J. M. Cocking is making a similar point when he observes that 'Proust's intellectual curiosity was as persistent as his aesthetic sensibility was delicate, and the speculations of his intelligence were not, as Baudelaire's, carried on outside the work of art but as part of its very substance.'[4] Where this is the case in *A la recherche* one finds an occasional echo of Proust's own probing in *Le Carnet de 1908*. As he considers the possibility of creative writing, for example, the Narrator is confronted with what he sees as his lack of artistic vocation:

Puisque je voulais un jour être un écrivain, il était temps de savoir ce que je comptais écrire. Mais dès que je me le demandais, tâchant de trouver un sujet où je pusse faire tenir une signification philosophique infinie, mon esprit s'arrêtait de fonctionner, je ne voyais plus que le vide en face de mon attention, je sentais que je n'avais pas de génie ou peut-être une maladie cérébrale l'empêchait de naître. (I, 172–3.)

It is worth noting that, as with the reference from *Le Carnet de 1908*, the Narrator sees his future work as having a decidedly philosophical bent. Again, however, one is uncertain as to what exactly 'une signification philosophique infinie' entails, other than that it remains an artistic prerequisite in the eyes of the Narrator. We do, nevertheless, get a very concrete indication of what is implied, as the Narrator continues to reflect dolefully on his lack of creative flair:

Alors, bien en dehors de toutes ces préoccupations littéraires et ne s'y rattachant en rien, tout d'un coup un toit, un reflet de soleil sur une pierre, l'odeur d'un chemin me faisaient arrêter par un plaisir particulier qu'ils me donnaient [...]. [Ces impressions] étaient toujours liées à un objet particulier dépourvu de valeur intellectuelle et ne se rapportant à aucune vérité abstraite. Mais du moins elles me donnaient un plaisir irraisonné, l'illusion d'une sorte de fécondité et par là me distrayaient de l'ennui, du sentiment de mon impuissance que j'avais éprouvés chaque fois que j'avais cherché un sujet philosophique pour une grande oeuvre littéraire. (I, 178–9.)

Clearly, the Narrator is setting the idea of a philosophical subject against what he believes to be its antonyms, 'un objet particulier dépourvu de valeur intellectuelle [...], un plaisir irraisonné'. From this series of oppositions, one can discern a parallel between the philosophical and what are intellectual and abstract truths. The latter would seem diametrically opposed to random sense-impressions. For the young Narrator, the ideal experience – and hence the one destined for the work of art – requires a conceptual framework. This accounts for the way in which he dismisses his own feelings and perceptions as being ultimately unsuitable for the great literary opus that he envisages.

In the overall context of *A la recherche*, one can quickly see the irony of this position, since what the young Narrator now disparages is to play a vital role in *Le Temps retrouvé*. There, the seemingly fortuitous accumulation of sense-impressions is central to the Narrator's growing awareness of a privileged state of extra-temporality.[5] But the evidence of *Du côté de chez Swann* tends to confirm the reverential manner in which the adolescent Narrator conceives of the philosophical. His view that it should be exclusively conceptual makes it all the more inaccessible to him.

It is a similar kind of almost exaggerated respect that dictates the Narrator's response to what is, in the context of Proust's work, the celebrated line of Racine 'La fille de Minos et de Pasiphaé'. In Chapter 1, I examined Jean Santeuil's enthusiasm for its non-conceptual appeal, and also referred briefly to an early version of *Du côté de chez Swann*, where the Narrator spoke of the line's enigmatic beauty (Chapter 1*f*). On closer analysis, one can see how this text has a direct bearing on the present question of the Narrator's philosophical preoccupation:

Je me rappelle mes angoisses en me promenant dans les champs du côté de Méséglise parce qu'on m'avait dit que pour Théophile Gautier le plus beau vers de Racine était 'La fille de Minos et de Pasiphaé'. Je ne pouvais alors laisser à l'art – bien au-dessous de la philosophie – quelque dignité qu'à condition qu'il contînt quelque grande idée. Que ce vers de Racine, que certains vers de Leconte de Lisle fussent plus beaux que des vers philosophiques de Sully Prudhomme, cela me troublait d'autant plus profondément que cette beauté que je ne pouvais légitimer je la ressentais. Moi qui aujourd'hui – pour de toutes autres raisons que Théophile Gautier – n'attache presque aucune importance au contenu intellectuel explicite d'une oeuvre d'art. Mais le temps n'était pas encore venu où je devais rencontrer l'idée de l'art que je me faisais aujourd'hui et que j'avais encore à passer par bien des chemins avant d'y arriver.[6]

One of the most striking revelations in this aesthetic judgement is the relegation of art to a position much inferior to that enjoyed by philosophy. The latter is for the young Narrator a much more imposing human achievement, and he feels as a result that the inclusion of concepts and ideas can only enhance the work of art. But on this occasion the Narrator's observation has even more important repercussions. For he introduces a double perspective, set neatly on the temporal opposition of 'alors' and 'aujourd'hui', showing not only his fascination with the philosophical, but also his subsequent reappraisal and upgrading of his own art. In some respects, this anticipates the process of self-realisation in art at the end of the *Recherche*. Yet the Narrator concedes how complicated this evolution of thought is, and his insistence on the need to 'passer par bien des chemins avant d'y arriver', is reflected in the wealth of tentative probing evident in *Du côté de chez Swann*.

Moving on from the early draft of the *Swann* text, one finds that in the definitive version it is Bloch who confounds the Narrator with his reference to the Racine line. Here the experience appears especially perplexing for a Narrator who is fired by the lofty ideal of 'la révélation de la vérité' (I, 91) and yet is simultaneously haunted by his own spiritual impoverishment. When Bloch introduces him to the work of Bergotte, the Narrator responds in a similar ambiguous way. One senses a strong note of idolatry in his admiration for the writer, and a concomitant self-deprecation.

Nevertheless, the surprise of finding an echo of his own thoughts in his reading of Bergotte helps bridge the gap between their opposite worlds: 'Il me sembla soudain que mon humble vie et les royaumes du vrai n'étaient pas aussi séparés que j'avais crus, qu'ils coïncidaient même sur certains points' (I, 96). Evidently, the grandiosity of 'les royaumes du vrai' derives to some extent from the irony of the mature Narrator's standpoint. Yet that makes the adolescent's preoccupation no less real, and he continues to languish in awe of what he sees as lofty conceptual truths. He goes on to describe the sense of assuagement that accompanies his concurring with Bergotte:

Aussi quand tout d'un coup je trouvais de telles phrases dans l'oeuvre d'un autre, c'est-à-dire sans plus avoir de scrupules, de sévérité, sans avoir à me tourmenter, je me laissais enfin aller avec délices au goût que j'avais pour elle, comme un cuisinier qui pour une fois où il n'a pas à faire la cuisine trouve enfin le temps d'être gourmand. (I, 96.)

The imagery that the Narrator uses to capture this dissolution of intellectual doubt is particularly apt. Not only does the passivity of 'je me laissais enfin aller' suggest a lessening of mental burdens, but the culinary frame of reference ushers in a reassuring, uncomplex order. More than that, it recalls the effortless enjoyment of gastronomic pleasures in *Jean Santeuil* (see above, Chapter I).

But what exactly is it in Bergotte that holds his attention? The Narrator is taken by what appear at first sight to be the novelist's Ecclesiastes-style borrowings: '[Bergotte] se mettait à parler du "vain songe de la vie", de "l'inépuisable torrent des belles apparences", du "tourment stérile et délicieux de comprendre et d'aimer"' (I, 94).

But one gains further insight into these allusions by correlating the Pléiade text with the parallel manuscript version. There, he attributes to Bergotte

une philosophie nouvelle pour moi et qui me parut sublime, une sorte de philosophie néo-bouddhiste, qui parlait sans cesse du vain songe de la vie, des vieux mythes qu'enrichit lentement la pensée des siècles, l'écoulement sans but, sans fin et sans vérité des illusoires, des splendides mensonges de l'amour, du tourment stérile de penser, de l'incurable mélancolie du beau. Ces pensées infinies si nouvelles pour moi donnaient aux chants si doux qui les accompagnaient quelque chose de sublime. J'étais presque déçu quand le fil du récit reprenait, quand Bergotte ne voulait plus faire de révélations sur l'éternelle illusion, sur la vanité de comprendre et la douleur d'aimer, de ces révélations que je cherchais dans ses livres. (*Cahier 14*, fo 80.)[7]

Not surprisingly, Bergotte, with his decrial of the 'tourment stérile de penser' and the 'vanité de comprendre', finds an eager disciple in the young Narrator. The latter, hopelessly uncertain of the merit of his own thinking, warms to a literary figure who announces the futility of human reason and understanding. In particular, the reference to a form of neo-Buddhism is informative of the direction in which the Narrator is leaning. He draws some sustenance from Bergotte's rejection of a *maya*-like state of illusion, consoling himself with the possibility of escape from human inadequacy. It is intriguing to examine the different aberrations that the Narrator sees this variation on oriental religion as highlighting. What one has is a whole catalogue of instances of misspent energy – a history of barren ideas, endless aesthetic speculation and obsession with love. The sense of futility in all this seems to strike a chord with the Narrator. When we look, much later in this study, at the music of Vinteuil, we find that, for the Narrator, part of the composer's greatness was that he avoided the road mistakenly taken by the rest of humanity, that leading to 'la formation des mots, l'analyse des idées' (III, 258; see below, Chapter 6a). Between this and Bergotte's neo-Buddhism, there would seem to be at least a measure of affinity.

But why should something as specific and undisguised as the reference to neo-Buddhism fail to reappear in the *Recherche* itself? Any attempted explanation will be necessarily tentative. Still, it is worth noting that many of the 'articles' in the neo-Buddhist code are also attributed, as we have seen, to the Bergotte of the *Recherche*. What is absent, however, is the possibly constricting label of neo-Buddhism itself. For were he to affiliate himself to that religion, the Narrator might run the risk of seeing his complex state of mind all too easily categorised. And by keeping the hero of the *Recherche* outside this religious sect, Proust spares him the pain of apostasy, which would inevitably come with the Narrator's formulation of his own, artistic credo. The value of the manuscript development lies in its naive enthusiasm. It suggests a mind briefly tempted by Buddhism but not won over to it. Elsewhere in this study, I shall be referring to manuscript passages where energetic experimentation with ideas can produce the same impression of a reality that is, in the final analysis, too clear-cut and inflexible to mirror faithfully the Narrator's position.

However much Bergotte's message may calm the Narrator's doubting, the episode is not totally representative of his intellectual conditioning and formation in *Du côté de chez Swann*. One recalls how his almost sacred respect for 'une signification philosophique infinie' quickly stifles any creative potential (I, 172). So too, he considers how sense-impressions fall far short of the conceptual absolutes that he sees as his ultimate goal. But of such impressions, he does concede: 'Du moins elles me donnaient un plaisir irraisonné [. . .] chaque fois que j'avais cherché un sujet philosophique pour une grande oeuvre littéraire' (I, 179). In this way, they come to assume a consolatory value for the Narrator.

Interestingly enough, they again rally round, as it were, when his mental world is thrown into confusion by Norpois. The old diplomat turns upside down the Narrator's carefully constructed hierarchy of artistic values, by dismissing Bergotte as a 'joueur de flûte' and in the same breath underlining the puerile character of the young Narrator's prose poem (I, 473–4). In spite of this great rebuff, the Narrator is comforted somewhat by the power of a musty smell to resurrect memories of his uncle's Combray home:

Il me sembla que je méritais vraiment le dédain de M. de Norpois: j'avais préféré jusqu'ici à tous les écrivains celui qu'il appelait un simple 'joueur de flûte' et une véritable exaltation m'avait été communiquée, non par quelque idée importante, mais par une odeur de moisi. (I, 494.)

Again, he notes the absence of any significant idea or concept that might enhance his exhilaration. But whereas he previously considered the elusive philosophical truth to be a *sine qua non* for the work of art, he now experiences 'une véritable exaltation' in the sense-impression. This becomes something more than a mere consolation, as the choice of 'véritable' clearly illustrates. Moreover, the Narrator comes near to overcoming the mental fixation that has him stick doggedly to the primacy of the conceptual in art.

Later, one finds a more resigned Narrator in conversation with Bergotte. The artist points to the pleasures of the intellect that he sees the Narrator as enjoying, but the latter can only reflect on what he sees as this misrepresentation of his own manner of feeling:

Je pensai, au moment de lui répondre, que j'aurais aimé une existence où j'aurais été lié avec la duchesse de Guermantes et où j'aurais souvent senti, comme dans l'ancien bureau d'octroi des Champs-Elysées, une fraîcheur qui m'eût rappelé Combray. Or, dans cet idéal de vie que je n'osais lui confier, les plaisirs de l'intelligence ne tenaient aucune place. (I, 569–70.)

As well as the joys of involuntary memory, the Narrator now also mentions life in the company of the Duchesse as easing his sense of intellectual inadequacy. For the Narrator, this new recruit to the side of non-intellectualism is a significant one. With this expression of interest in the Duchesse, we have an early indication of the search for elusive female beauty that is to dominate much of the *Recherche*.

Slightly later in the novel, an anonymous milkmaid is also associated with this disregard for philosophical complication. The letter that the Narrator excitedly believes to be hers is actually from Bergotte: 'L'idée qu'il était plus difficile et plus flatteur d'avoir une lettre de Bergotte ne me consolait en rien qu'elle ne fût pas de la laitière' (I, 714). In this brief and humorous insight, one finds a very neat reversal of a previous view expressed by the Narrator. Formerly, he had regretted his spiritual impoverishment and grudgingly acknowledged his purely sentient being. Now, by contrast, the prospect of a close spiritual relationship with his former artistic idol, Bergotte, in no way excites him. He would rather step into the unknown world of the milkmaid. Later I shall be dwelling at some length on how peasant girls and those of the Balbec beach appear to embody an instinctual primitivism for the Narrator (see Chapter 4). But for the present, it is sufficient to highlight the gulf separating the writer and the peasant, in the mind of the young Narrator, and to see how he breaks the spell of Bergotte's creative ability.

Nevertheless, throwing off this onerous admiration for Bergotte brings only a partial resolution of the conflict for the adolescent Narrator; there are many other ramifications to what I term his philosophical preoccupation. Thus, the self-doubt that is at the heart of his overvaluation of established artists also comes to pervade his own artistic judgement. A good illustration of this is his attempt to assess the merit of Berma's theatrical performance.

For the Narrator, much of his difficulty derives from the limitless expectation that he nurtures prior to his visit to the theatre. He sees Berma as some quasi-divine personage, embodying the absolute in theatrical perfection (I, 444–5). But the reality of his experience as an actual spectator runs contrary to this anticipation:

J'avais beau tendre vers la Berma mes yeux, mes oreilles, mon esprit, pour ne pas laisser échapper une miette des raisons qu'elle me donnerait de l'admirer, je ne parvenais pas à en recueillir une seule. Je ne pouvais même pas, comme pour ses camarades, distinguer dans sa diction et dans son jeu des intonations intelligentes, de beaux gestes. (I, 449.)

However intense his studious application, the Narrator seems incapable of appreciating the artistic merit of Berma's performance. If anything, this is due to the excessive scrupulousness of his approach:

J'aurais voulu – pour pouvoir l'approfondir, pour tâcher d'y découvrir ce qu'elle avait de beau – arrêter, immobiliser longtemps devant moi chaque intonation de l'artiste, chaque expression de sa physionomie; du moins, je tâchais, à force d'agilité mentale, en ayant avant un vers mon attention tout installée et mise au point, de ne pas distraire en préparatifs une parcelle de la durée de chaque mot, de chaque geste, et, grâce à l'intensité de mon attention, d'arriver à descendre en eux aussi profondément que j'aurais fait si j'avais eu de longues heures à moi. Mais que cette durée était brève! A peine un son était-il reçu dans mon oreille qu'il était remplacé par un autre. (I, 449.)

The description gives a very clear impression of the Narrator's almost intolerable state of hypersensitivity. He devotes his total mental energy to trying to freeze each and every aspect of Berma's diction and delivery. But such a minute dissection of her art is not feasible, and the actress's performance remains altogether tantalising for the Narrator.

Significantly, therefore, her genius proves so elusive for him precisely because of his renewed insistence on analytical and conceptual criteria. The doubt that overshadows the intuitively felt beauty of the line of Racine returns, then, in a slightly different guise. To that extent, the Narrator persists in this rigidly intellectual approach to art.

As the performance proceeds, he continues to be perplexed and uneasy. Even the mere use of opera-glasses becomes a burning philosophical issue for the Narrator, who now questions the reality of what he sees on looking through them. His scruple is that 'quand on croit à la réalité des choses, user d'un moyen artificiel pour se les faire montrer n'équivaut pas tout à fait à se sentir près d'elles' (I, 449). The irony is that without his grandmother's opera-glasses, he has a much poorer view of Berma! And indeed, in what becomes an increasingly comic scene, one senses a mildly satirical mature Narrator playfully allowing the adolescent to anguish about which of the two Bermas is the more real. Yet while conceding that the situation has this humorous dimension, it is equally important to see the doubt surrounding the young Narrator's use of the lorgnette. Taken in the context of his adolescent formation, it comes to represent yet another enigma for the anxious spectator of Berma's performance.

Overall then, the Narrator's experience of the theatre appears fraught with intellectual scruples. It comes as something of a surprise therefore when he finally breaks the grip of self-doubt that has been gaining hold of him: 'Enfin éclata mon premier sentiment d'admiration: il fut provoqué par les applaudissements frénétiques des spectateurs' (I, 450). The Narrator thus finds release from frustration in the spontaneous outburst of popular applause. By immersing himself in the general enthusiasm, he can shed the burden of his own problematic response to Berma. Reflecting on the audience's words of praise, however devoid of technical artistic insight they may be, he comments:

Et heureux de trouver ces raisons de la supériorité de la Berma, tout en me doutant qu'elles ne l'expliquaient pas plus que celle de la Joconde ou du Persée de Benvenuto, l'exclamation d'un paysan: 'C'est bien fait tout de même! c'est tout en or, et du beau! quel travail!', je partageai avec ivresse le vin grossier de cet enthousiasme populaire. (I, 451.)

Thus, the Narrator is happy to shelve his aesthetic scruples and to experience the delirium of frantic applause.

Nor is the judgement of the parterre necessarily erroneous, he argues. In fact he joyfully reports that the first outburst of applause coincides with one of Berma's finest touches (I, 450). This leads him to digress briefly, citing other instances where the common people can be equally discerning:

Il semble que certaines réalités transcendantes émettent autour d'elles des rayons auxquels la foule est sensible. C'est ainsi que, par exemple, quand un événement se produit, quand à la frontière une armée est en danger, ou battue, ou victorieuse, les nouvelles assez obscures qu'on reçoit et d'où l'homme cultivé ne sait pas tirer grand'chose, excitent dans la foule une émotion qui le surprend et dans laquelle, une fois que les experts l'ont mis au courant de la véritable situation militaire, il reconnaît la perception par le peuple de cette 'aura' qui entoure les grands événements et qui peut être visible à des centaines de kilomètres. On apprend la victoire, ou après coup quand la guerre est finie, ou tout de suite par la joie du concierge. (I, 450.)

What especially excites the Narrator's curiosity is the mysterious nature of these powers. As well as this, he insists that it is a discernment that cultured men do not enjoy. They seem incapable of divining the presence of this strange aura. In so far as this is the case – and one should not overlook the 'cent autres connaissances toutes erronées' (I, 450) that the Narrator also ascribes to the common people – it is clear that Proust is aware of an obscure cognitive potential in simple-minded folk. We have already seen a suggestion of this in the preface to *Jean Santeuil* (see above, Chapter 1a). As for the digression on the populace in the presentation of Berma, it is noteworthy that this development can be dated post-1914, since it does not appear in the 1914 Grasset galleys, nor prior to them.[8] Accordingly, one cannot dismiss the deliberations on primitive thought-processes in non-intellectuals as being of only passing interest in Proust's formative years. What appears in *Jean Santeuil* is also present in the great expansion of the *Recherche* during the war years. Returning briefly to the question of Berma's performance, we see the Narrator happy to share the instinctual popular approval, and to abandon any more difficult, conceptual appraisal of her art.

It is evident that the adolescent Narrator's mental horizons are constantly changing. On one level, he is conscious of a strong sentience that throws up scents and smells, as well as visual and auditory effects. But in some ways, the immediacy of such awareness is not sufficient for him. This stems from his insistence on the primacy of abstraction, a belief that enslaves him to the search for 'une signification philosophique infinie' (I, 173). As we have noted, for him the philosophical is synonymous with the conceptual, the intellectual. There is, therefore, an agonising gap between what he feels involuntarily and what he believes he should be discerning – the elusive philosophical subject. The discrepancy is perplexing for him, and his preoccupation will only diminish when he ceases to see conceptualisation as the great absolute. But any such demotion is dependent on the progress of the Narrator's self-disabusement, which is by turns rapid and slow. And perhaps it is as a reaction to the taxing nature of the experience generally that he responds so favourably to the theatre audience's spontaneous applause. The quality of the parterre's response is a far cry from the intellectual-isation on which the Narrator originally insisted. As a result, the taste that he acquires for 'le vin grossier de l'enthousiasme populaire' appears all the more striking.

(c) The primitivism of Françoise

One can see in the theatre description how the parterre enjoys what the Narrator considers to be a primitive consciousness – evidence that points to his interest in varying levels of human awareness.[9] In fact these powers that he so envies in others assume the value of near prescience when contrasted with the slow mental grasp of the intellectual (I, 450). Yet, as I have already pointed out, these common minds are frequently fallible.

In the case of Françoise, the archetypal simple soul of the *Recherche*, the defects in her spoken language provide an obvious illustration of this. One of her most delightful malapropisms is the use of 'le jambon de Nev'York' to denote 'jambon d'York' (I, 445). What captivates the Narrator is the absolute certainty with which Françoise uses the incorrect expression. The ham itself is one of the ingredients that she uses in the preparation of her 'boeuf mode' speciality. Here too, it is her unfaltering application to the culinary task in hand that fans the Narrator's imagination: 'Ce jour-là, si Françoise avait la brûlante certitude des grands créateurs, mon lot était la cruelle inquiétude du chercheur' (I, 446) – the particular anxiety to which he is referring is that prior to the Berma performance. There can be no mistaking the irony with which a more mature Narrator is looking back on the experience, deriding not only Françoise and her miraculous reincarnation as Michelangelo but also the young Narrator, now shackled with the onerous adult role of the 'chercheur'! The mock grandeur of the transformations effectively undercuts the descriptions. Yet for the adolescent Narrator, the emotion provoked by the whole Berma episode is inescapably serious, and it is curious that the character contrast should still run along the lines of 'certitude'/'inquiétude'; it is that opposition which explains his longing look back at the seemingly certain knowledge that Françoise enjoys. So whether in error or not, Françoise, with an unshakeable belief in her own words and ability, can still excite something of the Narrator's envy.

It becomes apparent very early in *Du côté de chez Swann* that Françoise falls into the mould of instinctualism in which the Narrator casts the parterre. Frequently, the child Narrator is distressed that his mother should be entertaining guests and be therefore unable to kiss him good night. His ploy is to have Françoise deliver a letter to his mother, claiming that it contains some information that she is anxiously awaiting. Nevertheless, the child feels that it is not possible to deceive Françoise:

Je pense que Françoise ne me crut pas, car, comme les hommes primitifs dont les sens étaient plus puissants que les nôtres, elle discernait immédiatement, à des signes insaisissables pour nous, toute vérité que nous voulions lui cacher. (I, 29.)

So in spite of her simplicity of mind, Françoise appears to enjoy a direct apprehension of reality, which frustrates the Narrator's intentions. In furtherance of this idea, Proust uses images relating to prehistory that seem especially effective. For such a register opens up a primitive stage of human consciousness that the Narrator cannot recapture. Accordingly, far from adopting a stance of superiority vis-à-vis Françoise, he chooses to marvel at her mysterious divining powers.

On another occasion, she almost surprises the Narrator and Albertine in a moment of sexual flirtation. Yet the Narrator does not doubt Françoise's spontaneous grasp of the situation, however quickly he and Albertine end their courting. He likens her discernment variously to the sailor's awareness of the sea or the sick man's intuitive sense of his own illness (II, 358), and goes on to draw an interesting parallel with the situation of the Ancients:

Tout ce qu'elle arrivait à savoir aurait pu stupéfier à aussi bon droit que l'état avancé de certaines connaissances chez les anciens, vu les moyens presque nuls d'information qu'ils possédaient (les siens n'étaient pas plus nombreux; c'était quelques propos, formant à peine le vingtième de notre conversation à dîner, recueillis à la volée par le maître d'hôtel et inexactement transmis à l'office). Encore ses erreurs tenaient-elles plutôt, comme les leurs, comme les fables auxquelles Platon croyait, à une fausse conception du monde et à des idées préconçues qu'à l'insuffisance des ressources matérielles. (II, 358.)

Here the Narrator is very much impressed by Françoise's uncanny knack of sensing the truth of a situation. Moreover, it is the same feeling that he experiences very often when in the company of the servant. This can be partly attributed to the fact that her presentation as a character remains largely constant throughout the *Recherche*.[10] One recalls how, at the very end of the novel, it is Françoise who faithfully collaborates with the Narrator in his work of composition. There too, she reveals an obscure understanding of his artistic creation:

A force de vivre de ma vie, elle s'était fait du travail littéraire une sorte de compréhension instinctive, plus juste que celle de bien des gens intelligents, à plus forte raison que celle des gens bêtes. (III, 1034.)

It is also worth remembering that to describe his work of art, the Narrator uses images that are drawn straight from Françoise's occupations. The work, he conjectures, might be like the stitching together of a dress that Françoise has made (III, 1033). Shortly afterwards, he compares its composition to her 'boeuf mode', which M. de Norpois so liked (III, 1035). In this way, these humble images taken from the servant's domestic pursuits gain a new importance and value when used in the context of the Narrator's own artistic creation.

We have seen different references, to ancient as well as prehistoric times, helping to reinforce the primitivism of Françoise's being. In addition to this, there is the very strong medieval peasant side to her character; the view of her as an embodiment of medieval tradition and of peasant simplicity serves as a useful adjunct to the notion of her primal consciousness. Accordingly, her peasant instinct is a sure one. With the departure of Albertine, she shares nothing of the Narrator's grief. But she immediately sees the latter's claim that his friend's absence is a temporary and prearranged one for the fabrication that it is. Likewise, when the butler terrorises her with talk of radical political change and other, similar evils, 'Françoise [...] sans pouvoir lire, regardait instinctivement et avidement le journal, comme si elle eût pu voir si c'était vraiment écrit' (III, 467). However resentful she has been of Albertine, she cannot ignore the Narrator's tears when he learns of the death of his former captive. In this, she is again 'servie par son instinct d'ancienne petite paysanne [...]. Son "coutumier" de Combray ne lui permettait pas de prendre légèrement les larmes' (III, 480–1). It is clear therefore that the Narrator sees medievalism as a further, important source of her instinctualism, and a suitable backdrop against which it can unfold.

The Narrator continues to forge a direct link between the peasant class and a pre-conceptual mode of existence, in what is one of the most developed descriptions of Françoise in the entire novel:

On n'aurait pu parler de pensée à propos de Françoise. Elle ne savait rien, dans ce sens total où ne rien savoir équivaut à ne rien comprendre, sauf les rares vérités que le coeur est capable d'atteindre directement. Le monde immense des idées n'existait pas pour elle. Mais devant la clarté de son regard, devant les lignes délicates de ce nez, de ces lèvres, devant tous ces témoignages, absents de tant d'êtres cultivés chez qui ils eussent signifié la distinction suprême, le noble détachement d'un esprit d'élite, on était troublé comme devant le regard intelligent et bon d'un chien à qui on sait pourtant que sont étrangères toutes les conceptions des hommes, et on pouvait se demander s'il n'y a pas parmi ces autres humbles frères, les paysans, des êtres [...] qui, condamnés par une injuste destinée à vivre parmi les simples d'esprit, privés de lumière, mais pourtant, plus naturellement, plus essentiellement apparentés aux natures d'élite que ne le sont la plupart des gens instruits, sont comme des membres dispersés, égarés, privés de raison, de la famille sainte, des parents, restés en enfance, des plus hautes intelligences, et auxquels – comme il apparaît dans la lueur impossible à méconnaître de leurs yeux où pourtant elle ne s'applique à rien – il n'a manqué, pour avoir du talent, que le savoir. (I, 650.)

Again we find highlighted the singular fascination that Françoise exerts on the Narrator. His sense of perplexity and bemusement in her presence is an important indication of this. In particular, the allusion to 'le regard intelligent et bon d'un chien', while signalling a note of some condescension on the part of the Narrator, perhaps more importantly confirms his profound interest in the nature of Françoise's consciousness. Although she is unmindful of the world of concepts, he judges this to be counterbalanced by another kind of elevation of which she is capable. To some extent, this corresponds to the instinctive powers she displays in frequently divining the truth of different situations.

The passage is doubly interesting in so far as it is a post-1914 addition to the text of *A l'ombre des jeunes filles en fleurs* (Winton, vol. 2, p. 39). It is therefore similar to the digression on popular intuition that Proust works into the description of Berma's performance at the theatre (see above, section *a*). It is easy to see the common thematic links that unite these two post-1914 expansions. They illustrate, significantly, how in his war-time development of the *Recherche*, Proust is seeking to define more clearly the quality of this primitive consciousness.

But there can be no escaping the essentially ambivalent tone in the description of Françoise inserted at 1, 650. Admittedly, the world of ideas passes her by. Yet she is still one of the straying, scattered members of the 'famille sainte', a long lost relative, so to speak, of the 'plus hautes intelligences'. What is more, he occasionally allows himself to speak of Françoise's culinary achievements in quasi-artistic terms. Thus, 'Françoise accepta les compliments de M. de Norpois avec la fière simplicité, le regard joyeux et – fût-ce momentanément – intelligent, d'un artiste à qui on parle de son art' (1, 484). The rush to qualify the use of 'intelligent' is perhaps an indication of Proust's own hesitation to attribute anything other than a fleeting intelligence to Françoise. Clearly the tentative nature of this reference echoes the caution of the lengthy portrayal that we have seen earlier, in which her ignorance is only total in a strictly limited sense: 'Elle ne savait rien, dans ce sens total où ne rien savoir équivaut à ne rien comprendre' (1, 650). As for the metaphor of the creative artist, it offers an indication of the warmth of feeling that the Narrator has for the servant, given the generally privileged position of artists in *A la recherche*. Like the common people sensitive to 'certaines réalités transcendantes' (1, 450), Françoise too may enjoy such divining powers in spite of her habitual simple-mindedness. And while her instinctive grasp of reality frequently frustrates the

Narrator's designs, he cannot cease to wonder at the nature and source of such intuitions. The certainty of these can be as fascinating for him as the spontaneous enthusiasm of the audience at the *Phèdre* performance. To this end, the occasional evocation of prehistoric or ancient times in descriptions of Françoise seems to confirm the absence of equivocation. But before drawing any further conclusions, it would be profitable to consider briefly the more general use that Proust makes of these distant periods in time.

(d)   Prehistoric and ancient times: eras of certainty

One of the most interesting aspects of this question is the wide temporal span that such a remote past is given in Proust. R. Bales, whose main concern is with Proust's medievalism, mentions in passing some pre-Christian images in an evocation of Françoise (*Proust and the Middle Ages*, p. 80). In addition to this, he alludes to the comparison that the Narrator makes between Françoise's archaic use of language and certain survivals from primitive stages of animal life (p. 86). The Narrator describes her language as being 'aussi curieux que ces animaux survivants des époques lointaines, comme la baleine ou la girafe, et qui nous montrent les états que la vie animale a traversés' (II, 737). As the Pléiade note reveals, however, 'lointaines' has replaced the earlier, manuscript use of 'tertiaires' (II, 1192). It would seem then that Proust was seeking an extremely remote age in which to set the evocation of animal life, in the belief that Françoise's own language would appear correspondingly more antiquated. Ultimately, however, he has rejected what might have been the harsh specificity of 'tertiaires', out of preference for the less technical 'lointaines' which still retains sufficient temporal distance.

Proust's use of such a prehistoric frame of reference is widespread. We recall how, at the beginning of the novel, the awakening Narrator is seen to savour the primal simplicity of 'le sentiment de l'existence comme il peut frémir au fond d'un animal; j'étais plus dénué que l'homme des cavernes' (I, 5). In many respects, the beauty of such an existence for the Narrator lies in its limitation and certainty. By the same token, he sees M. de Vaugoubert's attempts to rid himself of his homosexual inclinations in the interests of professional advancement, as a denial of his own, inner self:

M. de Vaugoubert, de même que l'homme civilisé qui ne serait plus capable des exercices de force, de la finesse d'ouïe de l'homme des cavernes, avait perdu la perspicacité spéciale qui se trouvait rarement en défaut chez M. de Charlus. (II, 664.)

The Narrator realistically describes the ability to 'spot' homo-sexuality as a 'perspicacité spéciale'. It is ironical then that this sophisticated attribute should be compared to a primitive's keen hearing. Yet in this analogy, we catch an interesting glimpse of Proust the dilettante, dabbling happily in theories of evolution. The point he is making is that civilised man has forfeited much of the developed sentient being that his primitive counterpart enjoyed before him. The added implication is that the era of the caveman is an age of instinctual authenticity, and one for which the Narrator feels a strong natural sympathy. In the case of the young Andrée, whom he meets at Balbec, the Narrator initially sees her as being 'une créature saine et primitive' (I, 943), and is favourably impressed by her as a result. But I shall be examining her role more fully in conjunction with that of the other girls at Balbec in Chapter 4.

This interest in prehistory again becomes prominent in the memorable portrayal of the Narrator's grandmother's illness. To convey the mortal character of her ailment – and hence the sureness of death – the Narrator adopts a by now familiar series of images:

Alors ma grand'mère éprouva la présence, en elle, d'une créature qui connaissait mieux le corps humain que ma grand'mère; la présence d'une contemporaine des races disparues, la présence du premier occupant – bien antérieur à la création de l'homme qui pense –; elle sentit cet allié millénaire qui la tâtait, un peu durement même, à la tête, au coeur, au coude; il reconnaissait les lieux, organisait tout pour le combat préhistorique qui eut lieu aussitôt après. (II, 300.)

The approach of death, dramatised as the unfolding of the 'combat préhistorique', is seen as the advent of something eternal and ineluctable. It immediately throws everything into a more ultimate perspective, stripping away the superimposed layers that have formed with the growth of civilisation. Death thus becomes a primordial force, in the Narrator's eyes, a force existing prior to the evolution of reflecting man. In the light of this, we can see how Proust uses prehistory to introduce a note of finality, as though the first man were somehow more conscious of and closer to the primary, elemental character of existence.

As well as drawing on this prehistoric era, Proust also bases images on less remote times. We have already seen Françoise's intuitive powers likened to those of Plato and the Ancient philosophers (II, 358). The Narrator himself frequently appears to be very much at home in this ancient world, as for example when he enthuses about an inspiring Celtic belief:

Je trouve très raisonnable la croyance celtique que les âmes de ceux que nous avons perdus sont captives dans quelque être inférieur, dans une bête, un végétal, une chose inanimée, perdues en effet pour nous jusqu'au jour, qui pour beaucoup ne vient jamais, où nous nous trouvons passer près de l'arbre, entrer en possession de l'objet qui est leur prison. (I, 44.)

This reference is just one example of the Narrator's interest in the notion of reincarnation. But he seems to reinforce the plausibility of this belief by grounding it in a notably ancient world. Proust actually uses this motif from Celtic lore to introduce the *madeleine* resurrection. One can readily appreciate why he should make such a *rapprochement*. But the complex reality that is retrieval through memory in *A la recherche* inevitably throws into relief the rudimentary quality of the Celtic tradition. In that sense, Proust may actually be impoverishing the belief he appears to cherish. But if he ultimately undermines it, he does so in spite of himself, for the Narrator enters the field of primitive reincarnation myths with evident enthusiasm and pleasure. It is also notable that at the end of the novel, the Narrator should again use a specifically Celtic image to refer to the possible reception that his work of art might have:

Je ne savais pas si ce serait une église où des fidèles sauraient peu à peu apprendre des vérités et découvrir des harmonies, le grand plan d'ensemble, ou si cela resterait, comme un monument druidique au sommet d'une île, quelque chose d'infréquenté à jamais. (III, 1040.)

The answer to the question of the book's popularity or otherwise will only emerge with time. Yet it is obvious that the Narrator reserves a very special place for the Christian and Celtic edifices alike, since both are associated with the sacrosanct work of art.

In casting a glance over these references to eras long past, one can see what it is that they have in common. Almost all of them are used with the intention of guaranteeing a sureness of cognition: Françoise instinctively discerning the truth of a situation; the real nature of the grandmother's illness or of M. de Vaugoubert's sexuality; the attraction of the Celtic doctrine of reincarnation. All these appear as incontestable realities, precisely because they are grounded in the certitude and necessity of distant epochs. Far from belonging to any factitious order, they mark an unadulterated and hence more authentic experience for the Narrator.

In the light of such evidence, one might recall the position of Françoise. Linked as she is to this remote past, she too enjoys some of the unfailing perceptions that the Narrator attributes to primordial being. More importantly, even in moments of comic aberration, Françoise still enjoys a sure belief that she is correct. And one cannot help contrasting her unquestioning acceptance of reality with the excessive doubting that plagues the Narrator (see above, section *b*). Moreover, as we have already seen, the Narrator himself jealously opposes his own position to that of Françoise: 'si Françoise avait la brûlante certitude des grands créateurs, mon lot était la cruelle inquiétude du chercheur' (I, 446).

It seems fair to say that a character such as Françoise acts largely as a foil to the Narrator's own complexity of being. In contemplating her, he sees more than a comic side to her character, and his joy may be partly the relief of having found in her an antidote to his own equivocation. While their existences remain radically different, the Narrator occasionally yearns for the quality of awareness that is hers, thus betraying a nostalgia for an instinctive apprehension of reality. The elemental simplicity of consciousness seems as assured for Françoise as it was for prehistoric, preconceptual man.

(e)   The grandmother's war on hypersensitivity

If Françoise is herself unaware of the impact that her instinctualism has on the Narrator, the same is not true of his grandmother and the influence that she exerts on him. Throughout his childhood, she wages a conscious campaign designed to combat the extreme frailty of mind and body that dogs him. Thus she will rebuke the Narrator's father, for instance, when the latter recommends that his son should do some reading on days of inclement weather:

Ce n'est pas comme cela que vous le rendrez robuste et énergique, disait-elle tristement, surtout ce petit qui a tant besoin de prendre des forces et de la volonté. (I, 11.)

Her concern is very obviously for her grandson's physical and psychological well-being, and close contact with Nature is, she believes, a guarantee of such a balance.

To appreciate her enthusiasm, one has only to recall the pleasurable associations that abound in the description of her in a rainswept garden:

Ma grand'mère, elle, par tous les temps, même quand la pluie faisait rage et que Françoise avait précipitamment rentré les précieux fauteuils d'osier de peur qu'ils ne fussent mouillés, on la voyait dans le jardin vide et fouetté par l'averse, relevant ses mèches désordonnées et grises pour que son front s'imbibât mieux de la salubrité du vent et de la pluie. Elle disait: 'Enfin, on respire!' (I, 11.)

The impression given is one of the grandmother's exhilarating intoxication with the experience. It is also significant that the language used is quite similar to that of a description of the

Narrator's own walk to Montjouvain. On that occasion, he enjoys 'une heure de pluie et de vent contre lesquels j'avais lutté avec allégresse' (I, 155). The Narrator himself is evidently aware of the kind of bracing pursuits that his grandmother is advocating.

Furthermore, the conflicting recommendations of grandmother and father on the Narrator's formation reflect a tension within the Narrator himself. For he does not feel only the attraction of a physical experience, such as that provoking the cries of 'Zut, zut, zut, zut' at Montjouvain (I, 155). As well as this, he may be perplexed by literature towards which his father is unwittingly turning him when he suggests that he should read. That perplexity can only increase when one remembers that, although here advocating reading, his father is often hostile to literature and the arts generally. The fact that the grandmother tends to be pro-culture – albeit culture of a certain kind – can only further fuel the Narrator's confusion.

The criss-crossing in the codes of both father and grandmother returns in the conflict arising from the Narrator's proposed visit to the theatre. His father, who normally dismisses theatre with all its 'inutilités', is quickly won over by Norpois' view that to see a performance of *Phèdre* would be a rich experience. The grandmother regretfully opposes the visit on the grounds that the nervous excitability that this might bring would be injurious to his health. Violent frustration with the complex debate is all the literal-minded father can express: 'Comment, c'est vous maintenant qui ne voulez pas qu'il y aille! C'est un peu fort, vous qui nous répétiez tout le temps que cela pouvait lui être utile' (I, 439). When we remember the perplexity of the Narrator's reaction to Berma, it becomes clear that the grandmother's fears are well-founded.

Part of her function in the novel, therefore, is to focus attention on the question of the Narrator's hypersensitivity. Occasionally the question is treated in a far from serious manner by the mature Narrator. He refers, for example, to the proposed trip of the young Narrator and his grandmother to Balbec, and to her conception of a holiday – rigid almost to the point of caricature. There is of course the cultural treasure of the Balbec church, but their vacation will consist largely of endless brisk walking and inhaling the fresh sea air (I, 129–30). Now the same fixation with breathing clean air is at the heart of the hilarious episode in the hotel dining-room, when menus and napkins are almost blown through the window that she had earlier insisted should be opened. Clearly, these humorous instances tend to accentuate the impracticability of what she recommends for the young Narrator.

But as well as this comic dimension to her character, there is also a solemn, admiring tone in many of the Narrator's descriptions of his grandmother. And with this introduction of a more serious note, her comments on the young Narrator's lack of willpower come to acquire a renewed gravity.

Hélas! je ne savais pas que, bien plus tristement que les petits écarts de régime de son mari, mon manque de volonté, ma santé délicate, l'incertitude qu'ils projetaient sur mon avenir, préoccupaient ma grand'mère au cours de ces déambulations incessantes de l'après-midi et du soir, où on voyait passer et repasser, obliquement levé vers le ciel, son beau visage aux joues brunes et sillonnées, devenues au retour de l'âge presque mauves comme les labours à l'automne, barrées, si elle sortait, par une voilette à demi relevée, et sur lesquelles, amené là par le froid ou quelque triste pensée, était toujours en train de sécher un pleur involontaire. (I, 12–13.)

It is noteworthy that in indicating his grandmother's very real preoccupation for her grandson, the Narrator should portray her as a noble and disinterested sufferer. The opening exclamation serves immediately to introduce a note of earnestness to the description, an earnestness that the reference to tilled fields in autumn reinforces. In that respect, the use of a chthonic image seems especially effective in imparting a sense of the grandmother's selflessness and modesty. Like the earth that yields fruit, the grandmother's overriding concern is to spend herself in an attempt to remedy the Narrator's debility.

One of the principal ways in which she endeavours to instruct the young Narrator is to prescribe certain reading material for him. In her enthusiasm to have him read what she deems to be the works of great authors – a contact that she considers to be as beneficial as the enjoyment of Nature's wide open spaces – she buys him works by Musset and Rousseau, and a copy of George Sand's *Indiana*. The Narrator's father judges these to be unsuitable for the child, whereupon the grandmother falls back on some of George Sand's pastoral novels (I, 39). Her reasoning in this is that her grandson will still be buoyed by the soothing tones of good French prose.

We get a fuller insight into how she makes her choice of authors when, on another occasion, her desire to guarantee the Narrator's emotional stability explains her invective against some contemporary writers. Among those outlawed are Baudelaire, Poe, Verlaine and Rimbaud:

C'était obscurément les exigences de mon bonheur menacé par le nervosisme, par mon penchant maladif à la tristesse, à l'isolement, qui lui faisaient donner le premier rang aux qualités de pondération et de jugement, particulières non seulement à Mme de Villeparisis, mais à une société où je pourrais trouver une distraction, un apaisement. (I, 727.)

Accordingly, the grandmother urges him to read those authors whose work she sees as reassuring and harmonious – Doudan, Rémusat, Mme de Beausergent, Joubert and Mme de Sévigné. Thus, there exists in the grandmother's mind a very sharp division between the 'pondération' of earlier writers and the disquieting imbalance so prevalent in more recent, Symbolist art. It is precisely the intellectual chaos and disharmony attributed to the latter from which she feels she must safeguard the Narrator.

Proust leads into the contrast between these two apparently different groups of writers by using a very thinly veiled borrowing from Schopenhauer:

> Comme on dit que c'est l'intérêt de l'espèce qui guide en amour les préférences de chacun et, pour que l'enfant soit constitué de la façon la plus normale, fait rechercher les femmes maigres aux hommes gras et les grasses aux maigres, de même c'était obscurément les exigences de mon bonheur menacé par le nervosisme, par mon penchant maladif à la tristesse, à l'isolement, qui lui faisaient donner [i.e., à ma grand'mère] le premier rang aux qualités de pondération et de jugement. (I, 727.)[11]

One can see that the movement of counterbalance that Schopenhauer is postulating is analogous to the antidotal function of the grandmother's recommended reading for the Narrator. The essence of her strategy is to restrict the range of his contact with literature in an attempt to assuage his hyperanxiety.

Our examination of *Jean Santeuil* has revealed a similar limitation of the self, deriving again perhaps from Schopenhauer – there it was Henri de Réveillon who enjoyed the calm of such restriction (see Chapter 1e). So in both *Jean Santeuil* and the *Recherche*, one finds evidence of a felicity achieved by fixing the parameters of consciousness in such a way as to exclude self-doubt.

Yet as he approaches maturity, the Narrator grows less heedful of his grandmother's counsel. Later in the novel, one has only to look at his enthusiastic quoting from the 'outlawed' Baudelaire to see how unmindful he has become of her exhortations in his adulthood.[12] Similarly, while pointing out the presence of a Schopenhauerian 'limitation of the self' notion in Proust, one cannot overlook the Narrator's conscious decision to abandon that philosophy (see below, Chapter 4a). Nevertheless, it would seem that for much of the Narrator's adolescence, this limitation of the person remains a distinct possibility for him. It is just possible that his extreme literary sensitivity will learn to restrict itself to easily accessible, uncomplicated authors; or again, he may throw himself open to the difficult imaginative world of other, more complex writers – a contact that the grandmother strongly resists.

Although the two principal ideas that she advocates are a close contact with Nature and the reading of certain authors, one finds the briefest of allusions to a third possible antidote, namely the niceties of high society. The reference occurs in *Cahier 41*, but does not feature in the *Recherche*. Speaking of 'les plaisirs mondains', the Narrator points out:

> Pour me faire à moi-même ce mensonge de les trouver intelligents, supérieurs, exquis, je trouvai des complices dans (mes parents) ma grand'mère qui sans doute heureuse que j'allasse dans un milieu qu'on jugeait distrayant, utile, destiné à développer en moi des points de vue qui s'opposent à la nervosité et à la bohème, non seulement rit de l'histoire: 'Donc j'ai acheté un chapeau' etc., mais approuva les principes de la Princesse de Parme. (*Cahier 41*, fo 59.)[13]

The grandmother, then, can again put the Narrator's scruples temporarily to rest. But it is the exacting nature of his self-analysis that explains the Narrator's anxiety to justify each and every experience. The fear that time spent in society is time wasted is temporarily allayed by the grandmother's words of approval. The Narrator is then happy to live the lie.

When seen as an escape into a more superficial self, therefore, socialising takes on a positive, although passing, value for the Narrator. His grandmother is quick to discern this. In the light of the informative manuscript development, it is somewhat surprising that in the *Recherche* itself, the Narrator seldom describes his excursions into high society in terms of their explicitly palliative value.[14] Yet certainly, the notion of a less introverted self that *Cahier 41* highlights is at least implicit in the portrayal of high society in the *Recherche* itself. It would of course be wrong to reduce Proust's extensive portrayal of the aristocracy to any one single concept, least of all an unstated one. Yet it is instructive to bear in mind the grandmother's view that society may be distracting, and in that sense salutary for the Narrator.

Elsewhere in the drafts, however, the same urge to socialise freely involves moral dilemma for the Narrator – a complication spawned, rather ironically, by the grandmother's declining health. Elated at the prospect of meeting certain girls at the Champs-Elysées, he can only feel acute resentment at the news that his grandmother, who was to accompany him, is now gravely ill and may not be able to travel. And there is a second case, also in *Cahier 47*, of this fascination with society leaving the Narrator insensitive to his dying grand-mother (see Bardèche, *Marcel Proust romancier*, vol. 2, pp. 154, 156). As Bardèche points out, these manuscript developments help explain the grief and moral guilt that overwhelms the Narrator long after her death (II, 758–9). The imperatives of his social life, then, harm the grandmother, causing her an anguish from which she desperately wanted her grandson to be free.

The irony is compounded when she herself begins to suffer from a psychic imbalance that is close to the adolescent's nervous debility. The family doctor, du Boulbon, makes the link all the more direct, when he groups grandmother, mother and Narrator together by attributing a similar disposition to them all (II, 303). He begins his diagnosis by speaking in eulogistic terms of the great family of hypersensitives, 'cette famille magnifique et lamentable qui est le sel de la terre' (II, 305). They have been principally responsible for the outstanding achievements in art, he acknowledges:

'Nous goûtons les fines musiques, les beaux tableaux, mille délicatesses, mais nous ne savons pas ce qu'elles ont coûté à ceux qui les inventèrent, d'insomnies, de pleurs, de rires spasmodiques.' (II, 305.)

The ambivalence of artistic achievement and self-destruction that comes across here mirrors the doctor's earlier use of 'magnifique et lamentable' (*ibid.*). This is consonant with the tension that the Narrator himself associates with the creative process, an activity that is simultaneously onerous and rewarding.

As du Boulbon proceeds with his advice, it is worth noting how he defines the nervous hypersensitivity that he has diagnosed:

'Je vois sur votre table un ouvrage de Bergotte. Guérie de votre nervosisme, vous ne l'aimeriez plus. Or, me sentirais-je le droit d'échanger les joies qu'il procure contre une intégrité nerveuse qui serait bien incapable de vous les donner? Mais ces joies mêmes, c'est un puissant remède, le plus puissant de tous peut-être. Non, je n'en veux pas à votre énergie nerveuse. Je lui demande seulement de m'écouter; je vous confie à elle. Qu'elle fasse machine en arrière. La force qu'elle mettait pour vous empêcher de vous promener, de prendre assez de nourriture, qu'elle l'emploie à vous faire manger, à vous faire lire, à vous faire sortir, à vous distraire de toutes façons.' (II, 306.)

In singling out his patient's literary pursuits to help explain his proposed remedy, du Boulbon is taking up a position very similar to the grandmother's, when she herself impresses upon her grandson the need to minimise his excitability. In both cases, immersion in the imaginative world of literature brings problems in its wake. And so du Boulbon surmises that, were she able to escape her nervous diathesis, the grandmother would feel a stability of self and a concomitant indifference to literary preoccupations. Of course, we are not meant to see du Boulbon's words as being oracular.[15] What is clear, however, is that his distinction between an integration of the self in simple pursuits and its fragmentation in the perplexities of literature can be linked to the Narrator's own development. In a manner recalling the doctor's own prognosis, the whole drift of the grandmother's campaign is that every opportunity should be taken to dull the kind of elaborate and to her mind potentially destructive mental activity that is sometimes the Narrator's. Not that she is closed to art. She is after all keen to introduce him to Berma's masterful performances, and is anxious for him to see the Balbec church. But in the case of Berma, the family is bemused when he speaks of an initial disappointment with her. And having arrived at Balbec and suffered 'la tyrannie du Particulier' on seeing the church, he cannot bring himself to deflate his exultant grandmother (I, 660–1). In both cases, the problem is that the Narrator's studious concentration on the art object rules out any 'easy' immediate response. Under pressure from family and Norpois, he concedes: 'Sans doute [la Berma] est très bien . . .' The father's retort confirms the gulf that separates these different levels of aesthetic awareness: 'Si elle est très bien, qu'est-ce qu'il te faut de plus?' (I, 457)!

Still, the discrepancy between the grandmother's views and those of the Narrator does not diminish the fact that their situations are in some ways parallel. Shortly after the former's death, the Narrator's mother recalls how the deceased was concerned first and foremost for the Narrator's health and 'équilibre nerveux' (II, 347). Her choice of words recalls the 'intégrité nerveuse' (II, 306) that the doctor envisages the grandmother enjoying.[16]

In addition to this, it is worth noting how Joubert – one of the grandmother's approved authors – is contrasted with Henri de Régnier, this time by the Narrator himself, in *Cahier 32*. I am quoting here from the *premier jet* of the *Cahier*, which was written about 1910:

Nous avons en nous de si vastes champs d'expérience psychologique, contenant à vrai dire presque tous les caractères humains qu'il est difficile souvent que nous disions quel est notre caractère. En lisant Joubert, nous vérifions en nous-même ce qu'il dit et tout l'être noble qu'il nous fait regarder en nous, nous fait honte du livre tout sensuel et vaniteux que nous écrivons. Mais vous lisez Régnier et il parle en vous à un être sensuel qui proclame que nous sommes plutôt lui que l'être noble de Joubert. Un philosophe du repos nous fait bannir les chagrins, un évocateur de la douleur montre en nous un être douloureux pour qui cette philosophie du repos et de l'oisiveté est une affectation. (*Cahier 32*, fo 23r.)

The Narrator's view that Joubert appeals to the noble side of one's being is evidently quite similar to the grandmother's assessment of the moralist (see above, p. 80). The favour with which she views his work can be related to the Narrator's warmth for the 'philosophe du repos'. By the same token, Régnier would thus join writers such as Baudelaire, Poe and Rimbaud whom the grandmother condemns as being arch-exponents of the grief and misery of the human condition (cf. I, 727).

It would seem important, then, to take into account the position of the grandmother vis-à-vis the Narrator. It is through her eyes that we gain further insight into an issue central to *A la recherche*, namely the Narrator's hypersensitivity. Moreover, she is sufficiently perceptive to realise how onerous the adolescent Narrator may find his teeming intellectual and imaginative activity. Yet her remedies are not always efficacious, and indeed may even appear quite exaggerated. Her insistent belief that the fresh air of Nature is some kind of panacea is a good illustration of this. The Narrator himself may enjoy the exhilaration of solitary Nature, but his is never a ritual worship.

Leaving aside the faint suspicion of caricature in the grandmother, however, it should be said that she is the careful exponent of a mode of consciousness to which the Narrator responds with some ambivalence. The lack of complication, for example, in her recommended authors can be consoling for the Narrator, even if he is later to steep himself in the world of the Symbolists. Yet he will remain sensitive to Mme de Sévigné, and is characteristically quick to uncover in her work innovation and challenge: 'Elle nous présente les choses, dans l'ordre de nos perceptions, au lieu de les expliquer d'abord par leur cause.' This he likens not only to Elstir; it suggests what is for him the delightful Dostoevskyan side to Mme de Sévigné (I, 654 and III, 378-9). The Narrator's drive towards a view of art as something complex and polyphonic can seem unrelenting.

And yet an attraction to limitation and security in literature still prevails. One can appreciate this by recalling how the child Narrator responds to his mother's reading to him:

Elle amortissait au passage toute crudité dans les temps des verbes, donnait à l'imparfait et au passé défini la douceur qu'il y a dans la bonté, la mélancolie qu'il y a dans la tendresse, dirigeait la phrase qui finissait vers celle qui allait commencer, tantôt pressant, tantôt ralentissant la marche des syllabes pour les faire entrer, quoique leurs quantités fussent différentes, dans un rythme uniforme, elle insufflait à cette prose si commune une sorte de vie sentimentale et continue. (I, 42-3.)

The predominant emphasis in the grandmother's approach is very similar to the mother's rendition of the stories in the child's bed-time books. Both rely heavily on what might be termed a 'euphemisation' of existence. Understandably, the child Narrator is won over by the soothing tones that seem to characterise the world his mother creates. But even the more adult Narrator is not averse from savouring the calming perspectives to which the grandmother introduces him. Her role gains in prominence when one remembers how she herself begins to develop some of the Narrator's own 'symptoms', thereby joining what du Boulbon sees as the family of hypersensitives. Clearly, she is closely linked to the main thread of the *Recherche*, namely the progress of the pilgrim Narrator.

In the character of the grandmother, therefore, we have an effective foil to the Narrator himself. Admittedly, she does not embody the primitive instinctualism that he sees in Françoise (see above, section *c*). She is literate, and indeed quite well-read; she also attends the theatre with the Narrator, whereas Françoise's simple-mindedness excludes her from all but the most banal melodrama (I, 447).[17] Yet in spite of some obvious contrasts, both women play an important part in throwing into relief the Narrator's own view of consciousness. The instinctive knowledge of the servant and the grandmother's war on hypersensitivity excite the Narrator's eager attention. In these minds, he sees possible alternatives to his own experience. To that extent, they form links in a chain of being which he glimpses only fleetingly, but which awakens his curiosity. From consciousness as seen by the Narrator in others, we might move on to examine the frequently primitive exhilaration that he sees as coming from within himself.

(f) The immanence of pleasurable sensation

We have seen in Chapter 2 how the opening few pages of the *Recherche* describe the Narrator awakening from the world of sleep. His enjoyment of that primitive level of being is evident from the sensuous detail in which it is described. But he does not restrict such pleasurable associations to his evocation of sleep. Recalling the different rooms in which he has lived, he enthuses about those

où, par un temps glacial, le plaisir qu'on goûte est de se sentir séparé du dehors (comme l'hirondelle de mer qui a son nid au fond d'un souterrain dans la chaleur de la terre) et où, le feu étant entretenu toute la nuit dans la cheminée, on dort dans un grand manteau d'air chaud et fumeux, traversé des lueurs des tisons qui se rallument, sorte d'impalpable alcôve, de chaude caverne creusée au sein de la chambre même, zone ardente et mobile en ses contours thermiques, aérée de souffles qui nous rafraîchissent la figure et viennent des angles, des parties voisines de la fenêtre ou éloignées du foyer, et qui se sont refroidies. (I, 7.)

J.-P. Richard sees in this and other evocations a desire for what he terms 'la nidification', with its movement towards 'l'uniformité lentement reconstituée, réparée, protégeante, d'un seul et vaste corps'.[18] In these moments of indolent reverie, with the self-sufficiency of the sentient experience, there is no trace of any intellectual awareness. The image of the swallow reinforces the process, for in pointing to the bird's concern with purely physical needs, Proust is indirectly echoing the life-force principle attributed to animals in *Jean Santeuil* (see above, Chapter 1c). Moreover, it is informative to contrast the chthonic images used in the description of the swallow with other ornithological references that are important for their suggestion of flight and ethereal being. The most obvious example of the latter category would be the gull-like and inaccessible girls on the beach at Balbec (I, 788), to whom I shall be returning in the next chapter. With the image of the swallow, however, secure in its subterranean recess, the Narrator's experience is set in an unrepentant sensualism.

Similarly, certain rooms evoke associations of summer for the Narrator, who enjoys the sense of being 'uni à la nuit tiède [...] où on dort presque en plein air, comme la mésange balancée par la brise à la pointe d'un rayon' (I, 7–8). Again, the image of the titmouse is a most appropriate one, reinforcing the strong instinctual dimension to the Narrator's happiness.

An important feature of this experience is the feeling of reassurance that it imparts to the Narrator. He senses himself to be insulated and secure, and totally untroubled. In another evocation, this time of a winter scene, the Narrator presents the pleasure of an unscrupulous self-preservation:

Avant que j'entrasse souhaiter le bonjour à ma tante, on me faisait attendre un instant dans la première pièce où le soleil, d'hiver encore, était venu se mettre au chaud devant le feu, déjà allumé entre les deux briques et qui badigeonnait toute la chambre d'une odeur de suie, en faisant comme un de ces grands 'devants de four' de campagne, ou de ces manteaux de cheminée de châteaux, sous lesquels on souhaite que se déclarent dehors la pluie, la neige, même quelque catastrophe diluvienne pour ajouter au confort de la réclusion la poésie de l'hivernage. (I, 50.)

While the continuation to this text shows a Narrator reverting to greedy communion with the 'odeur [...] poisseuse, fade, indigeste et fruitée du couvre-lit à fleurs', the passage quoted here exudes an atmosphere of solid, physical well-being. More important, perhaps, is the nice shifting of roles, whereby the winter sun seeks out the heat of the fireplace. In this beautifully simple reversal, one sees crystallised the process of interiorisation that is taking place. The effect of such a movement is to invert the normal position of the Narrator in relation to cosmic forces. His dependence on them gives way to their reliance on the warmth of his retreat. In a word, he not only enjoys the self-sufficiency of this existence of feeling but can also invite the sun to partake of it as well. An index of the Narrator's contentment with such experience is the fact that he should elevate it to the level of 'la poésie de l'hivernage'. The privilege that this imparts to the Narrator makes of him a latter-day Noah, shielded from all harshness and preoccupation.[19] He can, temporarily at least, see existence in terms of effortless sense-impressions.

We might now move from this type of sentient living, character-ised by its spatial restriction, to consider some of the Narrator's other experiences, when the emphasis is still on felt awareness, but where one finds a more outward-going Narrator. This involves switching from closed worlds, such as the swallow's underground nest, to the broader horizons of Montjouvain, for example, where the hero enjoys carefree walks in autumn.

In considering the episode that ends in the celebrated 'Zut, zut, zut, zut' cries, it is revealing to bear in mind the background given by the Narrator himself to the event. Only after a prolonged period of reading does the adolescent set out on his walk. Admittedly, we do not know the specific nature of the reading. But whatever this is, the pastime inevitably reduces the body to a state of inertia. The Narrator elaborates, however, on the not-total inactivity of the physical self:

Mon corps obligé depuis longtemps de garder l'immobilité, mais qui s'était chargé sur place d'animation et de vitesse accumulées, avait besoin ensuite, comme une toupie qu'on lâche, de les dépenser dans toutes les directions. Les murs des maisons, la haie de Tansonville, les arbres du bois de Roussainville, les buissons auxquels s'adosse Montjouvain, recevaient des coups de parapluie ou de canne, entendaient des cris joyeux, qui n'étaient, les uns et les autres, que des idées confuses qui m'exaltaient et qui n'ont pas atteint le repos dans la lumière, pour avoir préféré, à un lent et difficile éclaircisse-ment, le plaisir d'une dérivation plus aisée vers une issue immédiate. (I, 154–5.)

And so the body expresses itself in a totally random and carefree manner, released from its former stagnation when the Narrator had been reading. To this end, the image of the spinning top appears especially effective, capturing the gentle frenzy of the Narrator's bodily movement. His rapture is intensely lived, but is so overwhelming that he must acknowledge the ineffable nature of the emotion. He thus contents himself with an orgy of pre-verbal utterances, the immediacy of which compensates in part for the absence of any more coherent elucidation.[20] Language then disintegrates, its form broken; the Narrator frantically vocalises irrational forms reflecting the intensity of the experience, but also its intellectual opacity. As the episode reaches its climax, the Narrator shows himself to be aware of the ambivalent character of his enthusiasm:

Et voyant sur l'eau et à la face du mur un pâle sourire répondre au sourire du ciel, je m'écriai dans tout mon enthousiasme en brandissant mon parapluie refermé: 'Zut, zut, zut, zut.' Mais en même temps je sentis que mon devoir eût été de ne pas m'en tenir à ces mots opaques et de tâcher de voir plus clair dans mon ravissement. (I, 155.)

What is potentially a privileged moment becomes an abortive one in the eyes of the Narrator, owing to its over-reliance on the immediate, instinctual response. For the excited but also confused adolescent, the hermeneutic task seems too daunting a prospect. Consequently, he believes he has failed in the work of self-enlightenment.

The incident brings out not only the positive value of mental lucidity for the Narrator but also his intoxication with the obscurity of instinctual joys. It is not fortuitous, therefore, that he prefaces the description of his walk by referring to the long hours of reading that precede it. In going out by Montjouvain, he is leaving a mental, imaginative world, to enjoy the rush of bodily excitement that comes in its wake. Hand in hand with this is the explosion of mere sound that is the spontaneous 'Zut, zut, zut, zut' utterance (I, 155).

In assessing the import of the experience for the Narrator, one should avoid the danger of paying exclusive attention to his insistence on the intellectual duty of decoding his 'ravissement' (I, 155). While that is important to him, the present experience adequately shows how such duty does not always come first for the Narrator. Similarly, there can be no doubting the reality of his ecstasy, however inarticulate it may appear.

There is also interesting evidence in one of the early *Cahiers* that Proust had envisaged using the 'Zut, zut, zut, zut' exclamation in rather different circumstances:

Tout d'un coup, mon anxiété tomba, une félicité m'envahit comme quand un médicament puissant agit, nous enlève une douleur, je venais de prendre la résolution de ne plus essayer de m'endormir sans avoir revu maman, de l'embrasser au moment où elle monterait, je me levai, je m'assis, j'ouvris la fenêtre, le calme qui résultait de mes angoisses finies, la peur et la soif du danger me mettaient dans une allégresse extraordinaire. J'étais dans une disposition joyeuse, ces paroles insignifiantes que j'entendais [monter] mollement du jardin m'enchantaient. Je me répétais 'Zut! zut! zut! zut alors!' avec le même accent enivré que si ces mots avaient signifié quelque vérité délicieuse, je sautais seul dans ma chambre, je m'adressai un sourire dans ma glace, et ne sachant sur qui faire tomber ma tendresse et ma joie, je saisis mon propre bras avec transport et j'y déposai un baiser. Hélas, cette joie dura peu. C'était le moment où on allait monter. Il fallait envisager les choses en face. (*Cahier 8*, fo 37r.)[21]

In this particular passage, it is evident that the Narrator's concerns are not for any artistic duty. Hence, the joy accompanying his resolve to wait for his mother's kiss is totally unspoilt. As for the note of deflation on which the passage ends, this arises from what Proust sees as the frequent disappointment in moving from anticipation to realisation (see I, 13). It in no way derives from a dissatisfaction with the expression he gives to his felicity. Clearly, we are not to dismiss these utterances as being a mere preliminary to more coherent expression. In choosing to deliberate on them and on the body language of ecstasy, the Narrator reveals how entranced he is by a pre-verbal consciousness.[22]

Contrary to certain critical opinion (see note 22), the Narrator's enjoyment of an exclusively sentient existence is not infrequent in *A la recherche*. Descriptions of a state of inebriation form a regular source of such happiness. On the recommendation of the family doctor, the grandmother allows the Narrator to take some alcohol before heading off to Balbec. Such is the euphoria that he experiences as a result that he becomes a joyous prisoner of present sensation. The same cannot be said of his grandmother:

Alors je lui parlais, mais cela ne semblait pas lui être agréable. Et à moi pourtant ma propre voix me donnait du plaisir, et de même les mouvements les plus insensibles, les plus intérieurs de mon corps. Aussi je tâchais de les faire durer, je laissais chacune de mes inflexions s'attarder longtemps aux mots, je sentais chacun de mes regards se trouver bien là où il s'était posé et y rester au delà du temps habituel. (I, 652.)

The Narrator finds himself completely engaged by the immediacy of the situation, taking sensuous delight in his own voice and gaze. His grandmother offers him a volume of Mme de Sévigné, but he initially ignores this, preferring to allow his attention to focus on a blue window-blind in the carriage. Again, he gives himself over totally to the visual appeal of the experience:

La couleur bleue du store me semblait, non peut-être par sa beauté, mais par sa vivacité intense, effacer à tel point toutes les couleurs qui avaient été devant mes yeux depuis le jour de ma naissance jusqu'au moment où j'avais fini d'avaler ma boisson et où elle avait commencé de faire son effet, qu'à côté de ce bleu du store, elles étaient pour moi aussi ternes, aussi nulles, que peut l'être rétrospectivement l'obscurité où ils ont vécu pour les aveugles-nés qu'on opère sur le tard et qui voient enfin les couleurs. (1, 652.)

It is as though, through alcohol, the Narrator has been reborn into a new world of perception, where colour gains a fresh, exciting, virginal character. The naivety of vision that is his shows up in a very positive light, rendering the experience in every way replenishing for him. Thus it is that existence becomes temporarily reduced to a marvelling at the phenomenon of colour. Likewise, the silvery buttons on a railway employee's uniform can hold the Narrator spellbound (1, 652). He finds the intensity of their appeal totally satisfying. The scene becomes increasingly comic when in his drunken exuberance, the Narrator tries to invite the employee to join them. The stranger's escape into another carriage offers hilarious confirmation of the subjective quality of reality as experienced, however dimly on this occasion, by the Narrator![23]

These evocations of intoxication suggest the immanence of the Narrator's experience. Gone is any desire to transcend its present reality, for the Narrator is clearly captivated by the directness of elementary perceptions themselves. What is more, he sometimes describes drunkenness in a manner reminiscent of other moments of emotional upsurge. Thus, looking back on his intoxication of the day before, he elaborates on his state of awareness on that occasion:

Je ne pouvais cesser de remuer ni de parler, je n'avais plus de consistance, de centre de gravité, j'étais lancé, il me semblait que j'aurais pu continuer ma morne course jusque dans la lune. (1, 821.)

The way in which he is 'lancé' recalls especially the 'Zut, zut, zut, zut' moment, where the image of the spinning top conveys the Narrator's frantic movement (1, 155). Furthermore, the dispersal of self, implied by his loss of substance and of any central focus, seems particularly liberating for the Narrator. Needless to say, the many preoccupations that beset him now drop from his mind. In the euphoria of alcohol, he becomes immune to the problem of his literary vocation, for example, or to doubts about the validity of his own response to experience. For a period, there is nothing beyond pleasurable sense-perceptions.

But we have one of the clearest indications of alcohol's appeal for the Narrator when he recalls a trip to Rivebelle alone:

Tout en vidant une dernière coupe je regardais une rosace peinte sur le mur blanc, je reportais sur elle le plaisir que j'éprouvais. Elle seule au monde existait pour moi; je la poursuivais, la touchais et la perdais tour à tour de mon regard fuyant, et j'étais indifférent à l'avenir, me contentant de ma rosace comme un papillon qui tourne autour d'un papillon posé, avec lequel il va finir sa vie dans un acte de volupté suprême. (II, 1016–17.)

The all-engaging character of present sensation, as conveyed by the arresting image of the butterfly, seals tight the Narrator's own experience. His position becomes one of totally subjective idealism: 'Elle seule au monde existait pour moi.' Other indications of this are the Narrator's absorption in instantaneous pleasure, and the irrelevance of any sense of futurity. One final interesting detail is the use of the possessive in 'ma rosace', reinforcing as it does the idea that for the Narrator, solely the objects of his perception have existence, in what is a state of complete self-reference.

Nor is it solely with alcohol that consciousness may become reduced to these agreeable proportions. The Narrator's state of sexual arousal in the presence of Albertine is an obvious example of a broadly similar process:

La vue du cou nu d'Albertine, de ces joues trop roses, m'avait jeté dans une telle ivresse (c'est-à-dire avait tellement mis pour moi la réalité du monde non plus dans la nature, mais dans le torrent des sensations que j'avais peine à contenir) que cette vue avait rompu l'équilibre entre la vie immense, indestructible qui roulait dans mon être, et la vie de l'univers, si chétive en comparaison. (I, 933.)

The imperative of instant sexual gratification brings with it something of the radical self-concentration brought on by alcohol. He goes on to describe his enthusiasm for existence, all of which is no longer without him but within him; at the same time, he ridicules any philosopher who might insist on his mortality and the greater permanence of Nature. The Narrator's riposte is lively and self-assured:

'Comment cela eût-il été possible, comment le monde eût-il pu durer plus que moi, puisque je n'étais pas perdu en lui, puisque c'était lui qui était enclos en moi.' (I, 933.)

The Narrator has thrown off all subordination to a universal order. Paradoxically, his microcosmic world embraces the now insignificant, subsidiary macrocosm. One might compare this process of interiorisation with the image that I interpreted earlier of the winter sun coming to shelter in the Narrator's warm retreat. In both instances, the reduction of the universe to a position of dependence on the Narrator's own world of feeling reflects the immanence of his experience. His unreflecting sensationalism appears unchallengeable on each occasion.

To sum up, then, one can see that the Narrator in the *Recherche* attributes some value to an experience of sentient hedonism. Its beauty is that he savours instinctual joys in themselves, without seeking to give them any other, perhaps intellectual, significance. We have already seen the mental frustration of the Narrator's philosophical preoccupation. Yet here, that torment is conspicuously absent. What is more, one feels occasionally that for the Narrator, the whole-hearted living of sensations may counter any reflective doubts on the character of experience. The Narrator's intoxication on the Balbec train, for example, effectively dulls the intense mental activity of imagining the as yet unknown Balbec. Alcohol holds him securely in the present. The same applies to his desire for sexual gratification when with Albertine at the hotel in Balbec. The intrinsicality of that pleasure principle allows him to escape all doubt about her character and inclinations. For him, absorption in the present is here synonymous with freedom from self-questioning.

The aim of this chapter has been to examine the Narrator's childhood and adolescent development. Although centred predominantly on the Narrator, it also brings in two important figures from his immediate family circle. This is in an attempt to show that an interdependence of characters is in operation. For we have seen something of a cross-fertilisation between grandmother and Narrator. Although frequently poles apart temperamentally, the former's code of education for her grandson occasionally coincides with what he himself sees and admits to being his own urgent needs. As for Françoise, her belonging to a still extant race of primitives stimulates his attention, since it opens up the strange, obscure terrain of intuitivism for the Narrator. Whereas he himself may experience an isolated intuition of reality, it is that quality of cognisance which habitually belongs to Françoise. Both women characters, then, introduce him to modes of consciousness that are quite removed from his own. He in turn can reflect on the intriguing possibilities of a life-style like theirs, and enjoys turning over in the mind what is for him this virtual, other being.

But however much Françoise and the grandmother can be categorised (and their presentation as characters remains generally uniform throughout the *Recherche*), there can be no escaping the complexity of the adolescent's development. Within him, one sees simultaneously the pull of 'une signification philosophique infinie' (I, 172) and the haste to enjoy immediate instinctual delights. His self-deprecation and his idolatry of established artists may quickly give way to the assurance accompanying an undiluted sensationalism. From seeing conceptual truths as some remote and highly desirable goal, the Narrator can turn rapidly to enjoying limited sense-perceptions. Even more radical is his flirtation with a total dissolution of the self in a Bergottesque Nirvana (cf. *Cahier 14*, fo 80).

What sometimes spurs the Narrator on to make this quick change in course is the knowledge that sentient experience may allay intellectual scruples. But it would be wrong to suggest that this is his sole, or indeed primary, motivation. He is aware, for example, of the intrinsic interest of characters like Françoise or his grandmother. They are not mere foils to his own complexity, but rather have full roles to play in the novel. As for the appeal of sense-impressions, one should remember that these become intricately tied up with the Narrator's thinking on the 'moments bienheureux'. There, a taste or a smell becomes not a retreat from spiritual activity but a 'point de départ' for the careful probing of the intellect. But I shall come to the question of the privileged moments in Chapter 6.

For the present, we might note the developing Narrator's concern with the multifariousness of human awareness. Between his own complexity and the simplicity of others, there are many points of contact and significant dissimilarity. He may sense a nostalgia for the quality of existence that Françoise incarnates. But of course, in highlighting the peculiar nature of her being, he is implicitly asserting the fundamental difference in their dispositions. It is difficult for him to suppress that gap. Nevertheless, he occasionally experiences, within his own self, brief moments of a total reliance on the senses – a fleeting glimpse of a lost primitivism.

4

Characterisation: the Functioning of a Law of Opposites

Etait-ce qu'ayant vu auparavant de l'épine blanche, la vue d'une épine rose et dont les fleurs ne sont plus simples mais composées, le frappa à la fois de ces deux prestiges de l'analogie et de la différence qui ont tant de pouvoir sur notre esprit?

(*Jean Santeuil*, p. 331)

(a) Imaginative desires: limiting them or exploring them?

The impression that the Narrator gives of his childhood in Paris and Combray is generally one of a restricted number of human relationships, unfolding against a background of solid family order. Most of his daily contact is with his parents, his grandmother or Françoise. The Narrator's liaison with the young Gilberte, however, comes to disrupt this stability. The intense emotion that he feels for her tends radically to change his hitherto family-centred world. But with the death of his love for Gilberte and his growing indifference to her, the balance is restored.

By contrast, the Narrator's experience in Balbec has much greater repercussions on this unchanging domestic background. One is immediately impressed by how the stagnation of Combray is replaced by an atmosphere of change and newness and mobility in the seaside town. On his many excursions into the surrounding countryside with his grandmother and Mme de Villeparisis, the Narrator often glimpses anonymous young peasant women. He is at once seized with a sense of their beauty, and yet they remain unknown and inaccessible to him. The effect of their tantalising presence is to throw the Narrator's affective and mental self into disarray: 'La vue et la perte de toutes accroissaient l'état d'agitation où je vivais, et je trouvais quelque sagesse aux philosophes qui nous recommandent de borner nos désirs' (I, 714). The movement of intense expectation followed almost immediately by sharp disappointment troubles the Narrator emotionally. But one is left wondering quite which philosophers he has in mind. I mentioned in Chapter 1 how Henri de Réveillon's untroubled, limited existence is the envy of Jean Santeuil, and went on to draw some parallels with Schopenhauer's view of such a life-style in his *Aphorisms on the Wisdom of Life* (see Chapter 1e). This reference to the German philosopher is not a fortuitous one, since Proust himself alludes to the French translation of the work in his preface to Ruskin's *Sésame et les lys*. The point that Proust makes in that preface is that Schopenhauer is always happy to illustrate his own views with ample quotation from many and varied sources, both literary and philosophical. He continues by saying that, with more space,

j'aurais eu plaisir à compléter cette petite démonstration à l'aide des *Aphorismes sur la Sagesse dans la Vie*, qui est peut-être de tous les ouvrages que je connais celui qui suppose chez un auteur, avec le plus de lecture, le plus d'originalité, de sorte qu'en tête de ce livre, dont chaque page renferme plusieurs citations, Schopenhauer a pu écrire le plus sérieusement du monde: 'Compiler n'est pas mon fait.'[1]

It is evident here, and also from Proust's detailed annotation of the work in question (*CSB*, pp. 185–6), that he was extremely familiar with Schopenhauer.

Returning now to the reference in *A la recherche*, one finds that it is from the same work by Schopenhauer that Proust is borrowing when he speaks of the restriction of one's desires. The following is an extract from the sixth of the philosopher's 'Counsels and Maxims':

All limitations make us happy. The narrower our range of vision, our sphere of action, and our points of contact, the happier we are: the wider these are, the more often do we feel anxious and worried. For with them, our cares, desires, and terrors are increased and intensified [. . .]. Every limitation, even that of the mind, is conducive to our happiness. (*Parerga and Paralipomena*, vol. i, pp. 416–17.)

For the Narrator in his 'état d'agitation', these words do embody a very obvious wisdom.

One finds further, conclusive evidence that the Narrator is indeed drawing on Schopenhauer, in the parenthesis following the counsel of limitation in the *Recherche*. There, the Narrator qualifies his support for such philosophy by stipulating that the desire to be curbed can only be the

désir des êtres, car c'est le seul qui puisse laisser de l'anxiété, s'appliquant à de l'inconnu conscient. Supposer que la philosophie veut parler du désir des richesses serait trop absurde. (i, 714.)

The Narrator's reference to material wealth seems largely meaning-less, until one realises that it is a thinly disguised refutation of part of the *Aphorisms*. For Schopenhauer begins that study with a neat tripartite exposition of man's condition, having chapters on 'What a Man is', 'What a Man has', and 'What a Man represents'. The second of these sections deals with possessions and property (*Parerga and Paralipomena*, vol. I, pp. 346–52), an area of interest that the Narrator considers to be totally inappropriate for the philosopher. Thus, although Proust is vague in his allusion to philosophers, one can see the specifically Schopenhauerian frame of reference on this occasion. The general tenor of the *Aphorisms* provides the Narrator with a useful platform from which to launch his own ideas.

This becomes more apparent when one considers how the passage develops. Having stated his dissatisfaction that philosophy should concern itself with material wealth, the Narrator then graduates to a conscious rejection of the limitation notion itself. Significantly, it is his desire to explore the world of the young girls of Balbec that prompts his non-acceptance of the philosopher's suggestion:

Pourtant j'étais disposé à juger cette sagesse incomplète, car je me disais que ces rencontres me faisaient trouver encore plus beau un monde qui fait ainsi croître sur toutes les routes campagnardes des fleurs à la fois singulières et communes, trésors fugitifs de la journée, aubaines de la promenade. (I, 714–15.)

One sees simultaneously, therefore, the Narrator's sympathetic response to Schopenhauer's exhortation, and yet his impatience with a *modus vivendi* that does not allow for any imaginative adventure in the company of the 'jeunes filles en fleurs'. It is important that this ambivalent attitude should be borne in mind. Milton Hindus writes perceptively of Schopenhauer's influence on Proust, and indeed quotes a part of the same reference to limitation cited here (I, 714). Nevertheless, he commits the error of stating only one side of the case, namely the Narrator's acceptance of limitation, neglecting his subsequent resolve to abandon any such restriction of the self (Hindus, *The Proustian Vision*, p. 96). The critic's omission is a convenient one in the context of his own work, since it keeps intact his argument that the idea of pessimism is of primary importance in Proust's work. Yet he takes no account of the exhilaration that is to characterise much of the Narrator's experience with the little band of Balbec girls; as such, Hindus' appraisal appears one-sided and unduly sombre in tone.

At the outset then, the Narrator's reaction to these girls is one of hesitation. In him, the will to curb his interest in others is undercut by a desire to know the young women. We get a good illustration of this inner tension in the description of a girl cyclist. As she hurries elusively by, she excites a variety of emotions in the Narrator:

C'était par conséquent toute sa vie qui m'inspirait du désir; désir douloureux, parce que je le sentais irréalisable, mais enivrant, parce que ce qui avait été jusque-là ma vie ayant brusquement cessé d'être ma vie totale, n'étant plus qu'une petite partie de l'espace étendu devant moi que je brûlais de couvrir, et qui était fait de la vie de ces jeunes filles, m'offrait ce prolongement, cette multiplication possible de soi-même, qui est le bonheur. (I, 794.)

The Narrator's initial hesitancy now gives way to an unconditional enthusiasm for the girl whom he catches sight of. More importantly, he begins to develop the idea of broadening his own horizons, pointing out the limitless possibilities of virtual being that communication with the girl holds out to him. Indeed, he goes as far as to give such an extension of the self the character of happiness itself. This is significant in that it represents a clear reversal of the Schopenhauerian view that I considered just now (I, 714). The suggestion there was that the Narrator might find a contentment in limitation. Here, in contrast, happiness lies in the Narrator's throwing open the boundaries of his own individual self to experience the strange, unknown existence of the girls of Balbec. In view of the eudemonism associated with the exploration of new modes of consciousness, it is not surprising that the adolescent Narrator should feel inclined to pursue the host of new relationships that Balbec offers. In the imaginative flight sparked off by the 'petite bande', we see the Narrator's clear resolve to abandon the strategy of dull self-limitation. As well as enhancing the Narrator's happiness, contact with this tantalising female beauty has the added effect of sharpening his interest in existence generally: 'Pour les belles filles qui passaient, du jour où j'avais su que leurs joues pouvaient être embrassées, j'étais devenu curieux de leur âme. Et l'univers m'avait paru plus intéressant' (I, 712).

But in choosing this course of exploration, the Narrator still refers very perceptively to his role vis-à-vis the young women who excite his attention. From the outset, he is aware of the difficulty of totally penetrating that other world, and conveys this by use of an extended image relating to the situation of a deprived child:

Et dussé-je, maintenant que j'étais souffrant et ne sortais pas seul, ne jamais pouvoir faire l'amour avec elles, j'étais tout de même heureux comme un enfant né dans une prison ou dans un hôpital et qui, ayant cru longtemps que l'organisme humain ne peut digérer que du pain sec et des médicaments, a appris tout d'un coup que les pêches, les abricots, le raisin, ne sont pas une simple parure de la campagne, mais des aliments délicieux et assimilables. Même si son geôlier ou son garde-malade ne lui permettent pas de cueillir ces beaux fruits, le monde cependant lui paraît meilleur et l'existence plus clémente. (I, 711–12.)

The analogy that the Narrator draws between himself and the prison child sheds useful light on his own position. Prior to his discovery of a whole new world of reality, involving the vivacious, supple youth of Balbec, the Narrator has been restricted to what he considers to be the narrow confines of his own awareness. Now, new broader horizons throw open an exciting world of possibility. But it may be a possibility that never attains realisation if, like the child guarded by the gaoler, the Narrator is somehow unable to enjoy fully the beauty unfolding before him. In the course of the present chapter, I shall be considering what it is in the character of the 'jeunes filles', and of the Narrator himself indeed, that makes the transition seem to him at times so difficult (see below, section i).

We may conclude briefly by saying that, for the Narrator, the choice between limitation and exploration is not an easy one. He recognises that one possible result of his attraction for unknown girls is that his whole world would be thrown into chaos. Certainly, were he to heed the traditional admonitions of his grandmother, for example (cf. Chapter 3e), he would shy away from them. But seeing more and more of this evanescent beauty of Balbec has the effect of a heady wine on him. He then rushes quickly into this novel experience, disregarding any counsel that might recommend the control of his desires. While toying briefly with the idea of emotional confinement, he later abandons caution, fired by the prospect of an exciting, radically new awareness in the company of the 'jeunes filles en fleurs'.

(b) Regaining a lost enthusiasm – 'l'éternel regret de la vie'

Before coming to the little group of Balbec itself, it would be profitable to examine some of the Narrator's random encounters with other young women, who remain generally anonymous and underdeveloped as individual characters. I began Chapter 3 by referring to what is, in the eyes of the mature Narrator, the hilarious encounter of his youth with a young milkmaid. But in spite of this retrospective disavowal, the adolescent Narrator is too closely involved in that encounter to be anything other than earnest about the prospect of tripping along merrily with the girl. The immediate effect of her appearance is to reawaken in him a sense of exhilaration and enthusiaasm for living: 'Je ressentis devant elle ce désir de vivre qui renaît en nous chaque fois que nous prenons de nouveau conscience de la beauté et du bonheur' (I, 655). The Narrator can speak of a new sensitivity to this beauty and felicity. When the woman is not actually present, all he has are

des images abstraites qui sont languissantes et fades parce qu'il leur manque précisément ce caractère d'une chose nouvelle, différente de ce que nous avons connu, ce caractère qui est propre à la beauté et au bonheur. (I, 655–6.)

The appeal of an experience such as his meeting with the milkmaid seems to lie in its ability to unfold new experiential possibilities for the Narrator. Evidently, she embodies an essentially different quality of being. And so the Narrator is drawn towards a life-style that departs considerably from his more usual pursuits. For him, her world appears so alluring largely because it reveals a strongly instinctual, physical character. In the light of our earlier chapters, where distinctions between a cerebral realm and the area of felt, lived reality are frequent, it is notable that life should here seem devoid of intellectual preoccupations. To that extent, the image of the girl pursuing her pleasantly simple tasks against a background of rusticity is enormously assuaging for the young Narrator. Consequently, in savouring the idyllic world of the peasant woman, the Narrator feels himself to be sheltered from all metaphysical doubting. Her daily activity suggests a oneness and integrity of self that he does not normally enjoy.

Another indication of the impact that Proust sees her as making emerges in further manuscript variants. We might consider, for instance, how the sense of security deriving from her presence can be reinforced: 'Le petit arc noir qui dans son regard perçant était si fermement bordé, rendait aussitôt le monde aussi intéressant qu'elle-même' (*Cahier 32*, fo 21r).[2] At the same point in the manuscript, Proust also suggests that her company 'donnait confiance dans la vie'. Perhaps it was the openness of the comment and the totally unqualified assurance that it suggests that kept it out of the *Recherche*, where life with young girls can assume all kinds of other complexities. But the remark again throws up the possibility of life changing complexion dramatically for the Narrator.

We have already seen the Narrator saying of the milkmaid: 'Je ressentis devant elle ce désir de vivre' (I, 655). From context, it is clear this will to live comes with an injection of renewed vitality into existence. A similar language is used by Proust to describe the charm that three unknown girls exert on the Narrator: 'Elles m'avaient fait faire mille projets, aimer la vie' (III, 562). The same vitality even pervades the young Narrator's description of the marbles in the shop at the Champs-Elysées: '[Les billes d'agate] étaient souriantes et blondes comme des jeunes filles [...]. Elles avaient la transparence et le fondu de la vie' (I, 402). Clearly it is an exciting prospect for the Narrator that life should thus become endowed with a marvellous clarity.

One cannot help contrasting these qualities of transparency and pleasant continuity with the frequently oblique, troubled view of existence that is the Narrator's. What is more, almost every one of the girls whom he meets is described as being vivacious and carefree to the point of arousing his envy. Another young peasant, appearing this time in *La Prisonnière*, is described as showing 'un peu de ce qui fait l'éternel désir, *l'éternel regret de la vie*' (III, 141–2; italics mine). Even from this briefest of mentions, it is clear that she makes an impact similar to that of other adolescent women; again, the Narrator feels an undeniable nostalgia for some blissful lost world. A general feature, then, of these allusions to 'la vie' and its cognates is the tone of yearning underlying them all. The verve and sparkle in these girls appeals to the Narrator precisely because he himself is hopelessly lacking in such a vitality.

It comes as a sense of uplift to him, therefore, that life should have this energetic, positive character, untroubled by complication. Such is the quality of feeling in these anonymous women that existence now boasts an unchanging freshness for him. At first sight at least, they seem to promise a lost spontaneity and naturalness.

As for Combray and its environs, it is the habitat of a medieval peasant class. I have already considered the role of Françoise, who is perhaps the greatest representative of that tradition (see Chapter 3c). But for the Narrator there are also the very young 'paysannes' of the region. The fact that they are descended from a remote past is evident from the likeness that the Narrator sees between the statues of the medieval church of Saint-André-des-Champs and those women who now stand and take shelter under its porches. One saint in particular is portrayed as having

les joues pleines, le sein ferme et qui gonflait la draperie comme une grappe mûre dans un sac de crin, le front étroit, le nez court et mutin, les prunelles enfoncées, l'air valide, insensible et courageux des paysannes de la contrée. (I, 151.)

She thus appears robust and strong-willed, a resilience that favourably impresses the Narrator. More interestingly, we find Proust using the epithet 'insensible'. This suggests an impervious, unyield-

ing temperament, which at once excludes any of the effete characteristics that might be seen in the Narrator. I shall be looking at an
important development on this notion of insensitivity later in the
chapter, when speaking of the little band of girls at Balbec. But for
the present, it is sufficient to note the peasant-like appearance of the
medieval statues; they seem to project an image of inviolable mental
tranquillity.

One young woman whose medieval temperament is possibly
more in evidence in the manuscripts than in the published version of
the *Recherche* is Mme Putbus' chambermaid. There are several
references to her in the novel itself, most of which are linked to the
Narrator's strongly sexual desire for her.[3] That desire, however, is
never actually fulfilled. In the *Cahiers*, on the other hand, a quite
developed physical relationship exists between the Narrator and the
servant woman. In addition, there is an intriguing, if limited, affinity
between the latter and Françoise:

Je pensais à cette recommandation pour une domestique, telle que mes
parents la concevaient, quelle distance séparait la paysanne française
charmante comme Françoise et la paysanne pervertie comme elle était.
Paysanne française pervertie, mais paysanne française encore. Encore par
moments la paysanne française de toujours, celle qui s'est réfugiée contre les
pluies sous le porche de Saint-Jean-des-Bois. Cette courtoisie vis-à-vis de
l'étranger qu'avait Françoise, qui la faisait multiplier le nombre des poulets à
Combray et ne pas refuser un verre de vin à Borniche, ce respect de la couche
nuptiale qui lui faisait tenir pour sacrés les liens de la parenté, je les reconnus,
hélas, et pervertis chez cette belle fille. Dès le premier jour où nous
partageâmes le même lit, elle eut avec moi une politesse, une douceur qu'elle
considérait comme due au nom d'une superstition antique et à laquelle elle
eût cru manquer en ne me témoignant pas quelque sentiment, comme
Françoise aurait cru y manquer si elle n'avait pas été animée d'une gaieté
décente avec quelqu'un qui l'invitait à dîner, ou si elle n'avait pas parlé d'une
voix gémissante après la mort de ma grand'tante. (*Cahier 50*, fos 19r–20v.)[4]

And so the Narrator enjoys the reverential simplicity of manner that
Mme Putbus' maid shows him, savouring it almost as he does
Françoise's own way of comportment.

One question that comes to mind is why this developed description of the young servant should not appear in the *Recherche* itself. A
feature of the *Cahiers* generally is that they contain a considerable
number of developments, some of which were reworked and
modified, and perhaps transferred to other characters. There are also
passages that simply do not appear in the *Recherche*. It is impossible
to generalise about such absences, although Proust evidently wishes
to guard against any oversimplification of, say, the complex intellect-

ual and emotional forces at work in the Narrator. Nevertheless, in the intimacy of his own *Cahiers*, he must have felt free to assert boldly certain notions, however inarticulate or half-formed they were. And in spite of the problems of evaluating what could be ambiguously termed Proust's 'throw-away' manuscript statements, these do sometimes form the hard core that supports the finished surface of the *Recherche*.

In the particular case of the 'femme de chambre de Mme Putbus', we are fortunate to have a suggestion, in the *Cahiers* themselves, that some of the descriptions originally intended for her were later switched to Albertine. In *Cahier 53*, Albertine is presented as carrying on a medieval tradition (fo 8*v*), and Proust confirms this idea of a transposition in the following, extremely revealing memorandum:

Kapitalissimum [*sic*] à ce qui est au verso et ci-dessous quand je parle du donjon de Roussainville et quand je transporte à Albertine ce que je dis de la femme de chambre de Mme Putbus. (*Cahier 55*, fo 93*r*.)

Although I shall be looking at the role played by Albertine later on, we have an early indication, in these *Cahier* references to the 'paysanne pervertie française', of the kind of untroubled relationship that the Narrator is so anxious to secure. And in the maid's predictability and unchanging temperament, the Narrator sees a reassurance that is as great as the joy that her fellow peasant Françoise holds for him. The sad reality for him will be that the protracted love relationship with Albertine never recaptures the unadorned calm and sureness of the liaison with the 'femme de chambre de Mme Putbus'.

It becomes clear therefore that, for the Narrator, his meetings with unknown peasant women are occasions of exhilaration and reverie. His excitement is that of one eager to penetrate a new world opening before him, a world of limitless possibility and pleasure. In this mental and emotional utopia the Narrator's own self-doubt disappears. Now that I have examined these individual, isolated cases, we might turn to that group which provides the focal point for the Narrator's interest in a youthful female beauty, namely the little band of girls at Balbec.

(c) First impressions of the 'petite bande de Balbec'

When they first appear in the novel, these girls are immediately linked to the adolescent Narrator's quest for the great absolute of 'la Beauté' (I, 787; Proust's capitalisation). For the Narrator, such beauty satisfies in part his vague longing for an individual love that he has been unable to secure. Yet initially, the girls appear totally elusive. The provenance of this 'bande de mouettes' is as mysterious as the nature of its composition. For the ordinary folk who frequent the beach, it is impossible to gauge the motivation of such strange creatures. That sense of awe is also experienced by the Narrator, who describes the girls' ramble along the edge of the beach as 'une promenade dont le but semble aussi obscur aux baigneurs qu'elles ne paraissent pas voir, que clairement déterminé pour leur esprit d'oiseaux' (I, 788). He cannot fathom their internal, autochthonous logic, which seems closer to an ornithological sense of motivation than to any human reasoning.

Immediately then, the little band is set apart, and is seen to represent a curiously novel mode of being. Their sporting attire, constituting a distinctive form of dress in Balbec, helps to convey graphically this idea of a separate identity, thus heightening the disparity:

Leur accoutrement tranchait sur celui des autres jeunes filles de Balbec, parmi lesquelles quelques-unes, il est vrai, se livraient au sport, mais sans adopter pour cela une tenue spéciale. (I, 788.)

The effect of these distinguishing characteristics is to suggest that the girls enjoy a level of awareness that is markedly different from that of the Narrator. When one adds to this the nebulous atmosphere surrounding them and the Narrator's inability to project himself into their orbit, one is reminded somewhat of the presentation of the 'laitière' (I, 655). She too is strange and unknown, although in a very undefined way. But in the case of the 'jeunes filles', Proust develops the idea of their distinctive presence much further, and in a direction that has important repercussions for the Narrator himself. It is informative to recall the drift of the speculation on the Balbec girls:

Peut-être ces filles (dont l'attitude suffisait à révéler la nature hardie, frivole et dure), extrêmement sensibles à tout ridicule et à toute laideur, incapables de subir un attrait d'ordre intellectuel ou moral, s'étaient-elles naturellement trouvées, parmi les camarades de leur âge, éprouver de la répulsion pour toutes celles chez qui des dispositions pensives ou sensibles se trahissaient par de la timidité, de la gêne, de la gaucherie, par ce qu'elles devaient appeler 'un genre antipathique', et les avaient-elles tenues à l'écart. (I, 790.)

The impression quite clearly given here is that the young girls are primarily concerned with the cultivation of a physical beauty, and a frankness and self-assurance of manner. In consequence, any hint of reticence in conversation or of corporeal ugliness incurs their scorn. But the most striking comment, in the context of this chapter, is the

Narrator's surmising that they are 'incapables de subir un attrait d'ordre intellectuel ou moral'. The spiritual and ethical worlds are thus non-existent for them. The limitation of being that this indifference to self-analysis implies can only be contrasted with the Narrator's disposition.[5]

The gap separating the group and the Narrator widens further when one considers those girls 'chez qui des dispositions pensives ou sensibles se trahiss[ent] par de la timidité, de la gêne, de la gaucherie'. For it would not be forcing the parallel were one to point out that the fastidious, reflective temperament that the Narrator attributes to retiring young girls is really a carbon-copy of his own. Once again, he finds himself being made conscious of the gap between instinctual, pleasurable experience, on the one hand, and a very developed sensitivity, on the other. In their preference for the former, the girls appear nonchalant and free from doubt. In that sense, they have something in common with the insensitive peasant woman shown earlier in this chapter to be sculptured in the church of Saint-André-des-Champs (I, 151).

As the description develops, the impression of their indifference gains in intensity. They make no attempt to accommodate those of a more reflective nature:

Elles s'étaient liées au contraire avec d'autres vers qui les attirait un certain mélange de grâce, de souplesse et d'élégance physique, seule forme sous laquelle elles pussent se représenter la franchise d'un caractère séduisant et la promesse de bonnes heures à passer ensemble. Peut-être aussi la classe à laquelle elles appartenaient et que je n'aurais pu préciser, était-elle à ce point de son évolution où, soit grâce à l'enrichissement et au loisir, soit grâce aux habitudes nouvelles de sport, répandues même dans certains milieux populaires, et d'une culture physique à laquelle ne s'est pas encore ajoutée celle de l'intelligence, un milieu social pareil aux écoles de sculpture harmonieuses et fécondes qui ne recherchent pas encore l'expression tourmentée. (I, 790–1.)

The solely corporeal grace, suggested by the 'mélange de grâce, de souplesse et d'élégance physique', is developed in turn into a hymn of praise to the health and robustness of the human body, as exemplified in the 'jeunes filles'. The Narrator sees them as pursuing this cult to the exclusion of all intellectual and cerebral considerations. Indeed, the girls of Balbec may, the Narrator speculates, inhabit some primitive, pre-intellectual domain, founded on 'une culture physique à laquelle ne s'est pas encore ajoutée celle de l'intelligence' and where a markedly hedonistic bias is never very distant. In some respects, the Narrator is using terms remarkably similar to those which he has already applied to Françoise. As we have seen, she herself is oblivious to a whole world of intellectual reality: 'Le monde immense des idées n'existait pas pour elle' (I, 650; see above, Chapter 3c). Nor is the fascination that the girls of Balbec hold for the Narrator any less than that which he feels for Françoise. In this way, we are able to glimpse a world of non-reflection being intermittently represented in the *Recherche*.

It may well be that the Narrator's seeing the little group in this light strikes the reader as being somewhat idealised or even oversimplified. Granted, the Narrator himself is aware that much of the arguably exaggerated attraction felt for the standard-bearers of bodily health derives from his own physical debility: 'D'ailleurs, de plus en plus souffrant, j'étais tenté de surfaire les plaisirs les plus simples à cause des difficultés mêmes qu'il y avait pour moi à les atteindre' (I, 787). Nevertheless, the comfort and sustenance that are his as he looks at the girls are no less real. Nor do these characters serve merely to counteract the feeling of ill-health in him. To see how they are more than temperamental 'stop-gaps' for the Narrator, we might consider the important use that Proust makes of sculpture in descriptions of them.

In the Narrator's allusion to the plastic arts near the end of the lengthy passage that I have just quoted, one finds the stark juxtaposition of the 'écoles de sculpture harmonieuses et fécondes' and later schools developing 'l'expression tourmentée' (I, 791).[6] This amplifies the notion of 'une culture physique à laquelle ne s'est pas encore ajoutée celle de l'intelligence'. The pained facial expression of later sculpture, arising from the complex and taxing work of inner self-searching, has yet to darken the countenances of the young girls of Balbec; they continue to radiate an unsullied physical beauty. With this appreciation of serene beauty in the human form, there dawns an awareness of the calm and assuagement that this aesthetic ideal can impart:

Et n'était-ce pas de nobles et calmes modèles de beauté humaine que je voyais là, devant la mer, comme des statues exposées au soleil sur un rivage de la Grèce? (I, 791.)

The Narrator reinforces these Hellenic associations with the lofty description of the little band as being 'noble comme si elle était composée de vierges helléniques' (I, 796).

One important feature of the Narrator's tranquil contemplation of the human body is the absence of any need to go behind and beyond that form. This is because the ability to contemplate 'de beaux corps aux belles jambes, aux belles hanches, aux visages sains et reposés' acquires a beauteous sufficiency for the Narrator. It is as though the fullness of being might be found in savouring the reposeful contours of the body.

To that extent, the Narrator displays a strong liking for pleasant and full surfaces. His whole appreciation is directed towards the immediately visible, external dimensions of this beauty. Absent are all images of depth, which would only serve to introduce a disquieting perspective to what is a solid exteriority. One might make the obvious, but nevertheless important, point that, in describing himself, the Narrator frequently speaks of the interiority of the mind. And inevitably with such images of inner depth, there come associations of spiritual torment for him. Moreover, when illness or the advance of age forces him back onto his own bodily self, he conveys an impression of physical debility and an over-riding concern with the most elemental self-preservation (see III, 12). In marked contrast, when placing emphasis on the physical *superficies* of the 'petite bande', the Narrator throws light on their uninvolved and readily visible beauty. As he himself says of this youthful grace on one occasion: 'Elle nous retourne du dedans vers le dehors et change notre âme' (*Cahier 25*, fo 22v).[7] His regret is that, more often than not, he is tied to the interiorisation of thought and feeling.

In their initial presentation, the Balbec girls reveal how Proust has set much of his description on an axis linking a pre-intellectual domain, at one extreme, and the world of analysis and introspection, at the other. The total sentience that the girls embody is something new to the Narrator, and this awakens his keen interest. Equally unfamiliar to him is the sense of quiescence that he experiences in the company of the 'nobles et calmes modèles de beauté humaine'. To that extent, they play an important part in unfolding the Narrator's own sensibilities. Given the abundance of contrasts in disposition, both stated and implicit, it would seem appropriate to examine more fully the use that Proust makes of oppositions in his evocations of the 'jeunes filles'.

(d) Antithesis in the Narrator/'jeunes filles' presentation

As the Narrator reflects on how his discovery of the 'jeunes filles' has considerably altered his order of priorities, he examines the nature of his relationship with them. He regrets that the girl cyclist, for example, will forever remain inaccessible to him. Her sphere of activity seems permanently closed to his avid gaze. The reflections in her eyes are not caused solely by the material composition of 'ce disque réfléchissant',

que ce sont, inconnues de nous, les noires ombres des idées que cet être se fait, relativement aux gens et aux lieux qu'il connaît – pelouses des hippodromes, sable des chemins où, pédalant à travers champs et bois, m'eût entraîné cette petite péri, plus séduisante pour moi que celle du paradis persan. (I, 794.)

Mention of a genie and some mysterious oriental paradise introduces a note of the marvellous, which quickly sets the young girl in an elusive fairylike world. The effect is to throw into sharper relief the Narrator's exclusion from a mysterious, quasi-supernatural experience. One might recall in passing the description of a young girl cyclist in *La Prisonnière*, 'la jeune créature mi-humaine, mi-ailée, ange ou péri, poursuivant son voyage' (III, 172). Again, the stress that is laid on her mythical being tends to heighten the Narrator's sense of distanciation.[8] Furthermore, the ceaseless physical activity implied by the reference to the girls' sporting pursuits is in added contrast to the Narrator's own more sedentary life-style.

The Narrator finally pushes the distinction between their temperaments to the point where they become diametrical opposites. Here the life of the young girls is portrayed as being antithetical to his own:

Peut-être aussi c'était grâce à ces différences, à la conscience qu'il n'entrait pas, dans la composition de la nature et des actions de ces filles, un seul élément que je connusse ou possédasse, que venait en moi de succéder à la satiété, la soif – pareille à celle dont brûle une terre altérée – d'une vie que mon âme, parce qu'elle n'en avait jamais reçu jusqu'ici une seule goutte, absorberait d'autant plus avidement, à longs traits, dans une plus parfaite imbibition. (I, 794–5.)

It is as though the Narrator were a zealous convert to a radically new way of living – the very different consciousness promised by the 'petite bande'.

We gain further insight into the process in the preparatory manuscript drafts for these characters. Under the title 'A ajouter aux jeunes filles', Proust writes at some length on the new worlds that are constantly unfolding before us:

De même que nous disions hier: Ah! la lecture. Ah! un nouvel écrivain, mais simplement parce que nous l'imaginions pareil aux anciens, puis prenant le premier livre de d'Annunzio qui nous apporte autre chose et nous fait prendre goût aux Vierges des Rochers, ou Emilie Brontë qui nous fait prendre goût à une simple existence, de même dans l'ordre du goût physique la vertu d'une beauté nouvelle, c'est de nous donner le goût d'une nouvelle qualité de bonheur, c'est de nous ouvrir de nouvelles perspectives d'existence. Elle nous retourne du dedans vers le dehors et change notre âme. (*Cahier 25*, fo 22v.)[9]

One especially interesting feature is the parallel between the imaginative world opened up by literature and the world of the young girls. In both cases, the effect is similar, since each experience tends to project the Narrator out of himself onto another level of consciousness. In particular, the impact of Emily Brontë is to have made him sensitive to a life of simplicity and charm. We have already seen Proust attributing that same ability to George Eliot (see Introduction).

Yet for the Narrator, the desired integration into the world of the 'jeunes filles' is a difficult, if not indeed impossible, one to effect. It is worthwhile pondering just what it is that makes that world appear so inaccessible. René Girard, in his *Mensonge romantique et vérité romanesque*, suggests that the Narrator is implicitly willing separation between himself and the young girls. In that sense, he sees in Proust's hero a masochistic desire for non-acceptance and failure – 'seul cet échec peut lui révéler une divinité authentique'.[10] The critic's language is not extravagant when one remembers the allusions, cited above, to 'ange', 'péri' and 'Déesses' (p. 107). And certainly no one is quicker than the Narrator to see obstacles to his entering the world of the 'jeunes filles':

Cette supposition me paraissait enfermer en elle une contradiction aussi insoluble que si, devant quelque frise attique ou quelque fresque figurant un cortège, j'avais cru possible, moi spectateur, de prendre place, aimé d'elles, entre les divines processionnaires. (I, 795.)

What is of central importance here is the tension existing between the passivity of the Narrator's presence, as suggested by the 'moi spectateur', and the active participatory role given to the 'jeunes filles'. By placing them in the hermetically sealed work of art, the Narrator intensifies his feeling of exclusion. Also beyond his reach is the frenzy of pleasurable emotion associated with the young girls' ever physical and sensual pastimes. Again, what is being reflected (and, Girard argues, perversely overemphasised) is the Narrator's static, isolated self, merely looking in on their world.

One of the repercussions of the Narrator's non-participation is the strong note of idealisation in his evocation of the Balbec girls. The gap that this presupposes serves the very useful purpose of affording us insight into the Narrator's own consciousness. He may cherish the desire of living sentient experience to the full, yet ultimately he sees himself as being frustrated in his attempts by his own reflective and intellectual scruples.

Later one finds more explicit reference to such contrasting modes of awareness. As he reflects on the collective existence enjoyed by the members of the 'petite bande', the Narrator tries to conceive of the pleasure he might derive from entering into their sanctuary:

En devenant l'ami de l'une d'elles j'eusse pénétré – comme un païen raffiné ou un chrétien scrupuleux chez les barbares – dans une société rajeunissante où régnaient la santé, l'inconscience, la volupté, la cruauté, l'inintellectualité et la joie. (I, 830.)

The head-on clash between a religious scrupulosity and a barbaric lack of sensitivity reinforces the more significant juxtaposition of the young girls and the Narrator. Furthermore, it confirms the almost diametrical character of the opposition. One can thus surmise quite confidently that in such a world, the Narrator hopes to see his own traits of character negatived in a totally transformed register of human experience. 'La santé' and 'la volupté' point to a sentient, bodily living; the vigorous hedonism that this implies will shut out a troubled hypersensitivity. Moreover, the limitless joy that the girls radiate strengthens the Narrator's otherwise insecure happiness.

But what is perhaps most significant for the purposes of our present study is the allusion to 'l'inconscience' and 'l'inintellectual-ité'. In this, one can see how the Narrator is implicitly contrasting the absence of a reflective self in the 'jeunes filles' with his own, here unstated condition, which is arguably one of intellectual preoccupa-tion. Consequently, he treasures what he sees as the girls' liberation in an unreflecting, non-intellectual state. For him, theirs is a rejuvenating society, vibrant with sensuality. They trade in 'la volupté, la cruauté', and appear to do so with a totality of self that can only be contrasted with the Narrator's own inner fragmentation. Not that he is insensitive to the physicality of instinctual experience. But what he can never do is live this with the same fullness as the 'jeunes filles'. For the Narrator, the presence of the mind, however unobtrusive, still casts a shadow over his actions; for the girls of Balbec, there is no such shadow – not at least in the eyes of the Narrator, who in practising this cult so assiduously comes close to a masochistic sense of personal inadequacy and unworthiness.

Earlier, I mentioned the possibility of expanding Proust's group-ing of 'celles chez qui des dispositions pensives ou sensibles se trahissaient par de la timidité' to include the Narrator's own situation (p. 104). The stark contrast that we have just seen between the Narrator and the young women of Balbec would tend to confirm this association. In so far as this is the case, several characters seem to fall clearly on one side or the other of the 'sensible'/'insensible' fence. The latter therefore provides the Narrator with a framework in which he may conveniently set many of his character oppositions.

The accumulation of antithetical temperaments continues when the Narrator describes his next encounter with the voluptuous girls of the seaside town:

Je ramenais Elstir vers sa villa, quand tout d'un coup, tel Méphistophélès surgissant devant Faust, apparurent au bout de l'avenue – comme une simple objectivation irréelle et diabolique du tempérament opposé au mien, de la vitalité quasi barbare et cruelle dont était si dépourvue ma faiblesse, mon excès de sensibilité douloureuse et d'intellectualité – quelques taches de l'essence impossible à confondre avec rien d'autre, quelques sporades de la bande zoophytique des jeunes filles. (I, 855.)

The analogy with Faust, tending as it does to endow the relationship between the Narrator and the girls with an unusual degree of magnificence, has an obvious comic dimension. This is achieved by the sudden transformation in the characters involved. From being an anonymous holiday-maker in Balbec, the adolescent Narrator is quickly recast as a Faust figure. Likewise the 'jeunes filles' shake off their humble origins to assume, in the Narrator's mind, the gravity of a daunting Mephistophelean presence. The grandiosity of the image is as comic as is its arresting appearance.

Nevertheless, the juxtaposition of a 'vitalité quasi barbare et cruelle' and 'mon excès de sensibilité douloureuse et d'intellectualité' remains a very clear one. Its thematic import is very similar to that of the contrasts quoted a little earlier in the text (I, 830). Indeed, the existence of opposite temperaments is now stated quite categorically, with the Narrator seeing in the little band 'une simple objectivation irréelle et diabolique du tempérament opposé au [sien]'.

The basic premise that appears to underlie many of these dissimilarities, although itself not explicitly set forth, is that something akin to a partial attraction of opposites is in operation. Admittedly, the process is not a reciprocal one – we have no indication of the Balbec girls being drawn towards the Narrator. He refers in fact to 'ce monde inhumain qui enfermait la vie de cette petite tribu, inaccessible inconnu où l'idée de ce que j'étais ne pouvait certainement ni parvenir ni trouver place' (I, 794). But on the Narrator's side, there exists a strong fascination with the embodiment of a temperament alien to his own. Girard's reading of this as a subjacent urge in the Narrator to perpetuate that sense of alienation – and so protect the 'divinité authentique' – is in some ways persuasive. The situation with the 'jeunes filles' is never static however, and the Narrator later graduates from living in reverential awe of them to enjoying their intimate friendship. By penetrating their world, he transforms the relationship, so that deities become still attractive but essentially human companions. Moreover, for the Narrator, the movement away from deification is not a particularly painful one:

Il était arrivé d'elles comme de ces mythologies qui de loin paraissent si mystérieuses et qui sont au fond anthro[po]morphiques et où on retrouve les hommes et les femmes que nous connaissons. Mais malgré cela j'étais heureux de pouvoir les avoir, les retenir, les grouper autour de moi. (*Cahier* 26, fo 28r.)

Here the Narrator's perspicacity rules out any suggestion of an unabating self-delusion, and characters like Albertine and Andrée go on to provoke in him a complex of emotions that ultimately undermines the diagnosis of masochism.

Much of what we have seen in this chapter confirms the gap of consciousness separating the Narrator from girls such as the milkmaid (I, 655–7) or those of Balbec. Unlike the Narrator, who is conscious of both a physical and an intellectual reality, these women seem to advocate, albeit in an indirect way, an exclusively instinctual experience. They thus throw into relief the opposite, cerebral temperament of the Narrator, as well as drawing out of him a dormant will to live experience on a uniquely sentient level.

(e) From the collectivity of the 'petite bande' to individuation: Andrée and Albertine

At this point we might examine some of the repercussions deriving from the collective identity that groups the 'jeunes filles de Balbec' together. The text just quoted, introducing the story of Faust and Mephistopheles, refers to members of this restricted society as 'quelques sporades de la bande zoophytique des jeunes filles' (I, 855). This recalls an earlier description where again images of sea life are invoked to help convey something of its composite nature:

Comme ces organismes primitifs où l'individu n'existe guère par lui-même, est plutôt constitué par le polypier que par chacun des polypes qui le composent, elles restaient pressées les unes contre les autres. (I, 823.)

What is significant here is that the Narrator should liken the girls to a low order of marine life, from which individuality is largely excluded. A possible implication of this is that there is an accompanying absence of individual consciousness in the young girls themselves. To conceive of them in terms of a primitive, animal level of existence may have the effect of reducing their being to something approaching a mental nothingness in the eyes of the Narrator. And certainly this unchanging sameness could be linked to their non-intellectualism.[11]

When one remembers its polyp-like composition, the Balbec group thus appears to experience life on an obscure sentient level. Since at the outset, they are not individualised, these girls seem to lead a uniform existence. Unlike the Narrator's always complex and often unpredictable responses, we find a primitive standardisation among these characters who go to make up 'telle masse amorphe et délicieuse' (I, 823). Besides, by casting the girls in this restricting, collective light, the Narrator also seems to render them somehow more accessible to himself. In a sense, this affords him the necessary tranquillity in which to study at leisure the image of indolent sensationalism that they project.

With the passing of time, however, the Narrator grows more acquainted with the little band, and with this there comes a degree of demystification. Much of the imaginative energy that helped sustain the Narrator's fascination is now converted into a more objective, less idealised description of individuals in the group.

Andrée is an interesting case in point, especially since the Narrator's original impression of her is subsequently reversed, with the move towards individuation:

Andrée qu'à cause de cela j'avais crue le premier jour une créature si dionysiaque et qui était au contraire frêle, intellectuelle et, cette année-là, fort souffrante, mais qui obéissait malgré cela moins à l'état de sa santé qu'au génie de cet âge qui emporte tout et confond dans la gaîté les malades et les vigoureux. (I, 893.)

With this sudden metamorphosis, Andrée ceases to be the Dionysiac creature to whom the Narrator had become accustomed. Thus, he no longer sees her as pursuing a youthful hedonism. Rather she appears to experience something of the torment and perplexity of inner self that he himself lives. Almost immediately, she acquires many of his traits of character, described in a vocabulary now familiar in the context of this chapter – 'frêle, intellectuelle et, cette année-là, fort souffrante'. Youth, enthroned here as some superior goddess, ensures, however, that she partakes of the general merry-making in which all the other Balbec girls indulge. Still, with the disintegration of the group's collective identity, we find an unexpectedly Narrator-like Andrée.[12]

Once the idea of a new Andrée has been launched, the Narrator then proceeds to develop novel aspects of her character. Her delicate sensitivity is now contrasted with Albertine's occasionally undiluted pleasure-seeking:

Elle exprimait son amitié pour moi, pour Albertine, avec des nuances qui prouvaient la plus délicieuse intelligence des choses du coeur, laquelle était peut-être due en partie à son état maladif. Elle avait toujours un sourire gai pour excuser l'enfantillage d'Albertine qui exprimait avec une violence naïve la tentation irrésistible qu'offraient pour elle des parties de plaisir auxquelles elle ne savait pas, comme Andrée, préférer résolument de causer avec moi ... (I, 893–4.)

Andrée, it can be seen, has much in common with the Narrator. By contrast, Albertine seems to confirm the Narrator's earlier belief that the girls formed 'une société rajeunissante où régnaient la santé, l'inconscience, la volupté, la cruauté, l'inintellectualité et la joie' (I, 830).

While it is now Albertine and Andrée who are being contrasted, and not the Narrator and the composite grouping of the 'petite bande', it is striking nevertheless that the thrust and counterthrust of different temperaments continues. Thus, the narrative adheres to familiar polarities – a fine sensitivity, on the one hand, and the search for immediate gratification, on the other; or again Andrée's physical debility in confrontation with Albertine's uncomprehending, strongly assertive 'violence naïve'. In this way, Proust continues to exploit the possibilities that such radically divergent spheres of being and awareness can present, interweaving a multiplicity of comparisons and contrasts all the while. Andrée and the Narrator, formerly divided in temperament in the latter's mind, come to have important traits in common. Both in turn are set against Albertine. Clearly Proust realised the value for his characterisation of this dialectic of opposites.

The contrasts between Albertine and Andrée increase as the unity of the little band disintegrates further. Andrée's hands, for example, are described as being beautiful in a delicate, refined way, and are frequently the subject of Elstir's sketches. That in itself would seem to enhance them, in so far as they are thus drawn closer to a world of art and fine sensibility. In one such study, 'elles avaient sous l'éclairage la diaphanéité dorée de deux feuilles d'automne' (I, 919). If 'la diaphanéité' preserves a possibility of transcendence, there can, however, be no getting beyond the physical, sensuous solidity of Albertine's hands; and significantly it is for Albertine that the Narrator develops an individual attraction (I, 918).

The similarities in disposition between the Narrator and Andrée, on the other hand, continue to grow. Thus, she displays a keen sensitivity when the Narrator experiences aesthetic elation on seeing some hawthorns. This is so unlike the normally unfeeling response of others when the Narrator knows such exaltation.[13]

Autour de moi flottait une atmosphère d'anciens mois de Marie, d'après-midi du dimanche, de croyances, d'erreurs oubliées. J'aurais voulu la saisir. Je m'arrêtai une seconde et Andrée, avec une divination charmante, me laissa causer un instant avec les feuilles de l'arbuste. (I, 922.)

One has the impression that Andrée and the Narrator are, in some respects, kindred spirits sharing a common heightened sensitivity. In showing herself to be capable of a 'divination charmante' on this occasion, she is visibly free from Albertine's 'violence naïve' (I, 893) and the cult of unrestrained sensuality resulting from it.

But it would appear that it is precisely the similarity of mind between Andrée and the Narrator that militates against the birth of a love between them. We have already seen that he himself prefers to focus his attention on the sensual Albertine (I, 918). Now, the idea of a magnet-like attraction of opposite temperaments is taken a significant step further when the Narrator confesses: 'Mais pour que j'aimasse vraiment Andrée, elle était trop intellectuelle, trop nerveuse, trop maladive, trop semblable à moi' (I, 943). One sees, therefore, the re-emergence of the Narrator's salient traits of character in Andrée, and the exclusion of any love relationship as an immediate consequence of this. The implications of such an assertion are far-reaching, since the Narrator is intimating that his search for love is inextricably bound up with his quest for a nature that is in many respects the opposite of his own. From this, one can see that lying behind the thin veil of love for the Narrator is the longing to counteract his physical and nervous debility. One might say that in asking love to serve that curative function, he is unwittingly stacking the odds against its success. Certainly this would tally with the Narrator's pessimistic conclusions on love generally.

As he had originally believed Andrée to be 'une créature saine et primitive', the epitome of bodily health, the Narrator felt attracted to her:

J'avais cru, le premier jour, voir sur la plage une maîtresse de coureur, enivrée de l'amour des sports, et Andrée me disait que, si elle s'était mise à en faire, c'était sur l'ordre de son médecin pour soigner sa neurasthénie et ses troubles de nutrition, mais que ses meilleures heures étaient celles où elle traduisait un roman de George Eliot. (I, 943.)

By losing this mysterious fun-loving appearance, and showing herself to be more inclined to pursue intellectual pastimes, Andrée sheds much of the enchanting grace of the other, Dionysiac characters. The allusions to sporting activity, which by now form a *leitmotif* in the presentation of the 'jeunes filles' in Balbec, immediately suggest a cultivation of the physical body. For the Narrator, its beauty is that it casts into oblivion his own complex individual self. The corollary to this enthusiasm for a very different quality of consciousness is significant; he finds in Andrée a level of awareness similar to his own, but nothing of the sensual ecstasy that he automatically equates with life in the presence of her companions. As the Narrator says of Andrée, again setting her against Albertine: 'Si Albertine me semblait maintenant vide, Andrée était remplie de quelque chose que je connaissais trop' (I, 943).[14]

It is evident that the number of dissimilarities between the Narrator and the little band of Balbec is quite considerable. Such differences, we have seen, generally function on an axis running between a broad area of sensual, instinctual living at one end, and a thought domain at the other. Yet it is not possible to insist on a strict polarisation here, however much the Narrator may suggest this on occasions. Where for example would one position Andrée in such a binary classification, given her changing character? For even with the revelation that she is similar in temperament and mind to the Narrator, '[elle] obéissait malgré cela moins à l'état de sa santé qu'au génie de cet âge qui emporte tout et confond dans la gaîté les malades et les vigoureux' (I, 893). She can also share youth's exuberance, which expresses itself in a largely bodily living. Nor is the Narrator himself unaccustomed to such a way of comportment, if one remembers his own instinctual joys (see Chapter 3*f*). But the significance of the girls presented in *A l'ombre des jeunes filles en fleurs* is that almost all of them are motivated by purely sensual stimuli. They thus avoid the tension between sentient and intellectual experience that preoccupies the Narrator. It is principally on these grounds that he idealises the unicity of being in the 'petite bande'.

(f) The Duchesse de Guermantes as a similar case to the young girls

The same pattern of intellectual preoccupation followed by its negation is also visible in references to the Duchesse de Guermantes. The Narrator sees the way in which she expresses herself as forming part of that glorious, historical past that he finds so inaccessible: 'A l'accent, au choix des mots on sentait que le fond de conversation de la duchesse venait directement de Guermantes' (II, 502–3). But on this occasion, the Narrator does not restrict himself to delighting in her as the living embodiment of an almost sacred medieval tradition. For, as well as this, he attempts to gauge the quality of consciousness that her quaint use of language reflects. The outcome of this is a series of contrasts similar in some respects to those we have seen with the 'jeunes filles':

La duchesse différait profondément de son neveu Saint-Loup, envahi par tant d'idées et d'expressions nouvelles; il est difficile quand on est troublé par les idées de Kant et la nostalgie de Baudelaire, d'écrire le français exquis d'Henri IV, de sorte que la pureté même du langage de la duchesse était un signe de limitation, et qu'en elle l'intelligence et la sensibilité étaient restées fermées à toutes les nouveautés. Là encore l'esprit de Mme de Guermantes me plaisait justement par ce qu'il excluait (et qui composait précisément la matière de ma propre pensée) et tout ce qu'à cause de cela même il avait pu conserver, cette séduisante vigueur des corps souples qu'aucune épuisante réflexion, nul souci moral ou trouble nerveux n'ont altérée. (II, 503.)

The complexity that the Narrator attributes to Kant and Baudelaire stands in marked contrast to the serenity associated with the aristocratic lady's archaic, even-flowing French. Indeed, her diction is interpreted by the Narrator as a welcome 'signe de limitation'. This particular trait in some ways points back to the aphorisms of Schopenhauer. We have already examined these, especially the Narrator's view of the philosopher's theory that limitation of the self brings happiness to the individual (see above, section *a*). In the case of the Duchesse, her uncomplicated words speak volumes for her sedate, tranquil personality. By implication, this brings into play yet again the Narrator's own intellectual doubting and moral confusion; he can never quite experience the closed, and consequently more stable, mental world of his idol.

Once more, it is by virtue of their antithetical temperaments – the parenthesis in the passage just quoted confirms this – that he can enjoy the physical beauty, the 'séduisante vigueur des corps souples'. Yet that remains something that he may glimpse in others but not live within his own self. All this is, of course, very reminiscent of the 'jeunes filles' evocations. The parallel is strikingly obvious, with the renewed fantasising about a bodily suppleness and an absence of taxing self-examination – 'aucune épuisante réflexion, nul souci moral ou trouble nerveux'. The girls of Balbec, too, were seen to be 'incapables de subir un attrait d'ordre intellectuel ou moral' (I, 790).

Proust himself confirms the validity of this analogy by giving an explicit confirmation of the comparison in the text:

Son esprit d'une formation si antérieure au mien, était pour moi l'équivalent de ce que m'avait offert la démarche des jeunes filles de la petite bande au bord de la mer. (II, 503.)

In his reference to 'une formation si antérieure au mien', the Narrator is envisaging a more primitive level of consciousness, where one can escape the war of attrition with the mind. As for the enthusiasm with which he speaks of this peaceful awareness of experience, one detects a willingness to accept such a limitation of the thinking self. What is more, he is again speaking in terms of early and late stages of intellectual development. This he does in a significantly explicit and conscious way, and if we begin to think along these lines, we can trace the genealogy far back. At its most remote point, one finds Françoise, a living embodiment of primitive man (see Chapter 3c); the Duchesse de Guermantes and the girls of Balbec lie at some intermediary level; and the latest descendant is the Narrator, who reflects the fullest and most problematical development of human consciousness. Clearly then, Proust is making full use of these gradations of awareness in his work of characterisation. Their advantage is that they provide a series of temperament-categories, as it were, to which he conveniently and almost invariably returns.

A corollary to the young girls' 'inintellectualité' is their lack of sensitivity, which frequently expresses itself in a mildly cruel behaviour. The pattern recurs with the Duchesse. But while she is similarly insensitive, her hardness may grow into a ferocity, as this very graphic description reveals. She still retains

l'énergie et le charme d'une cruelle petite fille de l'aristocratie des environs de Combray, qui, dès son enfance, montait à cheval, cassait les reins aux chats, arrachait l'oeil aux lapins. (II, 503.)[15]

The self-indulgent manner in which she exerts such cruelty has the immediate effect of throwing into sharper focus the Narrator's own effeteness. This reinforces one's impression that the hypersensitive Narrator is forever set apart in the novel. While he lives in the solitude of his own mind, the 'jeunes filles' escape this, almost *en masse*. So too do the Duchesse and Françoise, with the result that a faltering Narrator looks with envy at what is for these characters the effortless process of self-realisation.

From this brief insight into the limited consciousness of the Duchesse de Guermantes, one may draw conclusions broadly similar in tone to those relating to the 'petite bande' of Balbec. The absence of any cerebral torment in the aristocratic lady excites the Narrator's keen interest. It is as though the burden of his excessive reflection were lightened in the limited and stable perspective on life that he sees her as enjoying.

(g) Life at Doncières

This might seem a strange point at which to consider the Narrator's enthusiasm for the military life in the garrison town of Doncières. Unlike the other subsections of this chapter, which deal with the adolescent Narrator's female acquaintances, the present one will be looking at his life in the company of soldiers. In spite of this very obvious contrast, the inclusion here of a commentary on Doncières can be justified on the grounds of strong thematic links. We shall be seeing presently how much of the Narrator's ecstatic experience in Balbec reappears, under a slightly different guise, in the evocations of Doncières.

In a letter that he receives from Saint-Loup, the Narrator reads his correspondent's description of the military 'ambiance'. This includes a statement of Saint-Loup's regret that he should have to forsake the Narrator's company, to return to

cette vie grossière, où hélas, je me sens bien exilé, n'ayant pas ce que j'ai laissé à Balbec; cette vie où je ne retrouve aucun souvenir d'affection, aucun charme d'intellectualité; vie dont vous mépriseriez sans doute l'ambiance et qui n'est pourtant pas sans charme. (I, 868.)

No doubt it is with the Narrator's temperament uppermost in mind that Saint-Loup concedes, almost apologetically, that Doncières has nothing to offer in the way of intellectual stimulation. Yet he remains unspecific about the joys that it may hold out in compensation for this. We have nevertheless, in the Narrator's own favourable reaction to life in the garrison town, perhaps some indication of what Saint-Loup means. In a way recalling life with the youth of Balbec, the Narrator marvels at the pleasurable experience that would be his, were he to lodge in the barracks:

Quel repos sans tristesse j'aurais goûté là, protégé par cette atmosphère de tranquillité, de vigilance et de gaîté qu'entretenaient mille volontés réglées et sans inquiétude, mille esprits insouciants, dans cette grande communauté qu'est une caserne où, le temps ayant pris la forme de l'action, la triste cloche des heures était remplacée par la même joyeuse fanfare de ces appels dont était perpétuellement tenu en suspens sur les pavés de la ville, émietté et pulvérulent, le souvenir sonore, – voix sûre d'être écoutée, et musicale, parce qu'elle n'était pas seulement le commandement de l'autorité à l'obéissance mais aussi de la sagesse au bonheur! (II, 78.)

On a structural level, the passage is essentially an accumulation of contrasts and oppositions. This pattern of construction is a significant one, in that it reflects a rhythm similar to that of the many passages on the 'jeunes filles' that we have examined. The Narrator sees military life as guaranteeing a pleasant tranquillity, a 'repos sans tristesse', which suggests an affective stability of which he himself is deprived. Evidence of this lies in the strongly conditional character of 'Quel repos [...] *j'aurais goûté*' (italics mine), crystallising the Narrator's sense of longing but also his status of mere onlooker.

It is equally noteworthy that the discipline of such a life ensures 'mille volontés réglées et sans inquiétude, mille esprits insouciants'. All reflective anguish seems to be allayed; in consequence, the Narrator is further drawn to this life-style. Moreover, he temporarily abandons his customary passivity in an attraction to the ceaseless physical activity of the troops. Hence, a pleasurable regimentation of the mind and a discipline imposed from without present themselves as alternatives to the Narrator's long hours of mental pondering and not infrequent melancholy. In the troops' unquestioning compliance with orders, the Narrator sees the effacement of the individual self, now subsumed into a pleasant, collective existence. For the Narrator, the end of self-responsibility brings relief from the burden of personal choice and reflection.[16]

So it is that he sings the praises of this disciplined, corporate living, which paints a picture of unmitigated happiness. And while the discipline of military life might be said to contrast with the anarchic band of indolent girls in Balbec, the two experiences are analogous in certain fundamental respects. The immediacy and self-sufficiency of the non-intellectual pleasure afforded by both would suggest a fair degree of consonance. In the eyes of the Narrator, the acquaintances of Balbec and Doncières are the unsung heroes and heroines who share a common limited awareness of existence.

Judging from Proust's work generally, the military life seems to have always held this potential. The treatment of the subject in his much earlier *Les Plaisirs et les jours* reveals a similar slant to that of the *Recherche*. He points out, for example, how the character of fellow soldiers can be refreshing in its idyllic simplicity (*JS*, pp. 130–1). In the same work, the first-person narrator recalls his untroubled enjoyment of

le calme d'une vie où les occupations sont plus réglées et l'imagination moins asservie que dans toute autre, où le plaisir nous accompagne d'autant plus continuellement que nous n'avons jamais le temps de le fuir en courant à sa recherche. (*JS*, pp. 130–1.)

This confirms the emphasis of the *Recherche*, where the inference is that in his contact with carefree living, the sting of the Narrator's reflective torment is drawn.

Still in *Les Plaisirs et les jours*, we see vivacious fellow soldiers, 'dont le corps était resté plus beau, plus agile, l'esprit plus original, le coeur plus spontané, le caractère plus naturel que chez les jeunes gens que j'avais fréquentés auparavant' (*JS*, p. 130). In this description of their body and mind, one gets a foretaste of the spontaneity and beauty of the 'jeunes filles en fleurs' in the later novel. Moreover, the young Proust insists that contentment in the garrison town results from the ability to pre-empt all reflection on the very character and source of the happiness itself: 'Nous n'avons jamais le temps de fuir [le plaisir] en courant à sa recherche' (*JS*, p. 131). Military life in *Jean Santeuil* is similarly portrayed (see *JS*, pp. 549–56).

Returning to *A la recherche*, one comes across further divergences between the Narrator and some of his military friends. He finds Saint-Loup's boundless energy and his active involvement in the military life to be quite contagious, and he quickly longs for an end to his own physical inertia:

A côté des occupations importantes qui le faisaient si pressé, si alerte, si content, les ennuis qui m'empêchaient tout à l'heure de rester un instant sans souffrir me semblaient, comme à lui, négligeables [. . .]. La vie me semblait si différente, si belle, j'étais inondé d'un tel trop-plein de force que je voulais agir. (II, 90.)

With the substitution then of mobility and action for a more normal passivity, the Narrator's attention is now happily focused on a total engagement of the self in the 'milieu vital fort différent de ma chambre' (II, 89).

The same savouring of bodily feeling marks the Narrator's description of the walks that he takes in order to view field manoeuvres. As he recalls how he needed to rest after his exertions, one can see what is almost the luxuriousness of his fatigue:

Au moment où je voulais me lever, j'en éprouvais délicieusement l'incapacité: je me sentais attaché à un sol invisible et profond par les articulations, que la fatigue me rendait sensibles, de radicelles musculeuses et nourricières. Je me sentais plein de force, la vie s'étendait plus longue devant moi. (II, 91.)

The renewed vitality engendered throughout this evocation serves to place the experience on the same instinctual register as that which marked the Narrator's praises of military life cited earlier.

Indeed, the sense of fullness becomes so all-pervading on occasions that it swells not only the Narrator but also the world of phenomena about him. Thus, the surfaces of objects assume a fuller, convex dimension. He himself sees their rotundity as mirroring the abundance of his own emotion:

Je gardais, dans mon logis, la même plénitude de sensation que j'avais eue dehors. Elle bombait de telle façon l'apparence de surfaces qui nous semblent si souvent plates et vides, la flamme jaune du feu, le papier gros bleu du ciel sur lequel le soir avait brouillonné, comme un collégien, les tire-bouchons d'un crayonnage rose [. . .]. Comme un plongeur respirant dans un tube qui monte jusqu'au-dessus de la surface de l'eau, c'était pour moi comme être relié à la vie salubre, à l'air libre. (II, 95–6.)

The image of the diver about to surface proves extremely suitable for the radical change of atmosphere that accompanies the Narrator's move to Doncières. For him, the transformation in the quality of human awareness is as great as that in the diver's respiratory supply.

The description that follows of Doncières' mysterious streets at night is vibrant with this new sensuality (II, 96–7). A useful indication of the Narrator's general inebriation with the experience is his changed attitude towards the Duchesse de Guermantes. His original motive in going to Doncières was of course to gain access to the Duchesse through her nephew, Saint-Loup; that plotting is now abandoned in the tranquillity of garrison life: 'Je songeais à l'avenir: essayer d'oublier Mme de Guermantes me semblait affreux, mais raisonnable et, pour la première fois, possible, facile peut-être' (II, 97). Slightly later, one finds that this concern for the Duchesse, once so prominent among his 'préoccupations extérieures', has slipped imperceptibly from his mind (II, 117).

The contentment with Doncières is strengthened, it would seem, with a significant choice of artist to explain further the Narrator's elation. This occurs in a portrayal of

des soldats balourds qui passaient sur le trottoir, la face peinturlurée par le froid; et elle faisait penser, dans cette cité que le brusque saut de l'automne dans ce commencement d'hiver semblait avoir entraînée plus avant dans le nord, à la face rubiconde que Breughel donne à ses paysans joyeux, ripailleurs et gelés. (II, 98.)

In view of our present considerations, the Narrator's selection of painter is extremely apposite. What Proust at any rate picks out in him is the suggestion of openness and transparency of emotion that his creations introduce. The assumption is that in the Flemish artist's work, there is a visible absence of any inner conflict, and that his normal subject-matter involves an unadorned, rustic simplicity. Moreover, the beauty of his compositions, Proust seems to imply, is that everything is visibly contained in his depiction of full surfaces.

Given this interpretation of Brueghel, the reference to him is not a gratuitous one. Rather it helps confirm the thesis that for the Narrator, his stay at Doncières is a frankly pleasurable experience.

We have already seen the successful use of a related art form to help expand and illuminate the Narrator's response to acquaintances. There was, for example, an evocation of the 'sculpture harmonieuse et féconde' of ancient Greek sculpture, which set the seal on the calming beauty of the 'jeunes filles' (see above, section *c*). Now Brueghel is introduced, his art helping to convey something of the simplicity and instinctual joys offered by the military life. If the aesthetics of the Greek and Flemish schools have anything in common for Proust's Narrator, it is perhaps that the untormented facial expression characteristic of both reflects an inner, undivided harmony. Indeed, it seems reasonable to assume that his fascination with a beautiful non-complication largely conditions the Narrator's choice of artists.

Further echoes of the 'jeunes filles' encounter also reach the description of life at Doncières. As with the little band of girls, of whom 'la santé, l'inconscience, la volupté, la cruauté, l'inintellectualité' (I, 830) appeared antithetical to the Narrator's temperament, so the young recruits of Doncières embody attributes that the Narrator lacks. Still, he seems capable of enjoying these vicariously: 'C'était de grand coeur que ces jeunes gens mettaient leur luxe, leur jeunesse, leur vigueur au service de ma faiblesse' (II, 128). Both soldiers and young girls mirror a oneness of being, without trace of inner fragmentation or conflict. The Narrator's haste to turn to these groups betrays a desire to share that freedom from a scrupulous self-criticism.

But it would be a misrepresentation to argue that the charm of the Narrator's stay at Doncières consists solely of an instinctual satisfaction. However much he is impressed by the newness of experience and environment, this does not exclude him from giving some attention to his own intellectual leanings. We have a concrete example of this when the Narrator applies himself to a serious evaluation of Saint-Loup's theorising on military strategy. This comes right out of the blue. Up until now, emphasis has been on the atmosphere of hedonism so prevalent in Doncières. Yet quite abruptly, the Narrator wonders if theorising on the art of warfare might redeem him intellectually:

Saint-Loup, par ce qu'il venait de me dire touchant l'art de la guerre, ajoutait un fondement intellectuel, d'une nature permanente, capable de m'attacher assez fortement pour que je pusse croire, sans essayer de me tromper moi-même, qu'une fois parti, je continuerais à m'intéresser aux travaux de mes amis de Doncières et ne tarderais pas à revenir parmi eux. (II, 113.)

The hope of permanence lying behind the search for a 'fondement intellectuel' marks quite a departure from other assessments of life in Doncières, where the predominant mood is one of *carpe diem*. The Narrator now alludes to the fugacious nature of many of the pleasures associated with Doncières; to counter this, he sets his sights on what is for him the gilt-edged intellectual justification of his stay in the town. He explains:

Ce qui me plaisait aujourd'hui ne me deviendrait peut-être pas indifférent demain, comme cela m'était toujours arrivé jusqu'ici, l'être que j'étais encore en ce moment n'était peut-être pas voué à une destruction prochaine, puisque, à la passion ardente et fugitive que je portais, ces quelques soirs, à tout ce qui concernait la vie militaire, Saint-Loup [. . .] ajoutait un fondement intellectuel. (II, 113.)

For the Narrator, who is constantly dogged by mental scruples, the effect of this cerebral sanction is to render more concrete and lasting some of the more ephemeral pursuits of barrack life. One can quickly see, then, how the reflective side to the Narrator's being comes to reassert itself; it finds a partial justification for the sojourn in the military theorising of Saint-Loup: 'Ces théories de Saint-Loup me rendaient heureux. Elles me faisaient espérer que peut-être je n'étais pas dupe dans ma vie de Doncières' (II, 112).

This is not the first time we have seen the Narrator concerned in this way. One might recall, for example, the enigmatic beauty of Racine and Leconte de Lisle, a beauty that he feels he must render conceptual if it is to be valid. His aesthetic scrupulosity on that occasion can be related to his present preoccupation with the academic merit of Saint-Loup's *exposé*.

The eleventh-hour insistence on intellectual criteria contrasts with the Narrator's general mood at Doncières. We have seen him warm to the atmosphere of 'bonhomie' among the soldiers; their generally tranquil, unthinking existence helps alleviate his own mental insecurity. In view of this, it is important to bear in mind the varying character of the Narrator's responses, for it guards against any diminution of what are complex questions in the *Recherche*. But what can be stated, and again quite categorically, is that the comparisons and contrasts, built up around the broad areas of instinctual and reflective experience, are fundamental to Proust's presentation of his Narrator.

(h) The young 'courrières' and a troubled Narrator

When one comes to *Sodome et Gomorrhe* and *La Prisonnière*, the Narrator's concern with love is so prominent as to produce a shift of emphasis in his preoccupations. In this respect, his quasi-philosophical doubting in adolescence becomes converted into the anguish that accompanies his liaison with Albertine.[17] Thus, whereas the impact of the 'jeunes filles' or life at Doncières was often to free the Narrator from the prison of metaphysical uncertainty, he now feels a need to calm the anguish and upheaval aroused by his relationship with Albertine. When seen against this background, the intercalation in *Sodome et Gomorrhe* of a description of two 'courrières' is doubly important.[18]

Throughout this late addition, the two young women are seen to be human extensions of their own rugged native environment: 'Nées au pied des hautes montagnes du centre de la France, au bord de ruisseaux et de torrents [...], elles semblaient en avoir gardé la nature' (II, 846). The natural and primitive character of their place of origin is important. Indeed, the reverential tone in which that mountainous retreat is described suggests something of the idyllic settings so common in Jean-Jacques Rousseau.[19] Further confirmation of the analogy lies in the serenity of mind enjoyed by the young women. This can only impress the Narrator, especially at a time of personal crisis in the relationship with Albertine.

Reinforcing his sense of calm is a reference to primordial man, which ushers in a remote period in human development, where primitive consciousness is but dawning:

On prétend que le liquide salé qu'est notre sang n'est que la survivance intérieure de l'élément marin primitif. Je crois de même que Céleste, non seulement dans ses fureurs, mais aussi dans ses heures de dépression, gardait le rythme des ruisseaux de son pays. (II, 850.)

I have already examined some of the implications attending Proust's use of a primitive frame of reference (Chapter 3); the particular way in which he exploits the theme here proves to be no exception. For hand in hand with the notion of a primordial consciousness is the suggestion that these women are oblivious of issues of an intellectual or literary nature. Indeed, it is from such an apparently blissful ignorance that a beautiful clarity in the person of Céleste comes about: 'L'eau coulait dans la transparence opaline de sa peau bleuâtre. Elle souriait au soleil et devenait plus bleue encore. Dans ces moments-là elle était vraiment céleste' (II, 850). The Narrator's undisguised enthusiasm for Céleste here takes off in this baroque and somewhat eccentric description. Yet in the diffusion of blues in the sketch, her lucid vision of things remains and is indeed fêted, reflecting as it does a total serenity of the self. For the Narrator, while her untroubled outlook is invigorating, it is nevertheless a way of viewing existence that he himself has never really known. His intensity of mind will continue to exclude that possibility.

The contrasts, then, existing between the Narrator and the two maids are clearly drawn, and one can detect a sentimental yearning in the former for the limpid, primitive existence that he sees in the young women. The calm that this brings becomes heightened if one remembers the position of this set-piece in the text. It is marked on either side by the growing tension provoked by suspicions of Albertine's lesbianism. Immediately before the 'courrières' sketch, we read of allegations concerning Bloch's sister, and scandalous revelations about Nissim-Bernard (II, 842); following the vignette, one finds a renewal of the Narrator's misgivings and doubts (II, 850 ff). Given its position, the portrayal affords the Narrator the opportunity to anaesthetise his assailed self, temporarily at least, against the anguish of his love for Albertine. In the unabating sea of amatory doubt, it stands out as a haven of calm and stability.

So it is that a glimpse of instinctual living enables the Narrator to escape not only reflective, intellectual uncertainty, as was the case with the 'petite bande', but also the imaginative onslaught of love. The liaison with Albertine is, of course, one of the central issues in *A la recherche*, and we shall be seeing the Narrator's hypersensitive response to that relationship in the next chapter. For the moment, however, it is sufficient to note the important role that the young peasant women again play in the Narrator's development.

(i) Idealisation: a major factor in the Narrator's fascination?

For the hero of the novel, it is the absence of any overwhelming intellectual gravity that explains the exhilaration of life with the 'jeunes filles' or the soldiers of Doncières. Yet he is at the same time aware that for himself, there can be no total escape from thought. This is what makes full integration with the 'jeunes filles' imposs-ible. And for the Narrator to describe the frivolity of Balbec or Doncières, he needs to feel contentment with the instinctual and yet ultimately sense its non-sufficiency. It is then his own temperament that provides the mental quotient, the 'dose de sérieux' (*Cahier 44*, fo 4) necessary to perceive the appeal of the light-hearted and the frivolous in others.

In some important respects, Proust's position is comparable with that of his own creation, Elstir. The latter's paintings are undeniably non-intellectual in their nature, since the aim of his art is to convey our primary, pre-conceptual vision of things. Yet this in no way diminishes the painter's intellectual capabilities:

L'effort qu'Elstir faisait pour se dépouiller en présence de la réalité de toutes les notions de son intelligence était d'autant plus admirable que cet homme qui avant de peindre se faisait ignorant, oubliait tout par probité (car ce qu'on sait n'est pas à soi), avait justement une intelligence exceptionnellement cultivée. (I, 840.)

Interestingly enough, the Narrator himself enjoys 'les joies intellectuelles dans cet atelier' (I, 842). And when in later years, the artist's work is in decline, the Narrator attributes this to Elstir's loss of 'la force de faire l'effort intellectuel qui seul peut produire son oeuvre' (I, 852.)

What is true of Elstir's development is, I suggest, similar to the Narrator's situation, and is equally applicable to Proust himself. The fact that the latter should choose to write of the girls in Balbec, or of the leisurely untroubled atmosphere of Doncières, does not preclude his own intellectual disposition. As for the Narrator, it would appear that his fascination with spontaneous, unreflecting youth is not so much in spite of his reflective temperament, but almost because of it. In so far as this is the case, one feels a drawing-together of opposite minds here.

One might push this notion slightly further by considering a manuscript passage that is no less significant for not appearing in the *Recherche*. In it, Mme de Guermantes chides the Narrator for frequenting what she believes to be the inferior social milieu of Mme d'Arpajon: the Narrator in turn rejects as stereotyped

les idées de Mme de Guermantes sur les esprits littéraires qu'elle croyait devoir se plaire uniquement avec des 'intellectuels' sans se rendre compte que pour eux, l'intelligence est quelque chose qu'ils produisent eux-mêmes et n'ont pas besoin d'aller chercher *les autres auxquels ils demandent plutôt le spectacle de ce qui diffère le plus de leur propre nature*. (n.a.fr. 16710:103; italics mine.)[20]

The Narrator is pointing, quite unequivocally, to the interest of the spiritually and literary-minded in experience that departs most radically from their own. The validity of his claim is fully endorsed when one recalls what is for him the central importance of the Balbec grouping, of peasant women generally, or the atmosphere of 'bonhomie' so prevalent in Doncières. Each of these experiences has the merit of drawing the Narrator out of his habitual self. And if the *Recherche* purports to describe his search in life, this element of quest is perhaps nowhere more in evidence than in his intrepid exploration of psychic and emotional states that are originally unknown to him. To take him into the zones of unintellectuality and pure sentience, he requires as viaticum what Proust terms 'une dose de sérieux dont une personne purement frivole eût été incapable' (*Cahier 44*, fo 4).

One significant aspect of the Narrator's portrayal of the 'jeunes filles' is the presence of a strong element of idolatry. In one sense, this is a consequence of the Narrator's eager imaginative involvement. Because he is unable to experience the oneness of being that he sees others enjoying, he will soon find their world an elusive, more privileged one than his own. As for the girls of Balbec, or the Duchesse de Guermantes, or the soldiers of Doncières, they of course have a less lofty view of their own existence than the exaggerated estimation given it by an ecstatic Narrator.

In one of his studies on Proust, Roger Shattuck refers to a question closely related to our present one when he speaks of the importance of 'soul error'. This he defines as 'the incapacity to give full value or status to one's own life and experience'.[21] His term is a translation of Montaigne's 'erreur d'âme', taken from the latter's essay on presumption. There Montaigne explains the nature of his error:

C'est que je diminue du juste prix les choses que je possede, de ce que je les possede; et hausse le prix aux choses, d'autant qu'elles sont estrangeres, absentes et non miennes [...]. Davantage que je suis tres ignorant en mon faict. J'admire l'asseurance et promesse que chacun a de soy, là où il n'est quasi rien que je sçache sçavoir, ny que j'ose me respondre pouvoir faire.[22]

Certainly, Shattuck's reference to Montaigne is enlightening. In the latter's confession of a fascination with what lies beyond his own reach, one finds echoes of the Narrator idolising the 'jeunes filles en fleurs', to cite but one example in Proust's work.

Differences arise however over the sameness or otherwise of our experience and that of others. Montaigne argues that we aim for the latter, even though there is no objective disparity between the respective worlds involved. And the contemporary critic René Girard takes the argument a step further, seeing in Proust's Narrator a perverse will to guarantee his exclusion from the world of the Balbec girls. But the charge of wilful self-delusion is not easily proven. The *Recherche* shows a very real gap existing between the Narrator's predominantly intellectual life-view and that of simpler minds – a situation that may be as inevitable for him as it is exciting:

Le charme du visage de la jeune fille de la montagne était bien de m'avoir donné le désir d'être auprès d'elle au soleil levant, de traire les vaches, de devenir l'un des siens, de ne plus même remarquer que cette vie était différente. Mais là, sans doute, je n'aurais rien trouvé de la particularité de sa beauté. (*Cahier 23*, fo 4.)[23]

Thus, the Narrator's desire to become totally integrated into the uncomplicated world of the young peasant is checked by the dawning of a sudden awareness. This is the realisation that it is precisely their fundamental difference of being that gives rise to the Narrator's attraction to the girl's instinctualism. It is important to remember that what the *Cahier* states categorically is no less true of the *Recherche* itself, although there it is more of an underlying assumption. Accordingly, the Narrator is not simply aware of the distance separating the girl from himself. More importantly, he insists that the beauty that he sees is conditional on their continuing unlikeness. His fascination feeds on this.

A similar situation arises when the Narrator speculates on the impact that his work of art might have on Albertine, especially the Albertine he first knew in Balbec:

Il était bien certain en effet que ces pages que j'écrirais, Albertine, surtout l'Albertine d'alors, ne les eût pas comprises. Mais c'est justement pour cela (et c'est une indication à ne pas vivre dans une atmosphère trop intellec-tuelle), parce qu'elle était si différente de moi, qu'elle m'avait fécondé par le chagrin, et même d'abord par le simple effort pour imaginer ce qui diffère de soi. Ces pages, si elle avait été capable de les comprendre, par cela même elle ne les eût pas inspirées. (III, 915n.)

Albertine's non-intellectualism, then, is again mentioned as con-tributing immeasurably to the Narrator's love for her. In addition to this, we find a renewed insistence on their different ways of apprehending reality. But the most significant fact is that this contrast should dominate the Narrator's own creative writing. The whole drift of his work on Albertine is such that it precludes her being able to understand it. Just as the mountain girl must retain her instinctualism if her influence on the Narrator is to persist (*Cahier 23*, fo 4), so too Albertine must remain insensitive to the art that she has inspired. Proust evidently wanted to stress this, for he reiterates the prerequisite, indicating how he sees this condition as being funda-mental to a proper understanding of the relationship with Albertine: 'Bien noter la formule du bas de cette page: ces pages, si elle avait été capable de les comprendre, par cela même elle ne les eût pas inspirées' (III, 1139, note 1 to III, 915).[24] In these observations of the mature Proust, one finds the author reaffirming yet again the essential difference between the Narrator and the most prominent of the 'jeunes filles', Albertine. In so far as this is the case, it marks a significant departure from Montaigne. For him, what we envy in others is no different in objective terms from what we are and have ourselves. On the other hand, Proust's Narrator is firm in his assertion of a very real newness of being in characters such as the girls of Balbec. Indeed, the novel quality of their perceptions becomes a veritable agent of fecundation for the work of art. Shattuck's notion of 'soul error' only partly explains the Narrator's reflections on others about him. In another sense, however, what the Narrator is seeking is contact with a quality of existence that is radically different from his own.

Idealisation, then, is only one factor in the Narrator's depiction of the inhabitants of Balbec, Doncières and Combray. Granted, it helps explain our impression that his appraisal of them is occasionally exaggerated. But when one examines their specific attributes, one finds the Narrator speaking of 'l'inconscience', 'l'inintellectualité' and 'la joie' – modes of feeling far removed from his own, and hence extolled by him.

At this point, it would be premature to sum up the full significance of the little band of girls for the Narrator, since we have yet to consider the very developed liaison between himself and the 'leader' of that group, Albertine. That will be the subject of the next chapter. For the present, we might recapitulate briefly, to gauge the collective impact made by the little band at the time of the Narrator's first visit to Balbec. In the early stages of his stay, the Narrator feels the need to take a conscious decision on whether or not to pursue the elusive girls of the region. His resolve to press on in a spirit of quest and imaginative adventure comes only after some deliberation. For a while, he sees the validity of Schopenhauer's counsel that the curbing of one's desires is enough to guarantee happiness. But he abandons that concept of limitation, preferring to risk possible deception and suffering in the hope that he might live some new and exhilarating experience. It is perhaps slightly paradoxical that in venturing to extend the horizons of his own life-view, the Narrator should choose the world of the 'jeunes filles' – one of uniformity and spiritual mediocrity. Yet even within these restricted parameters, he appears happy to taste the simple pleasures which that life offers. Besides, he succeeds in awakening within himself a keen enthusiasm for vigorous sensual living. He labels that attraction 'l'éternel désir, l'éternel regret de la vie' (III, 141–2).

The same desire lies behind his interest in unknown young women whom he happens to meet in the course of his excursions through the countryside. So too with the maids, Céleste and Marie, or again with Mme Putbus' servant woman. They all exert a similar kind of influence on the Narrator, inviting him to make the imaginative leap into their world. This is one free from self-doubt and introspection – and in the case of the Céleste intercalation in *La Prisonnière*, from a problematical experience of love. The discipline of military life holds a comparable fascination for him. What might otherwise be seen as the mental stagnation or the monotony of that life-style assumes for him the positive character of a constancy and a regularity. And yet in spite of the Narrator's contentment with this life, he still feels compelled to venture into the field of military strategy so that his stay might acquire a redeeming intellectual grace. By thus dabbling in military theories, he betrays his innate academic leanings. Still, the revivifying companionship of others eases the burden of that responsibility.

The present chapter has attempted to show that in his creation of characters, Proust is often playing off different temperaments one against the other. The description of the Balbec girls, for example, vis-à-vis the Narrator brings with it a steady pattern of polarities. At every point, it seems, the character of their own awareness is antithetical to that of the Narrator. Similarly, the qualities that we have seen in Saint-Loup and the Duchesse de Guermantes gain prominence by virtue of their oppositional value relative to the Narrator's traits of character. One might even venture to say that in the sections on Balbec and Doncières, a dialectic of contrasts is in operation, albeit as an unsung principle.

The same polarities also filter down into the internal composition of the Balbec grouping itself. The initial homogeneity of the 'petite bande' soon disappears, with Andrée showing herself to be joined in temperament to the Narrator. Both characters, together with Albertine, form a triangle of comparisons and contrasts. Significantly, the course of the Narrator's love is dependent on them. Andrée now moves in dovetail fashion between the remote group and the Narrator, acting out the frenzy of youth as well as providing an extension to the hero's own hypersensitivity. By attributing this awareness to another, chosen character, he gives wider exposure to the quality of his own consciousness.

As I have been trying to point out, it is not totally accurate to speak of an attraction of opposite temperaments here. Admittedly, the novel perceptions enjoyed by others exercise a strong pull on the Narrator. But the process is not necessarily a reciprocal one, although interestingly in *Le Temps retrouvé*, aristocrats are drawn out of social position by their interest in the intelligentsia – a movement of attraction felt by Mme de Guermantes, who, in her decline, grows interested in literary debate and welcomes bohemian artists (see III, 1004, 1026). Perhaps more strikingly, we find a new Albertine, grown fond of the Narrator's intellect (see below, p. 141–2). Still, Proust's claim remains that the intellectual may be drawn to that which departs most from his own experience. Recalling a discerning comment made in the manuscripts, one sees that what the reflective mind most appreciates in others is 'plutôt le spectacle de ce qui diffère le plus de leur propre nature' (n.a.fr. 16710:103).

It would be convenient in the following chapter to pay more attention to Albertine's increasingly prominent role, and consider what happens as the Narrator's fascination with her gains in intensity. To that end, I shall be paying particular attention to her captivity, and to the consciousness that the Narrator sees in her during that period. Though still limited, her awareness is to become very different from the pleasurable mindlessness that she flaunts at Balbec.

5

Albertine as Captive of the Narrator

Inconstance. – On croit toucher des orgues ordinaires en touchant l'homme. Ce sont des orgues, à la vérité, mais bizarres, changeantes, variables [dont les tuyaux ne se suivent pas par degrés conjoints]. Ceux qui ne savent toucher que les ordinaires ne feraient pas d'accords sur celles-là. Il faut savoir où sont les [touches].

Pascal[1]

In the preceding chapter, I referred briefly to the Narrator's increasingly anguished view of his relationship with Albertine. Much of his preoccupation derives from his suspicion that she is giving free rein to her lesbian inclinations. He finds such a liberty intolerable. When seen against such a troubled background, the manuscript insertion on the two 'courrières', Céleste and Marie (II, 845–50), serves as a useful emotional stop-gap, if only temporarily (see Chapter 4h). In his search for a more permanent remedy, the Narrator decides to bring Albertine to his Paris home, and to hold her there as a physical captive. His hope is that her imprisonment will put his emotional doubt to rest.

The aim of this chapter is to consider the many implications of Albertine's captivity, especially in view of what we have already seen to be the characteristics of the 'jeunes filles en fleurs' at Balbec. There, Albertine was one of the dominant members in a group of sensual, uncultured young women who seemed immune from the intellectual and moral scruples confronting the Narrator. The flightiness that she represented for the Narrator was immensely appealing to him. It will be interesting therefore to see how differently he responds to her when she comes to live in his home. But before examining the new Albertine of *La Prisonnière*, it would be informative to look briefly at the Narrator's other love experiences. For in his adolescent relationships, there are definite pointers to what is to follow in the protracted liaison with Albertine.

(a) A growing subjectivity in love

In much of the 'jeunes filles en fleurs' evocation, the Narrator allows himself room for imaginative play and speculation. He takes obvious delight, for example, in toying with the idea that they are somehow mythological creatures; the mystery that this provokes quickly excites his attention (see Chapter 4). But there can be little doubt that his joy is largely self-generated, as his inventive, fanciful mind moves into operation. Indeed, the Narrator is himself aware of the strongly subjective dimension to the attraction the girls have for him. Recalling his experience as an adolescent with Gilberte at the Champs-Elysées, he draws the following significant conclusion:

J'avais autrefois entrevu aux Champs-Elysées et je m'étais mieux rendu compte depuis, qu'en étant amoureux d'une femme nous projetons simplement en elle un état de notre âme; que par conséquent l'important n'est pas la valeur de la femme, mais la profondeur de l'état. (I, 833.)

Clearly, imaginative projections play a vital part in his love. In addition to this, however, the use of the generalising 'nous' points away from the particularity of the Narrator's case, making his own reaction appear a more universally applicable one. This is not an isolated case. We see the 'nous' device in a description of a woman as 'une poupée intérieure à notre cerveau' (II, 370), and again, in the final pages of the *Recherche*, 'il ne devrait y avoir [dans le visage d'une passante] qu'un espace vide sur lequel jouerait tout au plus le reflet de nos désirs' (III, 1045). The Narrator's suggestion that this is true of love generally becomes all the more arresting when one considers how it excludes any assertion of individual being on the part of the woman. The extreme subjectivity of that stance is thus thrown on us all, as it were.

This pattern of universalising needs to be kept in mind, as it is one that seems to become more and more applicable to the *Recherche* as a whole. After Albertine has left him, the Narrator reflects on the role of the woman whom he loves:

C'est qu'en effet sa personne même y est pour peu de chose; pour presque tout, le processus d'émotions, d'angoisses que tels hasards nous ont fait jadis éprouver à propos d'elle et que l'habitude a attachées à elle. (III, 433.)

Once more, we are made aware of how overshadowed the woman's individuality is. With the implanting of the Narrator's own 'processus d'émotions', and all the plurality of response which that suggests, woman serves a purely catalytic function. Although a source of emotional stimulus to the Narrator, she is almost nothing in herself; reference to her own being is incidental and peripheral.

In the period following Albertine's departure, the Narrator tries to find some consolation in the company of other, anonymous girls. The detail used to describe one such girl would seem especially interesting, in the light of these comments on woman's declining individuality. He tells, for example, of how he has found an innocent young girl standing at Albertine's door:

[Elle] avait l'air si bon que je lui demandai si elle ne voulait pas venir chez moi, comme j'eusse fait d'un chien au regard fidèle [...]. Bientôt après, la pensée d'avoir quelque autre petite fille près de moi, de ne jamais être seul sans le secours d'une présence innocente, fut le seul rêve qui me permît de supporter l'idée que peut-être Albertine resterait quelque temps sans revenir. (III, 432n.)

The significance of this is that the Narrator should liken her presence to that of a submissive animal, for this tends to diminish her own sense of independent being. However tender the emotion that he feels for her, she remains first and foremost a constant source of reassurance for him; evidently, he is looking to the impact she has on his own sensibility.

The same is true of another of these encounters, this time in Venice. There, it is an unknown Austrian girl who captures his imagination. But her candid beauty does not prevent him from being troubled by the belief that she is perhaps a lesbian: 'L'air qu'elle prenait pour éviter qu'on crût cela d'elle était comme cet éloignement révélateur que les animaux ont des êtres qui les ont battus' (III, 649–50). With the Narrator invoking yet again the image of a peculiarly animal reaction, one has an impression of the woman's dwarfed consciousness, in contrast with his own intense living of the experience.

In La Prisonnière itself, one of the Narrator's joys is to reflect on Albertine's unobtrusive presence, which he compares to that of a domestic pet

qui venait – c'était pour moi un repos profond – se jeter sur mon lit à côté de moi, s'y faire une place d'où elle ne bougeait plus, sans gêner comme eût fait une personne. (III, 15.)

The more non-human her appearance, the more comforting she is for him. As a general observation, one might say that the Narrator finds assuagement in his ability to relegate woman to this lower, animal register of awareness.

By the same token, he is quick to respond to any suggestion that the love partner is capable of an autonomous existence. His immediate reaction is one of alarm at this self-assertion in the other person:

Ces obstacles contre lesquels les amants ont à lutter et que leur imagination surexcitée par la souffrance cherche en vain à deviner, résident parfois dans quelque singularité de caractère de la femme qu'ils ne peuvent ramener à eux, dans sa bêtise, dans l'influence qu'ont prise sur elle et les craintes que lui ont suggérées des êtres que l'amant ne connaît pas. (I, 501.)

The Narrator presumes that the sense of powerlessness to influence a myriad of human relationships is damaging for lovers generally. We are, he argues, unable to assimilate the woman's individual being, the menacing 'singularité de caractère' that she embodies. It is hardly surprising that this independence of self should preoccupy him, especially when one considers the hypersensitive character of his emotional involvement. Accordingly, he feels that by penetrating the sanctuary of the woman's mind, he might relieve his affective torment.

The will to suppress a woman's awareness expresses itself in many different and interesting forms. We see the young Narrator, for example, enjoying what is a thinly disguised sexual experience with Gilberte. In keeping with the tradition of battle as established in 'ces obstacles contre lesquels les amants ont à lutter' (I, 501), the episode is likened to a struggle for dominance. The 'war' with Gilberte, however, is decidedly mock heroic in tone, with both waging it in an evidently playful, amicable spirit. But most important is the nature of the consciousness that the Narrator attributes to Gilberte herself:

Nous luttions, arcboutés. Je tâchais de l'attirer, elle résistait; ses pommettes enflammées par l'effort étaient rouges et rondes comme des cerises; elle riait comme si je l'eusse chatouillée; je la tenais serrée entre mes jambes comme un arbuste après lequel j'aurais voulu grimper; et, au mileu de la gymnas- tique que je faisais, sans qu'en fût à peine augmenté l'essoufflement que me donnaient l'exercice musculaire et l'ardeur du jeu, je répandis, comme quelques gouttes de sueur arrachées par l'effort, mon plaisir auquel je ne pus pas même m'attarder le temps d'en connaître le goût; aussitôt je pris la lettre. (I, 493–4.)

Perhaps the most striking feature of the episode is the plant-like appearance of Gilberte. Reduced to the dimensions of a bush, her presence becomes purely functional. She is the instrument facili- tating the Narrator's physical exertion – for it is mainly in these terms that he speaks of his sexual gratification. Furthermore, the absence of any conscious response on her part again contrasts with the Narrator's emotional and imaginative excitement.

In the continuation to the text just quoted, his principal aim remains that of conveying his own exhilaration, while Gilberte is only vaguely cognisant of the purpose of his physical wrestling: 'Peut-être avait-elle obscurément senti que mon jeu avait un autre objet que celui que j'avais avoué, mais n'avait-elle pas su remarquer que je l'avais atteint' (I, 494). Gilberte's passive stance goes hand in hand with her low level of cognisance. We might keep that passivity in mind for, as we shall be seeing, the same inert qualities are also prominent in descriptions of the imprisoned Albertine. Likewise, Gilberte's submissiveness on this occasion adumbrates Albertine's quiescent being in *La Prisonnière*. But before examining the overt restrictions that the Narrator imposes on his captive, I want first to consider an earlier sexual experience with Albertine.

This occurs when she calls unexpectedly at the Narrator's home in Paris. Interestingly enough, the Narrator himself likens his pleasure to that which he enjoyed with Gilberte in the Champs-Elysées. And what fascinates him is that Albertine has now lost the prudery of Balbec:

Une [modification] plus étonnante se produisit en Albertine, ce soir-là même, aussitôt que ses caresses eurent amené chez moi la satisfaction dont elle dut bien s'apercevoir [...]. Albertine avait pris un air que je ne lui connaissais pas, de bonne volonté docile, de simplicité presque puérile. Effaçant d'elle toutes préoccupations, toutes prétentions habituelles, le moment qui précède le plaisir, pareil en cela à celui qui suit la mort, avait rendu à ses traits rajeunis comme l'innocence du premier âge. (II, 366.)

In showing herself to be more responsive to the Narrator's sexual advances, Albertine has acquired a more compliant disposition, which is uncomplicated and thus appealing to him. It is as if her own escape from cares in a moment of voluptuous ecstasy is inviting him to enjoy similar release from doubt.

Essentially, therefore, it is her willingness to yield to the Narrator that the latter finds immensely satisfying. In this respect, her behaviour reflects something of the docile traits in Gilberte's character. Since the effect of this is to strip her of any perplexing individual consciousness, she can then be confined within the parameters of a 'simplicité presque puérile'. Moreover, although Albertine does not take on the purely botanical form of Gilberte (I, 494), she does share the latter's accessibility. As such, she appears increasingly attractive to the Narrator.

The evidence of these introductory remarks points to the frequently subjective nature of the Narrator's love encounters.[2] An important consequence of this is the subsidiary role assigned to his partner. On occasions, she is no more than an appendage to the Narrator's own being, and habitually shows nothing of the involved consciousness that one comes to associate with him. Indeed, in the event of a woman revealing a similar complexity, he interprets this as an obstacle to his enjoyment of the liaison. But of course, the phenomenon of subjective love is in no way unique to Proust. One need only look to one of the fathers of the modern novel, Cervantes, to see Don Quixote's gross distortion of Dulcinea. At the other end of the spectrum, chronologically speaking, Robbe-Grillet's presentation of the loved one in the *nouveau roman* reveals the autistic world of the main protagonist.[3] But what seems particularly significant in Proust's work, and indeed gives it its *sui generis* character, is the striking use of animal and plant imagery, for example, in descriptions of the woman the Narrator is attracted to. When we come to consider in some detail certain descriptions in *La Prisonnière*, we shall see what can only be termed radical departures from more traditional and indeed more contemporary treatments of love.

(b) The new Albertine: from Balbec to Paris

Once he is convinced of Albertine's lesbianism, the Narrator decides to bring her back to his Paris home. He believes that by holding her a physical prisoner there, he can prevent her from enjoying the company of the 'Gomorrhéennes'. He does not doubt the magnitude of his task. Yet so great is his hypersensitivity – now aggravated by incessant uncertainty about Albertine's sexuality – that he feels impelled to find some immediate solution. Since the mystery surrounding her has become intolerable for him, his great imperative is to break down this impenetrability and to become fully cognisant of even her most intimate thoughts and feelings.

Just how necessary this is becomes clear if, anticipating slightly, we look ahead to when the Narrator seems to have achieved what he set out to do. This is a moment in *La Prisonnière* when he can enjoy Albertine's presence in total tranquillity:

L'image que je cherchais, où je me reposais, contre laquelle j'aurais voulu mourir, ce n'était plus l'Albertine ayant une vie inconnue, c'était une Albertine aussi connue de moi qu'il était possible (et c'est pour cela que cet amour ne pouvait être durable à moins de rester malheureux, car par définition il ne contentait pas le besoin de mystère), c'était une Albertine ne reflétant pas un monde lointain, mais ne désirant rien d'autre – il y avait des instants où, en effet, cela semblait être ainsi – qu'être avec moi, toute pareille à moi, une Albertine image de ce qui précisément était mien et non de l'inconnu. (III, 75.)

Here, the Narrator is mainly seeking to substitute what is visible and tangible for the unknowable, the distant, the now cruelly inaccessible aspects of Albertine's character. He thus emphasises the work of demystifying and elucidating everything related to Albertine. When compared to the evocations in *A l'ombre des jeunes filles en fleurs*, this marks a significant shift in attitude to her. By expressing a wish to police her every moment, the Narrator is clearly abandoning many of his earlier fantasies and imaginative projections on the quality of Albertine's existence. Albertine displayed 'la cruauté, l'inintellectualité et la joie' (I, 830), all positive, enviable attributes in the eyes of a seemingly deprived Narrator. What is more, he earlier saw this disparity as being essential to the birth of any love, and for that very reason felt unattracted to Andrée, who was so like himself in temperament. Now, in sharp contrast, the Narrator's heartfelt yearning is for 'une Albertine image de ce qui précisément était mien et non de l'inconnu' (III, 75).

In view of this, her move to Paris involves much more than a physical displacement, for the light in which he chooses to see her has changed considerably. The tendency to idealise that marks his first encounter with the little band in Balbec is no longer in evidence. Now he is committed to surveillance, albeit reluctantly, since reducing Albertine to totally known proportions robs her of the attraction born of the mystery surrounding her. This helps explain why the dominant mood of *La Prisonnière* is quite distinct from the atmosphere of expectation in *A l'ombre*. In his initial encounter with the 'jeunes filles', the Narrator glimpses a world of motion, changeability and newness. With *La Prisonnière*, however, the trend is towards a more safe, unadventurous 'recueillement'. For the Narrator, the watchword in the affair with Albertine has become caution and self-protection. The movement of approximation, therefore, between the Narrator and Albertine is one of the main features of *La Prisonnière*. Its aim is clearly that of counteracting the former's sense of suspicion and anguish.

One characteristic common to the presentation of the 'petite bande' and other, less prominent girls in the novel is the frenzy of physical activity and mobility frequently associated with them. We saw in Chapter 4, for example, how those who appear on the Balbec beach are constantly engaging in sporting pursuits from which the Narrator is excluded. But on those occasions, the feeling of being barred in this way actually intensifies his imaginative enjoyment. The more mysterious the girls appear, the more enhanced their existence becomes in the Narrator's mind. A good illustration of this comes in an image of girls on bicycles that I mentioned in the preceding chapter:

trois jeunes filles étaient assises à côté de l'arc immense de leurs bicyclettes posées à côté d'elles, comme trois immortelles accoudées au nuage ou au coursier fabuleux sur lesquels elles accomplissent leurs voyages mythologiques. (III, 170.)

Their elusive and tantalising beauty, then, excites him. In particular, the mythological aura surrounding the girls makes their travel and destination seem all the more fascinating. Concomitant with this perpetual movement and mystery is the ever-changing perspective that he has of many such characters. Unable to ground them, he contents himself with lightning shots of the 'beauté fluide, collective et mobile' that is the Balbec set (I, 790). Albertine contributes a great deal to this impression of unceasing flux. But with the birth of the Narrator's suspicions, he is happy to salvage any glimpse of quiet domesticity or fidelity on her part.

Once, speaking of a reconciliation with Albertine, he boasts a measure of success in this. Granted, his respite is only temporary. Yet he longs to consolidate this passing felicity, and thereby stabilise his changing emotional fortunes:

J'aurais dû quitter Balbec, m'enfermer dans la solitude, y rester en harmonie avec les dernières vibrations de la voix que j'avais su rendre un instant amoureuse, et de qui je n'aurais plus rien exigé que de ne pas s'adresser davantage à moi; de peur que, par une parole nouvelle qui n'eût pu désormais être que différente, elle vînt blesser d'une dissonance le silence sensitif où, comme grâce à quelque pédale, aurait pu survivre longtemps en moi la tonalité du bonheur. (II, 835.)

However earnest the desire for a 'silence sensitif', it cannot influence the exceedingly tenuous nature of the motionless, unchanging utopia envisaged by the Narrator. But by wishing for her compliant voice to vibrate gently and indefinitely, he is indirectly cherishing a state of ideal stasis. Yet these vibrations are short-lived, threatened as they are by the harshness of 'une dissonance'; to that extent, they reflect the frailty of the Narrator's hope.

We have more obvious illustrations of the calming potential in Albertine's presence when she is actually a prisoner in the Narrator's home. There, he contrasts the woman he now guards with the Albertine of Balbec:

Elle était si bien encagée que, certains soirs même, je ne faisais pas demander qu'elle quittât sa chambre pour la mienne, elle que jadis tout le monde suivait, que j'avais tant de peine à rattraper, filant sur sa bicyclette. (III, 68.)

It is, then, with some contentment that he reflects on how his endeavours to check the motion of Balbec have borne fruit. The movement of flight – again symbolised by Albertine's bicycle – has been halted in the soothing inertia of imprisonment. With the once ethereal and elusive bird brought to ground, the Narrator's affective calm increases.

His joy may even approach that of the diligent horticulturist who has carefully effected a transplantation:

J'étais fier aussi d'avoir coupé à la racine, d'avoir cueilli, d'avoir dérobé à tous les autres qui maintenant la cherchaient vainement à Balbec, la plus belle rose d'entre les jeunes filles en fleurs. (III, 1069, note 1 to III, 68.)[4]

In the suggestion of stealth and furtiveness, one has an indication of the intensity of the whole experience for the Narrator. So great is the prize to be won that he feels justified in this 'unlawful' possession. It is also worth noting the reappearance of botanical imagery here; we shall be seeing other instances of this later in the chapter.

An added feature of the contrasts between the Albertine of his Paris home and the young girl of Balbec is how the Narrator speaks in terms of her now tangible self:

Le plaisir fait de mystère et de sensualité que j'avais éprouvé, fugitif et fragmentaire, à Balbec, le soir où elle était venue coucher à l'hôtel, s'était complété, stabilisé, remplissait ma demeure, jadis vide, d'une permanente provision de douceur domestique, presque familiale, rayonnant jusque dans les couloirs, et de laquelle tous mes sens, tantôt effectivement, tantôt, dans les moments où j'étais seul, en imagination et par l'attente du retour, se nourrissaient paisiblement. (III, 58–9.)

In this way, the evanescent pleasures associated with Balbec are more firmly guaranteed. The immateriality suggested by 'mystère' and 'fugitif' now disappears, weighed under by a cluster of images evoking fullness and substantiality. A striking instance of the latter is the reference to the Narrator's senses unhurriedly enjoying Albertine's new, stable presence.

We have already seen Proust using a similar language at a much earlier stage in his career. In *Jean Santeuil*, for example, the hero expresses his liking for the hospitable surroundings of the garrison town in words similar to those of the contented Narrator in *La Prisonnière* (see above, Chapter 1). In his hotel room, Jean's feeling of satisfaction echoes the Narrator's security in *La Prisonnière*:

Une allégresse inouïe remplissait son être. La porte refermée sur le portier et sur le monde, il ôta ses bottines pour mieux fouler les doux tapis, les sentir chauds, doux, fermes et silencieux sous ses sauts et sous ses bonds. Il [...] s'assura de la docilité de tous les boutons électriques à sa toute-puissance, reconnaissant aux lieux qui [...] lui avaient ôté le poids de ces soucis et communiqué cette ivresse. (*JS*, p. 555.)

If Jean's constant desire is to be securing pleasurable, limited sensations, it is fair to say that so critical has the Narrator's relationship with Albertine become that he adopts a similar standpoint in *La Prisonnière*. For him, the great consolation is that the vacuum of the emotional experience of Balbec has been filled with an abundance of 'douceur domestique, presque familiale' (III, 59).

So it is that the Narrator can to some extent purge himself of his over-sensitivised response to Albertine. Yet if these safeguards are to be viable, he must simultaneously accept a limitation of his own conscious self. Perhaps more alarmingly, his plans for a work of art may also have to be shelved. Indeed, it should be said that the *leitmotif* of his faltering artistic vocation is conspicuously absent from much of *La Prisonnière*.[5] But while his love for Albertine distracts him from art, this is not to say that he sees the relationship as being inconsequential. He judges it in fact to be a personal experience more valid than society living or even the friendship of Saint-Loup or Bloch: 'Une sensualité venue des régions plus profondes de mon être mettait en Albertine une consistance que sont incapables de créer les plaisirs de la vanité et de la conversation' (III, 1068, note 1 to III, 67). Nothing could be more inaccurate than to say of the experience with Albertine that it is casual and superficial.

In addition to this, there are other new sides to Albertine's personality as she is portrayed in captivity. One such modification involves her steady acquisition of culture under the watchful eye of the Narrator. This becomes especially revealing when one remembers how he originally conceived of her. At Balbec, what set his imagination alight was the certainty that she was a creature of the senses, oblivious of mind and intellect. As such, she embodied a new experiential possibility for him, that of 'l'inintellectualité', of freedom from reflective doubting (I, 830). In *La Prisonnière*, however, she gradually emerges in a quite novel light. We might now examine this aspect of her transformation, and consider how the Narrator himself interprets it.

Very early in *La Prisonnière*, he remarks that Albertine has undergone an important mental change. To his request that no one should enter his room in the morning until he is ready to receive him, she replies by likening this to the story of Ahasuerus as interpreted by Racine. The Narrator is immediately struck by this literary-mindedness (III, 18).[6] Similarly, she has now taken up painting in her captivity, and appears quite accomplished in this new artistic pursuit; the Narrator expresses admiration for what he terms 'les touchantes distractions de la captive' (III, 180). Evidently, she has come a long way from the original Albertine of Balbec – uncultured and even barbaric in the mind of the Narrator. He himself stresses this metamorphosis:

Elle n'était pas frivole, du reste, lisait beaucoup quand elle était seule et me faisait la lecture quand elle était avec moi. Elle était devenue extrêmement intelligente. Elle disait, en se trompant d'ailleurs: 'Je suis épouvantée en pensant que sans vous je serais restée stupide. Ne le niez pas, vous m'avez ouvert un monde d'idées que je ne soupçonnais pas, et le peu que je suis devenue, je ne le dois qu'à vous.' (III, 64.)

Although he suggests that Albertine is mistaken in expressing her gratitude in this way, one suspects that the Narrator is unavowedly elated that she should state her dependence on him in such a forthright way. Certainly, in the case of her musical talents, to which I shall be turning presently, he expresses his satisfaction that she has 'inherited' so much from him (III, 382).

We know that her expression of indebtedness to the Narrator originally took on a much more elaborate form (cf. III, 1067, note 3 to III, 64). In an earlier typescript, one reads how Andrée realised immediately when Albertine had been with the Narrator, on account of her changed diction or because she bore the smell of fumigations so particular to the Narrator's home.[7] The same reference now appears at the beginning of *La Prisonnière*, this time with the roles of Andrée and Albertine reversed. Yet there too, we find an indication of how the Narrator has imposed his personality on these girls. The curious details that Albertine chooses to highlight are significant, in that they reinforce the sense of her dependence on him:

'Un meunier n'a pas besoin de dire qu'il est meunier, on voit bien toute la farine qu'il a sur lui, il y a encore la place des sacs qu'il a portés. Andrée, c'était la même chose, elle tournait ses sourcils comme vous, et puis son grand cou, enfin je ne peux pas vous dire. Quand je prends un livre qui a été dans votre chambre, je peux le lire dehors, on sait tout de même qu'il vient de chez vous, parce qu'il garde quelque chose de vos sales fumigations.. C'est un rien, je ne peux vous dire, mais c'est un rien, au fond, qui est assez gentil.' (III, 20.)

For the purposes of the present study, the main point of interest is not that Andrée now adopts a role that was originally intended for Albertine (see III, 1067). What is important is that we appreciate how the Narrator has come to implant something of his own self in the 'jeunes filles'. A mere smell or a particular use of language may be sufficient to symbolise that reassuring contact. As Albertine herself observes rather shyly, 'C'est un rien, au fond, qui est assez gentil' (III, 20). The Narrator's reaction to the idea that he can influence others is equally enthusiastic, however much he may feign indifference.

It is this same sense of a woman's dependence on him which explains his untroubled acceptance of her newfound culture. In this respect, her literary and artistic ability is not symbolic of any individuality or independence of mind. That could only be alarming to the Narrator. Rather, these talents are what one might perhaps call totems of her attachment to him. This seems especially true of her musical skills, which the Narrator totally approves. He marvels at how Albertine has become the 'bête sauvage domestiquée, rosier à qui j'avais fourni le tuteur, le cadre, l'espalier de sa vie' (III, 382). And in describing her at the pianola, he disguises nothing of his joy that she now conforms to the moulds that he himself creates, and not those of Balbec:

Ses épaules, que j'avais vues baissées et sournoises quánd elle rapportait les clubs de golf, s'appuyaient à mes livres. Ses belles jambes, que le premier jour j'avais imaginées avec raison avoir manoeuvré pendant toute son adolescence les pédales d'une bicyclette, montaient et descendaient tour 6a tour))) celles du pianola, où Albertine, devenue d'une élégance qui me la faisait sentir plus à moi, parce que c'était de moi qu'elle lui venait, posait ses souliers en toile d'or. Ses doigts, jadis familiers du guidon, se posaient maintenant sur les *touches* comme ceux d'une Sainte Cécile. (III, 382.)

So it is with great acumen and economy of language that the Narrator effects the transition from bicycle to pianola. The feet that once drove the pedals of what for the Narrator is a machine of fugacity and mystery, now tread the pedals of a musical instrument.[8] Likewise her hands shift from handle-bar to keyboard. The movement of escape is checked and indeed reversed.

Most significant of all of course is that he should see in Albertine an elegance and artistry that he himself has nurtured. His sense of achievement reaches its culminating point in the reference to Albertine as a Saint Cecilia-like figure. Although arguably too flattering an image to use of Albertine, it sets her up in the Narrator's mind as protectress of the world of harmony and music. The value of this is that it effectively distances her from the uncultured world of Balbec, with the result that she becomes endearing to the music-loving Narrator. By extension, it placates his jealousy and suspicion. It is without trepidation therefore that the Narrator observes his captive's cultural development. Her artistic activity now keeps her within his jealously guarded sphere of influence.

(c) Albertine's sleep: its anaesthetising effect on the Narrator

Defending that influence is never easy for the Narrator. Indeed, in *La Prisonnière*, one sees him buffeted by wave upon wave of emotional crisis. His suspicions concerning Albertine often find a convenient focal point in references to her eyes and to her field of vision generally. The more uncontrollable and vast this appears to him, the more powerless the Narrator is to control and restrict Albertine. She has only to watch a woman pass by to awaken in the Narrator a violent feeling of extreme vulnerability:

Dans ce dernier cas, au contraire, son regard étroit et velouté se fixait, se collait sur la passante, si adhérent, si corrosif qu'il semblait qu'en se retirant il aurait dû emporter la peau. (III, 150.)

The unrelenting destruction of which Albertine's look is capable sounds a note of warning to the Narrator. For a start it undermines his whole elaborate scheme of imprisonment. And as he himself observes plaintively, 'A ces êtres de fuite [...], leur regard semble nous dire qu'ils vont s'envoler' (III, 93). Only by limiting Albertine's field of vision can the Narrator feel emotionally protected.[9] But if such restriction of her is impossible to secure, his hypersensitivity prompts another reaction, the move to deny himself a visual apprehension of reality. This too is aimed at guaranteeing his own felicity:

Quelquefois j'éteignais la lumière avant qu'elle entrât. C'était dans l'obscurité, à peine guidée par la lumière d'un tison, qu'elle se couchait à mon côté. Mes mains, mes joues seules la reconnaissaient sans que mes yeux la vissent, mes yeux qui souvent avaient peur de la trouver changée. (III, 76.)

Conscious of his desire to see no imperfection in the relationship with Albertine, the Narrator is anxious not only to control the functioning of her eyes, but equally to deny what is perhaps evident to his own. This points to a strong will on his part to euphemise his reactions; the resort to prettifying reality is an important part of his armoury. But even that may prove taxing. An important indication of just how intense an effort this self-delusion may require occurs after Albertine's death, when the Narrator devotes his whole energy to effecting a partial amputation of the thinking self:

Ce n'était plus assez de fermer les rideaux, je tâchais de boucher les yeux et les oreilles de ma mémoire [...] pour ne pas entendre ces invisibles oiseaux qui se répondaient d'un arbre à l'autre de chaque côté de moi qu'embrassait alors si tendrement celle qui maintenant était morte. (III, 480.)

In this way, the Narrator tries to dull the blow of painstaking realisation. Long after Albertine's death, his consciousness of their relationship, then, remains fraught with doubts. For him, the possibility of consolation lies less in the finality of her death than in a temporary absence of life – the eclipse of mind in sleep.

Those passages that deal with the Narrator's enjoyment of

Albertine's sleep are important for the strange existence that he then sees in her. Alison Winton points out that the descriptions do not form part of the *premier jet* of the continuous text of *La Prisonnière*, but appear either in layers added to this manuscript, or at the later typescript stage (Winton, vol. 1, p. 45). The interest of this is that the author presumably realised the possible impact that a portrayal of the sleeping Albertine might have.[10] In an attempt to see just what that impact is, we might now turn to the relevant passages.

For the Narrator the obvious beauty of Albertine's dormant form is that it is motionless and still. A hint of external movement and bustle can heighten this atmosphere of calm silence as Albertine sleeps: 'Des voitures passaient bruyamment dans la rue, son front restait aussi immobile, aussi pur, son souffle aussi léger, réduit à la simple expiration de l'air nécessaire' (III, 71). It is as if the Narrator were satisfied that his captive should barely reach living form. What is especially alluring to him is the state of unconsciousness to which sleep delivers her:

En fermant les yeux, en perdant la conscience, Albertine avait dépouillé, l'un après l'autre, ces différents caractères d'humanité qui m'avaient déçu depuis le jour où j'avais fait sa connaissance. Elle n'était plus animée que de la vie inconsciente des végétaux, des arbres, vie plus différente de la mienne, plus étrange, et qui cependant m'appartenait davantage. (III, 70.)

The reference to what are for him the disquieting 'caractères d'humanité' is less an expression of misanthropic venom than a fear of her resilient individuality. On first seeing Albertine at Balbec, the Narrator had been happy to speculate on her background and pastimes. Indeed, he allowed his imagination free rein, a licence unchecked by any actual contact with her. In that way, she became the carefree, instinctual creature for him. Now, in contrast, although he still insists on a fundamental difference of being between himself and Albertine, the Narrator delights in her inanimacy. Presented in these vegetal terms, she becomes more easily assimilable to him.

Even the Albertine who placates the Narrator's jealousy by contentedly playing various card-games with him cannot equal the sleeping 'prisonnière': 'C'était un naturel plus profond, un naturel au deuxième degré que m'offrait son sommeil' (III, 71). The notion of gradations of calm adds an interesting new dimension to these evocations, and possibly offers an indication of what Proust himself had in mind as he built up additions on the theme of sleep (cf. Winton, vol. 1, p. 113). The greater the depth of 'le naturel' – and sleep would seem ideal for offering that quality of living – the further removed the Narrator is from exposure to doubt and suspicion.

In this context, one might recall briefly some references in Proust's earlier work to what is a not-unrelated psychological trait. We saw in Chapter 2 the significant confession in the allusion to 'les moments où on a besoin de se verser dans l'âme du potage chaud' (*Le Carnet de 1908*, p. 99). The pleasure of immersion that this implies is analogous to the warmth with which the Narrator of the *Contre Sainte-Beuve* speaks of 'la délicieuse insensibilité des autres pots de confiture' (*CSB/NM*, p. 68). On both occasions, the mood is one of a need to take refuge in a reassuringly non-human world. The case of Albertine, with the added complication of jealousy, is clearly different from the context of these earlier quotations. But where there is a close affinity is in the Narrator's path of retreat in *La Prisonnière*. The desire to embrace Albertine's vegetal form in sleep is not unlike the longing, expressed earlier in Proust, for the mindless-ness of the material world.

The same desire will prompt the Narrator to consider any way in which she may be scrutinised. Hence his contentment on seeing Albertine's physical body abandoned to the unconsciousness of sleep. Moreover, he reflects that were that form to constitute her whole being, then in no way could she escape him. This is eventually realised:

Elle avait rappelé à soi tout ce qui d'elle était au dehors; elle s'était réfugiée, enclose, résumée, dans son corps. En le tenant sous mon regard, dans mes mains, j'avais cette impression de la posséder tout entière que je n'avais pas quand elle était réveillée. Sa vie m'était soumise, exhalait vers moi son léger souffle. (III, 70.)

In sleep, Albertine's otherwise pervious and multiple self, linked to divergent points in space and time, is now securely held in her bodily presence. This is conveyed syntactically in the subtle change of object pronouns, with all that she represents being subsumed into her tangible form.

Likewise, the celestial sound of her breathing is interpreted by the Narrator not as a mere symbol of her presence there but rather as equalling her total self:

Au moment où mon oreille recueillait ce bruit divin, il me semblait que c'était, condensée en lui, toute la personne, toute la vie de la charmante captive, étendue là sous mes yeux. (III, 71.)

The concentration of Albertine's being into her sleeping body affords him great emotional security – a clear contrast with the torment aroused by her absence.

The Narrator is most assured when able to look in all tranquillity at the plant-like Albertine, without fear of her interrupting him. In fact the very first reference to her asleep gives one an impression of her completely unobtrusive role: 'Je lui trouvais l'air d'une longue tige en fleur qu'on aurait disposée là' (III, 69). Seeing this ingratiating passivity, the Narrator then glimpses the possibility of love that this opens up for him. For when she is absent, he can only think of her; when she is awake and present, it is only on a surface level that they can communicate. Seeing her asleep, on the other hand, allows him to escape that superficiality and helps his unhurried contemplation: 'Quand elle dormait, je n'avais plus à parler, je savais que je n'étais plus regardé par elle, je n'avais plus besoin de vivre à la surface de moi-même' (III, 70). Again it is her inability to look at the Narrator that explains his untroubled self-indulgence.

There is another occasion where a similar desire for meditation and contemplation lingers in the Narrator's mind. The object of his keen attention is a young milkmaid and, as with Albertine, he speaks of how disconcerting her conscious presence is to him. Even more informative are the contrasts that he introduces between himself and Elstir, who has been working on different floral motifs:

Elstir, quand il les regardait, n'avait pas à se préoccuper de ce que faisaient les violettes. L'entrée de la petite laitière m'ôta aussitôt mon calme de contemplateur, je ne songeai plus qu'à rendre vraisemblable la fable de la lettre à lui faire porter. (III, 141.)

If the painter's inanimate subject explains his tranquil visual study, the same is no less true of the Narrator's contemplation of the 'longue tige en fleur' that is Albertine (III, 69). With the conscious and animate milkmaid, however, he cannot enjoy an unbroken concentration. Indeed when she arrives, he has quickly to resort to fabrication about why he has asked her to come.

He finds no difficulty, however, in justifying the contemplative dimension to his enjoyment of Albertine. At one point, he confidently defines his study of her in sleep in terms of its medicative function: 'Bientôt je commençai à entendre sa respiration égale. J'allai m'asseoir au bord de son lit pour faire cette cure calmante de brise et de contemplation' (III, 360). But this will to freeze Albertine, so that he may studiously observe her, has inevitable repercussions. The greatest of these is the atrophy of her individual consciousness. It seems that only in being reduced to a primitive life-form can Albertine allay her partner's suspicions. From the unintellectual being who excited the Narrator's wildest enthusiasm at Balbec, she has 'progressed' to the inanimacy of *La Prisonnière*. Here, there are times when only the total absence of human awareness and perceptions in Albertine will appease him.

One sees an intensification of this process in more radical expressions of the Narrator's desire to palliate his doubting. He is often overwhelmed by the sense of mystery that accompanies the pleasure of Albertine's presence. Kissing her as she sleeps, for example, appears as a source of frail, virtually poetic delight: 'Ce que j'éprouvais alors, c'était un amour aussi pur, aussi immatériel, aussi mystérieux que si j'avais été devant ces créatures inanimées que sont les beautés de la nature' (III, 70). However disinterested the Narrator's devotion may seem here, it is clear that Albertine's sense of individuality is becoming steadily more remote and distant. When he quickly graduates to experiencing a more material, physical pleasure, the fact that she is submissive like Nature itself acts as a further excitant to the Narrator. The form his gratification takes is revealing:

Sentant que son sommeil était dans son plein, que je ne me heurterais pas à des écueils de conscience recouverts maintenant par la pleine mer du sommeil profond, délibérément je sautais sans bruit sur le lit, je me couchais au long d'elle, je prenais sa taille d'un de mes bras, je posais mes lèvres sur sa joue et sur son coeur, puis, sur toutes les parties de son corps, ma seule main restée libre et qui était soulevée aussi, comme les perles, par la respiration de la dormeuse; moi-même, j'étais déplacé légèrement par son mouvement régulier: je m'étais embarqué sur le sommeil d'Albertine. (III, 72.)

The suggestion of impending danger and crisis announced by the use of 'écueils' reflects how cautious the Narrator is in his advances. The reference is doubly interesting in the light of what qualifies it. For it is Albertine's consciousness itself on which he would founder. But again the Narrator is encouraged with images of depth, with Albertine's falling away from mind. Significantly too, the imaginative flights so evident in descriptions of the Albertine of Balbec return, though this time more restrained, and carefully controlled by the Narrator. In the extended use of marine metaphors, the gentle movement of the woman as she breathes is interpreted by the sensitive Narrator as a soothing, lilting 'invitation au voyage'. Just as Elstir's contemplation of the flowers precedes artistic creation (III, 141), so the Narrator finds in Albertine's stillness a useful stimulant to his inventive fantasising.

If the description implies a strong sensual enjoyment on the part of the Narrator, he himself goes on to confess to an overtly sexual pleasure. He reveals how Albertine's sleep

me faisait goûter un plaisir moins pur. Je n'avais besoin pour cela de nul mouvement, je faisais pendre ma jambe contre la sienne, comme une rame qu'on laisse traîner et à laquelle on imprime de temps à autre une oscillation légère, pareille au battement intermittent de l'aile qu'ont les oiseaux qui dorment en l'air. (III, 72.)

The avowedly more physical act that the Narrator now recalls takes place in the presence of the object-like Albertine. The same is true of an earlier encounter with Gilberte, where he is again sexually aroused: 'Je la tenais serrée entre mes jambes comme un arbuste après lequel j'aurais voulu grimper' (I, 494; see above, section a). Granted, the mood of frantic, adolescent exhilaration with Gilberte gives way to the greater placidity and calm of the experience with Albertine. Yet neither woman is fully cognisant of what is happening. As for the Narrator, he is happy to associate one with the other, believing that 'la personnalité sensuelle et volontaire de Gilberte avait émigré dans le corps d'Albertine' (III, 502).

But where they diverge considerably is in the case of the sleeping Albertine. There, the Narrator usurps every aspect of her limited existence. More specifically, in describing his sexual joys, he exercises what can only be called the tyranny of his own imagination. Accordingly, if the only sound emanating from Albertine's body is that of her breathing, this is immediately appropriated by the Narrator, and transformed by him in an inner world of reverie:

Le bruit de sa respiration devenant plus fort pouvait donner l'illusion de l'essoufflement du plaisir et quand le mien était à son terme, je pouvais l'embrasser sans avoir interrompu son sommeil. (III, 73.)

However tranquil the Narrator's enjoyment, it does not diminish the fact that Albertine is the unknowing object of his physical advances. Her human make-up thus undergoes radical transformation, as a result of his will to dominate and contain her.

In the preparatory *Cahiers*, one finds references similar to those which I have been quoting from the *Recherche*. Others, however, are more explicit. And it is often because of their lack of subtlety or reworking that they offer very clear indication of the Narrator's desire to usurp the woman's consciousness. One such reference occurs in *Cahier 50* (*c.* 1911), and has to do with the Narrator's interest in an unnamed peasant woman. Some of the details of this early description might not appear out of place in evocations of Albertine's sleep in the *Recherche*. But the manuscript passage shows the Narrator making even bolder assertions:

Et si son corps ne me plaisait pas, il avait du moins ce charme des corps de femmes faciles et maniables qui finissent par nous 5evoquer toujours les plaisirs de la nature parce que ce sont les seuls qui sont toujours prêts à venir les partager avec nous, parce qu'en eux il ne reste aucune personnalité qui nous résiste, qui n'abdique pas dans la solitude, et que nous pouvons nous coucher sur eux comme sur le rocher ou sur l'herbe, ou rester[?] à penser à rien dans la solitude sans nous sentir seuls en les mâchonnant, en les chiffonnant comme une fleur. (*Cahier 50*, fo 12v.)

Perhaps it was the starkness of these images that convinced Proust of the need to suppress them; or again, he may have rejected them on the grounds that they were unrounded and stylistically crude. Whatever the reasons for their absence from the *Recherche*, they point nevertheless to the same intensity of emotion as that described in *La Prisonnière*. What is more, they leave one in no doubt as to the general character of the Narrator's feelings towards Albertine. By choosing to single out 'aucune personnalité qui nous résiste', he is reiterating his fear that a woman's self-awareness is detrimental to his love.

Still in the experimental world of the manuscripts, we find further insight into the character of the Narrator's anxiety in love in another passage. Here, he is contemplating suicide as a possible escape from the complexity of his relationship with Albertine. These reflections appear in the fifth of seven *Cahiers* that go to make up the original continuous text of *Sodome et Gomorrhe* (n.a.fr. 16708–14). The images used reveal the ultimate nature of the human situation involved:

Il y eut alors des jours où je voulus me noyer, me pendre, la tuer (car on aime une femme comme on aime le poulet à qui on est heureux de tordre le cou pour en manger à dîner, seulement pour les femmes on veut les tuer non pour en avoir du plaisir, mais pour qu'elles n'en prennent pas avec d'autres). (n.a.fr. 16712:1.)[11]

The image is admittedly an unpolished one. And yet in spite of its unsubtlety and menacingly primitive emotion, it announces something of the extremeness of the Narrator's feeling and his insatiable will to dominate. Again, this manuscript passage provides a useful back-up to the *Recherche* itself, showing just how the Narrator's anxieties and preoccupations are taking shape.

If Proust chose not to 'redeploy' these manuscript images of strangulation, or of woman as being elemental like grass, one might ask how – if indeed at all – he manages to convey the almost paranoiac emotions that they point to. Perhaps it is fair to say that in the descriptions of the sleeping Albertine that he added to his original text, Proust found a medium for channelling some of the Narrator's most inflexible desires. Certainly, the evidence of passages on 'le sommeil d'Albertine' is that the Narrator sees in her sleep the delightful and almost total subjugation of her individual consciousness.

With the suppression of Albertine's reflective self, the Narrator's sense of assuagement seems complete. It should be said that the value of her company lies in her capacity to calm his doubt. Thus, we find Proust inserting into the final typescript of *La Prisonnière* what looks as much a memorandum for himself as an emphasis for the benefit of his reader: 'Je ne le redirai jamais assez, c'était un apaisement plus que tout' (III, 77). Generally speaking, therefore, the Narrator is stressing the reduction of Albertine's conscious living form to an inanimate, and for him more readily accessible, mode of existence. With the resistance of her individual selfhood now waning, the Narrator enjoys a great quietude.

The same will to dominate underlies the Narrator's deliberation on the letters that he finds in Albertine's kimono Here, however, the emotion that he feels is complicated by overtones of stealth and secrecy. These tend to reflect a certain culpability on the part of the Narrator:

Quand je sentais le sommeil d'Albertine bien profond, quittant le pied de son lit où je contemplais depuis longtemps sans faire un mouvement, je hasardais un pas, pris d'une curiosité ardente, sentant le secret de cette vie offert, floche et sans défense, dans ce fauteuil [...]. Mais (et peut-être j'ai eu tort) jamais je n'ai touché au kimono, mis ma main dans la poche, regardé les lettres. A la fin, voyant que je ne me déciderais pas, je repartais à pas de loup, revenais près du lit d'Albertine. (III, 73-4.)

The extreme vulnerability of Albertine's situation is reflected in the Narrator's attraction for what is 'floche et sans défense'. This sense of superiority in him confirms what we have already seen of his desire for sexual dominance. Yet there is an inescapable ambivalence in his attitude. A strong inner tension ensures that the desire to press home his advantage is checked by a fear of what lies within Albertine. The contradiction in his situation is clearly visible, and we are left with the paradox of his being as it were 'willing to wound and yet afraid to strike'.[12] This hesitation can be attributed to the Narrator's need to remain ignorant of the potentially damaging revelations contained in her letters. As he once says of such knowledge: 'Il vaut mieux ne pas savoir, penser le moins possible, ne pas fournir à la jalousie le moindre détail concret' (III, 24-5). Clearly he finds euphemising a pleasurable alternative to the apprehension of an unpalatable reality.

Indeed, it is essentially his attempt to make reality more livable that explains many of his responses in *La Prisonnière*. For, undoubtedly, his fluctuating emotional fortunes can be closely linked to the success or failure of his efforts to chisel out a new, idealised Albertine.

The second main passage on Albertine's sleep is largely similar in tonality to the one just examined. Again, one finds the Narrator manipulating her receptacle-like being. She is variously likened to a watch, a creeper plant and a convolvulus, but most strikingly of all, perhaps, to a musical instrument:

Seul son souffle était modifié par chacun de mes attouchements, comme si elle eût été un instrument dont j'eusse joué et à qui je faisais exécuter des modulations en tirant de l'une, puis de l'autre de ses cordes, des notes différentes. (III, 113.)

Seen as the relationship of an instrument to its player, Albertine's role vis-à-vis the Narrator acquires all the characteristics of earlier descriptions. Once more, her presence is a totally passive one. More fascinating than this, however, is that, as a musical instrument, she is reliant on the Narrator's manipulation for her very *raison d'être*. Previously, she was an unwittingly compliant sexual accomplice. Now she is equally submissive, although this time as the hollow receptacle that is the stringed instrument. The melody that this plays creates an atmosphere of Edenic bliss for the Narrator. Not surprisingly,

ma jalousie s'apaisait, car je sentais Albertine devenue un être qui respire, qui n'est pas autre chose, comme le signifiait le souffle régulier par où s'exprime cette pure fonction physiologique, qui, tout fluide, n'a l'épaisseur ni de la parole, ni du silence et, dans son ignorance de tout mal, haleine tirée plutôt d'un roseau creusé que d'un être humain, vraiment paradisiaque pour moi qui dans ces moments-là sentais Albertine soustraite à tout, non pas seulement matériellement, mais moralement, était le pur chant des Anges. (III, 113–14.)

The opening of the passage, with its use yet again of the seemingly ubiquitous *s'apaiser*, is of key significance. It expresses precisely that relief from an extreme state of emotional overburdening which the Narrator is seeking. Once more, his affective calm comes with the solely biological functioning of Albertine's body. The activity of the mind and the will announced by 'la parole' and 'le silence' is entirely absent. In their place is a paradisiacal melody issuing forth from the 'roseau creusé' which Albertine has become.

It is hard not to think of that other, more celebrated reed, the 'roseau pensant' that Pascal sees man as being. The author of the *Pensées* uses this image of course to convey simultaneously man's greatness, through thought, and the inconsequentiality of his existence. Proust's use of the reed image is quite different. For his Narrator, Albertine's beauty as the 'roseau creusé' lies in the fact that she is incapable of thought and reflection; her hollowness ensures that she remains totally at the disposition of her manipulator. In addition, given her position of complete dependence and mere instrumentality, we have another neat reversal of Pascal's dictum on the quality of human relationships. The latter argues that these are subject to the unpredictable individuality that is for ever functioning in others: 'On croit toucher des orgues ordinaires en touchant l'homme. Ce sont des orgues, à la vérité, mais bizarres, changeantes, variables.'[13] In contrast, the Narrator's joy in *La Prisonnière* is to have made of Albertine's sleeping body something as regular, faithful and consoling as an enchanting musical instrument.

Unlike Pascal's impression of bemusement when face to face with 'orgues bizarres, changeantes, variables', the Narrator's mood may even become one of unshakeable self-assurance. There is a time when he fears that Albertine might depart without warning, but his happiness returns when he sees her motionless in her room:

Dans la pénombre les draps étaient gonflés en demi-cercle, ce devait être Albertine qui, le corps incurvé, dormait les pieds et la tête au mur [...]. Je sentis ce demi-cercle immobile et vivant, où tenait toute une vie humaine, et qui était la seule chose à laquelle j'attachais du prix; je sentis qu'il était là, en ma possession dominatrice. (III, 365–6n.)

It is notable that the image of the static semi-circle should dominate the passage, a process that renders the person of Albertine altogether less prominent. This is reflected syntactically, with the use of the pronoun 'il' referring the reader back not to Albertine but to the semi-circular form of which the Narrator is more immediately aware. She is, then, in some sense abstracted behind 'ce demi-cercle immobile et vivant', so that her own complex individuality grows increasingly remote. And there is further evidence of this in the process of recognition that leads him to identify Albertine: 'les draps étaient gonflés [...], ce devait être Albertine qui, le corps incurvé, dormait'. The conjectural note of 'ce devait être' implies no more than a probable interconnection. 'C'était Albertine' would have marked a more categorical assertion in the Narrator's mind. As it stands, the suppositional value of the reference makes Albertine's presence a less immediately visible reality. Hence, language itself can reflect this distancing of the captive Albertine, by bringing to the forefront the depersonalised 'demi-cercle'.

This confirms the more general conclusions that can be drawn from the other descriptions of Albertine's sleep in *La Prisonnière*. On such occasions, the independence and complexity of her being is subverted by the Narrator, the effect being to allay the incessant doubting generated by his jealousy. Moreover, his joy is largely that of the demiurge. For, by likening her to the stem of a flower, or a musical instrument, he succeeds in making of her an act of his own mind and fantasy.

(d)   The symbols of harmony

For the Narrator, Albertine's sleep is an ideal way of conveying the continuum of joy that he anxiously seeks to achieve. Interestingly, to describe this state, he draws on a variety of images and devices, some of which, by their frequency, help articulate certain predilections that he has been carefully nurturing. One such group of symbols consists of a varied crop of references to closed, restricted forms. It is easy to see how these may form a suitable backdrop to the scene of Albertine's close confinement.

One finds an indication of the fullness and solidity of Albertine's presence in the description of a coach journey back to the Narrator's home. On that occasion, he freely enjoys the sense of her containment,

présence qui nous acheminait non au vide des heures où l'on est séparé, mais à la réunion plus stable encore et mieux enclose dans mon chez-moi, qui était aussi son chez-elle, symbole matériel de la possession que j'avais d'elle. (III, 175.)

We are immediately made to see the pleasurable implications of claustration for the Narrator in the 'réunion plus stable encore et mieux enclose'. In *A l'ombre des jeunes filles en fleurs*, by contrast, the spatial perspective was seemingly infinite, something that harmonised with his joyful reflection on the mysterious existence of the 'jeunes filles'. The movement of restricting and immuring that dominates *La Prisonnière*, however, strengthens the atmosphere of suppression:

Mes regards l'enveloppaient encore tandis qu'elle s'enfonçait devant moi sous la voûte, et c'était toujours ce même calme inerte et domestique que je goûtais à la voir ainsi lourde, empourprée, opulente et captive, rentrer tout naturellement avec moi, comme une femme que j'avais à moi, et, protégée par les murs, disparaître dans notre maison. (III, 176.)

The cluster of epithets used to describe Albertine gives her a physical presence that the Narrator can enjoy unhurriedly. Similarly, the enclosing movement of *envelopper* and *s'enfoncer* is in turn reinforced by the smothering implicit in *protéger* and *disparaître*. The cumulative effect of this is to seal the experience emotionally for the Narrator. In that sense, the image of the arch, with its unbroken, enveloping form, serves as a symbol of his calm.

The clearest indication of the Narrator's attraction for claustral forms comes in descriptions of Albertine's naked body:

Son ventre (dissimulant la place qui chez l'homme s'enlaidit comme du crampon resté fiché dans une statue descellée) se refermait, à la jonction des cuisses, par deux valves d'une courbe aussi assoupie, aussi reposante, aussi claustrale que celle de l'horizon quand le soleil a disparu. (III, 79.)

The male anatomy, incomplete and unrounded, offers disquieting images of fragmentation; Albertine's body, on the other hand, reveals a closed form in which the Narrator finds contentment. One cannot but contrast such a depiction with other, menacing images of Albertine that re-activate the Narrator's hypersensitivity. Now, however, she seems capable of guaranteeing an emotionally secure world where he can share her activity. Indeed the effect of the anaphora in 'une courbe aussi assoupie, aussi reposante, aussi claustrale' is to convey an impression of abundant and growing repose. The added beauty of this closed world is that the Narrator throws off any lingering desire to go beyond it. The oneness of the experience pre-empts any need to transcend it and crowds out his self-doubting.

Speaking immediately after this of the sexual union between man and woman, the Narrator suggests that such a coming-together marks a return to the original unity that creation itself has fragmented:

O grandes attitudes de l'Homme et de la Femme où cherchent à se joindre, dans l'innocence des premiers jours et avec l'humilité de l'argile, ce que la Création a séparé, où Eve est étonnée et soumise devant l'Homme au côté de qui elle s'éveille, comme lui-même, encore seul, devant Dieu qui l'a formé. (III, 79.)

The mood is clearly one of aspiration to some primal unicity. As such, it bears some affinity with the completeness of Albertine's naked body, in that a desire to escape dispersal and to regain wholeness is common to both. As for Albertine, what pleases the Narrator is that he has now linked together the formerly disparate facets of her being. To this end, the allusion to Adam and Eve is valuable for the archetypal frame of reference that it introduces. This evokes a significantly atemporal setting, the Narrator's hope presumably being that the same timelessness may somehow permeate his own relationship with Albertine. Proust's affection for primeval man has already been noted (see Chapter 3d). With the creation of Adam, however, we are stepping back even further into the sureness of the archetypal order. When seen against such a background, the calm that the Narrator enjoys with Albertine seems eternal.

Likewise, on rainy overcast days, he savours the security of home in her company, a home assuming all the characteristics of Noah's Ark: 'Rien que la résidence dans la maison située au milieu d'une pluie égale et continue, avait la glissante douceur, le silence calmant, tout l'intérêt d'une navigation' (III, 82). The pleasant lilting sensation that he experiences in the confines of his retreat gently anaesthetises the Narrator against the anguish of jealousy. Like the biblical father, he remains sheltered from the evil without.

By consciously linking life with Albertine to this unchanging order of things, the Narrator is giving expression, as we have seen, to a desire for greater permanence in their relationship. It is a desire that conditions so many of his perceptions. A simple description of daylight, for example, becomes influenced by this drive to perpetuate their love. This occurs in a manuscript passage, where the Narrator speaks of the confinement with Albertine and of 'la journée [. . .] occupée pour plusieurs heures encore à sa tâche immémoriale'.[14] He has only to mention the sense of a 'tâche immémoriale' to endow the long days of bliss spent with Albertine with soothing primordial qualities. The effect is similar to that of earlier references to original man or the biblical flood. Each of these helps reinforce the impression of a static world nurtured by the Narrator in *La Prisonnière*.

It would seem appropriate to follow up these references to archetypes by looking at the many comparisons between the relationship with Albertine and works of art. For in Proust's work, a beautiful unchangeableness is as much a feature of artistic creation as it is of certain primitive human activities. There is, for a start, an effective series of sculptural references that reinforce this notion of a continuum.

In *Cahier 60*, which contains notes and sketches for *La Prisonnière*, we come across a significant comment on the effects of sleep:

Pour ajouter au sommeil d'Albertine: sans regards [?] elle était immobile, comme un marbre. Le sommeil est un grand sculpteur. Mais quel surcroît d'ivresse ajouté à l'admiration que ce marbre, aux fossettes si bien ciselées, à la splendeur inanimée, sans mouvement, était pourtant vivant, et quand je le voudrais, je saurais enfin éveiller la déesse endormie, la changer en une créature aux caresses agiles. (*Cahier 60*, fos 123–4.)[15]

For the Narrator, the beauty of sculpture would seem to lie in the hermetically sealed world that it represents. Hence his emotional security when he sees his captive as being part of it. Art itself now contains her.

But it is not solely when Albertine sleeps that she appears statuesque to the Narrator. Describing her visit to his home shortly after the death of his grandmother, he makes frequent use of sculptural motifs there also (see II, 350–4). If one looks at the original drafts of these evocations, one finds the Narrator confidently asserting that he has Albertine beside him, 'contenue dans son corps comme dans une statuette' (*Cahier 46*, fo 41). Later, in a mood of unchallenged tranquillity, he reflects on how she is

fine et ciselée, [elle] semblait résumer toutes les heures heureuses que j'avais passé[es] à l'attendre sur la digue à Balbec comme une délicieuse statuette à qui elles donnaient une sorte de pâleur voluptueuse. (*Cahier 46*, fo 52.)

That the Narrator should draw upon the plastic arts is not unexpected, given his general interest in things artistic. Yet these sculptural images are far from being purely decorative. The Narrator is aware of art's capacity to preserve and embalm. And when one bears in mind how incessant his suspicions of Albertine are, it is fitting that he should employ the language of art to convey the delicate calm that he would gladly see made permanent.

In the same context, the Narrator also mentions the art-form of music. The first of the seven *Cahiers* that go to make up the continuous text of *Sodome et Gomorrhe* (n.a.fr. 16708–14) begins with him returning from the Guermantes residence.[16] The sense of void that he feels in his contact with the elusive women of the *soirée* is soon dispelled when he reflects on the secure female presence that awaits him in his home:

J'aurais le sentiment tout opposé aux longues et vides attentes de ceux que la réalité ne récompense d'aucun retour, d'une richesse de réalisations complexes, d'une plénitude comme une musique substantielle ne laissant de place pour aucun creux. (n.a.fr. 16708:5.)

In this passage, the words 'comme une musique substantielle' have been added above the line, indicating a reinforcement of the idea of fullness in the experience. That it should be compared to that all-engaging art makes life with his captive totally self-sufficient for the Narrator. It is as though its solidity and its ubiquity banish doubt, for the fullness of 'une musique substantielle' leaves no room for self-questioning.

Here again, Proust has chosen a musical frame of reference to convey the Narrator's unspoilt happiness. Earlier, we saw Albertine herself likened to a musical instrument. In both cases, harmony is used to dispel the inner discord of suspicion and jealousy. These examples of music, then, impart an impression of security to the Narrator. The question of music will be returned to in the next chapter, since it is intimately bound up with the Narrator's self-realisation in *Le Temps retrouvé*.

But in spite of carefully worked images based on music and sculpture, the impact of Albertine's presence is perhaps best illustrated in an almost casual reference that the Narrator makes to her untidiness. He returns home on one occasion to find her clothing scattered all over the apartment. No sooner has he seen this than he realises he is not condemned to being alone with his own anguished self:

Dès qu'en entrant je les apercevais [i.e., ses vêtements], l'atmosphère de la maison devenait respirable. Je sentais qu'au lieu d'un air raréfié, le bonheur la remplissait. J'étais sauvé de ma tristesse. (III, 56.)

Much of what is conjured up by the reference to 'un air raréfié' has been foreshadowed in earlier chapters of the present study. For the Narrator has appeared oversensitive in his response to most human situations; there is the adolescent, grappling with intellectual questions, the young theatre-goer excessively scrupulous in his attempts to define the artistic merit of a work of dramatic art, the lover who must analyse his relationship to the point of dangerously dissecting it. With the fullness of Albertine's presence, however, the Narrator escapes the refined atmosphere of his own mind. Just as the 'musique substantielle' dispenses with any need to reflect on its merit, the Narrator occasionally finds experience with Albertine so full as to render its analysis superflous.

These images of stasis, of claustration and fullness, together with references to archetypes and art, have one very important point in common. Each represents an attempt to make more permanent an ideal liaison with Albertine – ideal, that is, to an over-cautious Narrator, who has buried all dreams of a fun-loving, vivacious Albertine. Although the complexity of her own person is an obvious casualty, he is happy to prettify the situation.[17] It is with the diligence of the sculptor, for example, that he attempts to create a new Albertine. For him, she is not, like the promiscuous Rachel, 'une vaine poussière de chair et d'étoffe' (III, 175). Rather he can look at her with the detachment an artist feels for the permanence of his creation:

L'imagination de mes yeux, de mes lèvres, de mes mains, avait, à Balbec, si solidement construit, si tendrement poli son corps que maintenant [...] je . n'avais pas besoin de me serrer contre Albertine. (III, 175–6.)

(e) The break-up of the liaison and its consequences

In *La Prisonnière*, it is very often clear that the Narrator cannot
guarantee Albertine's total insulation. Many of the references to this
inability to protect her only appear as additions to the manuscript, or
are inserted at the later typescript stage. This confirms Alison
Winton's observation that the original evocation of life with
Albertine was generally very relaxed: 'The basic seventy pages of the
MS "life with Albertine" seem, without the weight of these later
pieces, to centre, far more than the text we now have, on Marcel's
calmness, and his enjoyment of the world outside, perceived from
his room' (Winton, vol. 1, p. 45).

The effect of the additions, then, is to undermine the security that
he feels when she is physically present. One such late passage points
to a very obvious threat:

Et maintenant qu'elle m'avait dit un jour 'Mlle Vinteuil', j'aurais voulu non
pas arracher sa robe pour voir son corps, mais, à travers son corps, voir tout
ce bloc-notes de ses souvenirs et de ses prochains et ardents rendez-vous. (III,
94.)[18]

Remembering how she was totally present in her sleeping form, one
can now see what is for the Narrator the disturbing failure of her
physical self to envelop her whole being. Thus he must get beyond
this body if he is to find her scattered self. Another late appendage
has similar thematic implications, with the Narrator now reflecting
on

l'impossibilité où se heurte l'amour. Nous nous imaginons qu'il a pour objet
un être qui peut être couché devant nous, enfermé dans un corps. Hélas! Il est
l'extension de cet être à tous les points de l'espace et du temps que cet être a
occupés et occupera. (III, 100.)[19]

The spatial and temporal fragmentation that this introduces
explodes the motionless world in which Albertine has previously
remained. The stasis envisaged by the Narrator now seems an
illusory one.

This essentially ambivalent view of 'la prisonnière' is nowhere
more apparent than in an arresting image of Albertine as a stone
being touched by the Narrator. His joy is tinged with the fear that
she is not quite present, 'comme si j'eusse manié une pierre qui
enferme la salure des océans immémoriaux ou le rayon d'une étoile'
(III, 386). Sea and sky connote an infinity that allows Albertine an
inviolable freedom. Their elemental greatness dwarfs the Narrator's
solely human efforts to contain her.

But the lover's secure world does not disintegrate simply because it is an impracticable one. His own waning enthusiasm also becomes an important contributory factor. Conscious of Albertine's development from the mysterious girl of Balbec to the largely known inhabitant of his Paris home, he speaks of this contrast, and of how it led to an amphibious love:

> Et ainsi alternait, avec l'ennui un peu lourd que j'avais auprès d'elle, un désir frémissant, plein d'images magnifiques et de regrets, selon qu'elle était à côté de moi dans ma chambre ou que je lui rendais sa liberté dans ma mémoire, sur la digue, dans ses gais costumes de plage, au jeu des instruments de musique de la mer. (III, 174.)

Offsetting the 'ennui un peu lourd' of her captivity is the ecstatic vision of her former liberty – enhanced, incidentally, by yet another reference to musical instruments, albeit of a metaphorical kind. This dual view of Albertine throws into relief the essential paradox of her imprisonment. The captor's original desire is to win exclusive enjoyment of the vivacious, semi-mythological creature that Albertine is at Balbec. Yet by constantly scrutinising her, he unwittingly suppresses the very ethereal qualities he wants to preserve. Sartre – speaking about love generally – touches on a similar kind of ambivalence when commenting: '[L'amant] réclame un type spécial d'appropriation. Il veut posséder une liberté comme liberté' (*L'Etre et le Néant*, p. 434). The contradiction that this enshrines echoes the Narrator's own ambiguous response to Albertine.

In the *Recherche*, however, one can also detect a lessening enthusiasm for Albertine in the nostalgia the Narrator feels for the freedom that he himself has lost. This he has seen steadily eroded by his obsessive concern for her. He is momentarily distracted from this preoccupation at the sight of an aircraft flying overhead:

> Je pensais à ma grand'mère qui aimait, dans l'art humain, dans la nature, la grandeur, et qui se plaisait à regarder monter dans ce même bleu le clocher de Saint-Hilaire. Soudain, j'éprouvai de nouveau la nostalgie de ma liberté perdue en entendant un bruit que je ne reconnus pas d'abord et que ma grand'mère eût, lui aussi, tant aimé. C'était comme le bourdonnement d'une guêpe. 'Tiens, me dit Albertine, il y a un aéroplane, il est très haut, très haut.' (III, 406.)

The limitless spatial perspective that so attracted his grandmother contrasts sharply with the claustrophobia of his involvement with Albertine. Now the desire to break with her takes a great leap forward, with the note of self-realisation evident in 'la nostalgie de ma liberté perdue'. And indeed earlier, he refers to his meeting with a pilot as 'la rencontre quasi mythologique d'un aviateur [. . . qui] avait été pour moi comme une image de la liberté' (III, 105).

Quite clearly, the elation aroused by these visits to aerodromes takes us far from the sedentary world of the Narrator's home. Moreover, it is notable that the sight of this feverish activity, and the intoxication with perpetual motion that it brings, is not unlike the frenzy of movement characteristic of descriptions of the 'jeunes filles'. Formerly, the Narrator's imagination was as much fired by a view of the budding Albertine at Balbec as it now is on seeing the airman. One can, then, see a fine symmetry between the events prior to Albertine's stay in Paris and those near the time of her departure. In sharing captivity with her, he tries to check the evasive movement of the 'jeunes filles'. In turn, the period of stasis in his home begins to decline, only now the centrifugal movement is being generated by the Narrator himself. As the aircraft overcomes the weight of gravitational pull – 'il s'élevait lentement dans l'extase raidie' – so the Narrator aspires to flight from the heaviness of Albertine's company. Thus a time of stability and calm lies between two periods of frantic motion and transformation. But whereas it was previously Albertine who was a creature of flight, it is now the Narrator who experiences a longing for emotional and imaginative freedom.

Striking testimony of what this newfound liberty means to him is contained in an admission of just what he has sacrificed by persisting in the affair with Albertine. He says of the shutters on her window:

Certes, ces lumineuses rayures que j'apercevais d'en bas et qui à un autre eussent semblé toutes superficielles, je leur donnais une consistance, une plénitude, une solidité extrêmes, à cause de toute la signification que je mettais derrière elles, en un trésor insoupçonné des autres, que j'avais caché là et dont émanaient ces rayons horizontaux, mais un trésor en échange duquel j'avais aliéné ma liberté, la solitude, la pensée. (III, 331.)

Admittedly, the Narrator is conscious of the palliative impact that her company exerts. But against this, he feels alienated from his own reflective self. Intent on appeasing his hypersensitive reactions to Albertine, he had imprisoned her; now, by contrast, the imperative of spiritual freedom reasserts itself. And if it is mainly Albertine who suffers a diminution in her human individuality, the Narrator reflects that he himself is not totally unscathed. The eclipse of his artistic vocation is evidence of this. How he reverses that trend is seen in the final volume of the *Recherche*. Once free from the tie to Albertine, he may rechannel the great mental energy that has gone into preserving the relationship with her. The result is a return to important artistic speculation. In the following chapter, I shall be looking at the course which that reflection is to take in *Le Temps retrouvé*.

This chapter has attempted to show how the Narrator combats the extreme nature of his suspicions relating to Albertine. As we have seen, his earliest references to women contain the embryo of a strongly subjective view of love. That egocentricity develops, and leads to an almost complete overshadowing of Albertine's consciousness in *La Prisonnière*. There, the Narrator can delight in the 'thing-ness' and passivity of her new self. No longer the ethereal half-presence of *A l'ombre des jeunes filles en fleurs*, she now shows a qualitatively different being as captive. Out of this, the Narrator constructs what is a comforting poetry of solid, tangible forms; the result is a calming of his emotional upheaval. The joy of being able to assimilate her sustains this. Even in her new cultural achievements, the indelible stamp of his influence is discernible. For him, her reading and music-playing are not the apotheosis of any individual expression but rather symbols of her dependence on him.

These more immediate conclusions also have a strong relevance to the present study overall. If the Narrator's concern in *La Prisonnière* is his love for Albertine, his earlier preoccupation was of a philosophical and artistic nature. But what emerges through all this is that the effects of intellectual and amatory crisis are closely related in Proust. This is also illustrated in the somewhat naive assertions of Jean Santeuil. What links him to the hero of *A la recherche* is his comparable hypersensitive temperament. In addition, both are quick to seek antidotes to this. In the earlier novel, the troubled thinker is seen to envy the fullness of sentient living in the animal world. The young Narrator of *Du côté de chez Swann*, too, can sidestep artistic inadequacy by nurturing seemingly banal sense-perceptions. The movement is in some ways repeated in *La Prisonnière*, where Albertine's solid, tangible form is sufficient to dispel her partner's insecurity.

Yet in the final analysis, it is not a question of the Narrator simply escaping his too-active imagination and mind. With Albertine, he ends up by conceding that it is impossible to control her in any total sense. He comes to a realisation of something approaching Pascal's view that others are individual and unpredictable; their inner harmony is not consonant with our own. However keenly he may desire to perpetuate Albertine's presence, the bliss that the Narrator envisages is always tenuous and finally illusory. One might recall his anxious steps in *Sodome et Gomorrhe*, when he longs to preserve a fleeting, evanescent moment in which Albertine has shown him an unconditional love. Yet the fear that she 'vînt blesser d'une dissonance le silence sensitif' is inescapable (II, 835).

If the Narrator's initial reaction is to want to deny that Albertine is a complex, individual being, he is quickly lulled into that security by factors such as his ability to nurture the inanimacy of her sleeping body. But of course Proust's work does occasionally offer such 'easy solutions'. Already in Chapter 2, we have seen the hero of the *Contre Sainte-Beuve* trying to capture 'la délicieuse insensibilité des autres pots de confiture' (*CSB/NM*, p. 68). The reference is an interesting precursor of much of the experience with the sleeping Albertine. Common to both is this solace in an appealing mindlessness.

Ultimately, however, any negation of reflection by the Narrator is only provisional, a postponement of the inevitable return to the problems of his art and thought. As he himself concludes, the imbroglio with Albertine offers 'un trésor en échange duquel j'avais aliéné ma liberté, la solitude, la pensée'. It remains to be seen if the now more mature Narrator is as perplexed by the exigencies of his rekindled artistic vocation as he was as an adolescent. Will he, for example, sense the enigma facing the younger Narrator, who marvels that 'une véritable exaltation m'avait été communiquée, non par quelque idée importante, mais par une odeur de moisi' (I, 494)? In fact, it emerges that the adult Narrator does not live in awe of the conceptual. But although disabused in this way, he is still to give an important place to intellectual values in the artistic projections of *Le Temps retrouvé*.

6

The Realisation of an Artistic Vocation

The denouement of the *Recherche* has been one of the main subjects of discussion in Proust criticism. This seems due, in large part, to the self-conscious character of the closing volume, *Le Temps retrouvé*. There, it is a question of a book about writing a book. The Narrator assumes the role of art-critic, attempting to define the respective merits of different art-forms. More particularly, he speculates on the genre his own literary work will most easily fall into. What I hope to do in this final chapter is to examine the conclusions that the Narrator is now drawing, and to interpret them in the light of the present study. This will be complemented by a general over-view in the Conclusion proper.

Our most immediate concern, however, is to see the nature of the link between the self-realisation at the end of the novel and what I have been singling out in characters such as the Narrator's grand-mother, Françoise and the 'jeunes filles', especially Albertine. The chapter will also be asking how his hyperactive mind is appeased and satisfied. Much of this will depend on his ability to harmonise what is, in broad terms, intellectual and non-intellectual experience. In addition, it will be of interest to see if what dogged him as an adolescent, and indeed what also perplexed Jean Santeuil, can be resolved at all permanently.

One possible pitfall is to allow the Narrator's decisive-sounding judgements to condition our own response to the work and blind us to its complexity. Commonly quoted from Proust's work for example is the view that friendship is an inadequate human experience in so far as it militates against any artistic calling. The Narrator's frequently unequivocal pronouncements on the subject lend themselves to such an interpretation. But on other occasions, blanket assertions give way to something much more polyfaceted and subtle. So it is that he sees his relationship with the 'jeunes filles', and more specifically with Albertine, as having greater substance than the friendship that links him to Saint-Loup or Bloch (see above,

p. 141). One does then need to guard against overpromoting the Narrator's stated opinion that interpersonal relationships and art are mutually exclusive. Granted, he attributes his estrangement from art to the prolonged liaison with Albertine, for he speaks of this as 'un trésor en échange duquel j'avais aliéné ma liberté, la solitude, la pensée' (III, 331). But closer examination of *Le Temps retrouvé* reveals a less unilinear view of artistic awareness than certain of the Narrator's aphorisms and value judgements might lead us to believe. Literary theory and practice may, then, diverge.

Roger Shattuck advocates a similar reappraisal in this field, when he makes some perceptive and, I think, brave comments on the course of Proust criticism: 'The much touted "moments bienheureux" do not bring Marcel to his vocation or confer on him any lasting happiness [...]. The attitude of passivity on which they rely, and the tendency which they have to encourage substitution of pleasure for effort, and objects for people, prevent them from offering the key to Marcel's salvation.'[1] This call for re-evaluation encourages one to cast a fresh critical eye on the novel's conclusions generally.

(a) Music: a sublime artistic experience for the Narrator

In *La Prisonnière*, one of the chief sources of artistic impetus for the Narrator is the music by Vinteuil performed at the Verdurin evening. His joy seems all the more ecstatic when seen against the background of his troubled relationship with Albertine. Not that he closely links the musical experience to his love for this girl; Swann is more given to that kind of aesthetic indiscretion, adopting the Vinteuil sonata as the anthem of his love for Odette. Now, in the Verdurin home, the Narrator delights in comparing and contrasting the familiar sonata with the newly-performed septet. In spite of differences of mood and tone, both pieces, he insists, belong to the singular world of the composer's artistic creation. He refers to them as

ces deux interrogations si dissemblables [...], l'une [i.e., la sonate] si calme et timide, presque détachée et comme philosophique, l'autre si pressante, anxieuse, implorante, c'était pourtant une même prière, jaillie devant différents levers de soleil intérieurs. (III, 255.)

Thus, Vinteuil's art takes the form of 'une interrogation', 'une prière'. Later, we see a reference to 'les éternelles investigations de Vinteuil' (III, 256). These are all pointers to the fact that his work is essentially exploratory and questioning in its nature. Nevertheless, the Narrator is careful to point out that Vinteuil's probing is far from being of an intellectual kind. Significantly, his artistic activity is

aussi débarrassée des formes analytiques du raisonnement que si elle s'était exercée dans le monde des anges, de sorte que nous pouvons en mesurer la profondeur, mais pas plus la traduire en langage humain que ne le peuvent les esprits désincarnés quand, évoqués par un médium, celui-ci les interroge sur les secrets de la mort. (III, 256.)

Any verbal medium is inadequate for the artist; the non-intellectual quality of his feeling demands another, more apposite channel of expression. Indeed, the gap separating them seems no less than the fundamental divide between life and an indefinable after-life.

As the Narrator develops his reaction to Vinteuil, he gives increasing attention to defining the character of the musical experience generally. He seems particularly fascinated by its other-worldly dimension. The reference to hosts of angels just quoted is quickly returned to, when the Narrator expresses his sense of disappointment on falling back into the world of banal human conversations: 'J'étais vraiment comme un ange qui, déchu des ivresses du Paradis, tombe dans la plus insignifiante réalité' (III, 258). He goes on to expand his view of this lost paradise, using a language that is perhaps not altogether new in the context of this present study:

Et de même que certains êtres sont les derniers témoins d'une forme de vie que la nature a abandonnée, je me demandais si la Musique n'était pas l'exemple unique de ce qu'aurait pu être – s'il n'y avait pas eu l'invention du langage, la formation des mots, l'analyse des idées – la communication des âmes. Elle est comme une possibilité qui n'a pas eu de suites; l'humanité s'est engagée dans d'autres voies, celle du langage parlé et écrit. (III, 258.)[2]

The direction in which the Narrator projects his regret is of singular importance here. Man has totally committed himself to the structures of language, to verbal and conceptual forms. For this reason, it is with a very real sense of nostalgia that the Narrator looks on music and reflects on how it guarantees an important pre-intellectual order. His reaction is somewhat ambivalent, however, for he is aware of the potential in this reality beyond analysis and intellectual scrutiny, and yet feels it to be underdeveloped. Hence his interest in this 'possibilité qui n'a pas eu de suites'. One also feels that if humanity has erred, the Narrator is somehow excluded from that general deviation by virtue of his sensitivity to musical experience.

Another intriguing aspect of the passage concerns the comparison made at the outset. What is one to make of the assertion that 'certains êtres sont les derniers témoins d'une forme de vie que la nature a abandonnée'? Perhaps it is the same regressive movement that is in evidence in other parts of the *Recherche*. We recall how Françoise, for example, is seen by the Narrator as the living embodiment of a primitive, prehistoric era (see above, Chapter 3c). And while it is evident that the Narrator's contact with Françoise and his communion with Vinteuil's art are poles apart, he refers, coincidentally in both cases, to the absence of all intellectualising. Another form of life that captures the Narrator's attention is that represented by the 'jeunes filles en fleurs'. Earlier in life, he had asserted that this little group was at a certain, very definite stage in its evolution: in his eyes it stood for 'une culture physique à laquelle ne s'est pas encore ajoutée celle de l'intelligence' (see Chapter 4c). As in the case with Françoise, one must insist straightaway on the gulf separating the Narrator's flirtation with the band of Balbec and his experience of the septet. The former points towards a pleasurable sentience, whereas his contact with Vinteuil's work leads the Narrator to the highest aesthetic contemplation. Yet there is a point of contact between these divergent experiences. Just as he initially believed that by knowing the girls of Balbec he would glimpse a world of unreflection, he now describes listening to Vinteuil in slightly similar terms: 'Ce retour à l'inanalysé était si enivrant, qu'au sortir de ce paradis le contact des êtres plus ou moins intelligents me semblait d'une insignifiance extraordinaire' (III, 258–9). Quite clearly, the world of the septet lies beyond that of everyday communication. It represents a supreme artistic moment transcending individual human relationships. But of course for the adolescent Narrator of Balbec, the 'jeunes filles' are no ordinary mortals either. Initially, they appear on the beach like semi-mythological creatures, the children of a world free from taxing intellectual activity.

My point is that the Narrator's desire for 'ce retour à l'inanalysé' is asserting itself – albeit more crudely – long before his acquaintance with the Vinteuil septet. For it is this same desire that leads him to insist so much on the non-reflecting character of the Balbec girls. That, for him, was the source of their beauty and appeal. But, as he acknowledges afterwards, what he had imagined these girls to be clashes with the reality of their situation. Andrée, for example, emerges as a thinker and intellectual – just like himself. Yet with the musical experience, there can be no such disappointing reversal. Accordingly it satisfies the Narrator in so far as it offers a more adequate and permanent satisfaction of his longing for 'l'inanalysé'. Not that this diminishes the experience at Balbec; that adolescent flirtation throws early valuable light on the unintellectuality towards which he is leaning. To that extent, it prepares the way for the greater aesthetic experience of music.

Faint echoes of this same process occur at the very beginning of *A la recherche*. We have seen in Chapter 2 how the Narrator delights in hovering between consciousness and the oblivion of total sleep. One reference in particular has an immediate bearing on the impact made by Vinteuil. It is related to how the Narrator conceives of the darkness surrounding him:

Je recouvrais la vue et j'étais bien étonné de trouver autour de moi une obscurité, douce et reposante pour mes yeux, mais peut-être plus encore pour mon esprit, à qui elle apparaissait comme une chose sans cause, incompréhensible, comme une chose vraiment obscure. (I, 3.)

The absence of any need to comprehend or to establish causal links has the soothing effect of releasing the mind from its rational ties. To that extent, the Narrator's reaction then is comparable with his response to Vinteuil. But of course unlike the atmosphere of slumber and mindlessness at the opening of the *Recherche*, the effect of the Vinteuil performance is to awaken and stimulate the Narrator's artistic curiosity.

In his efforts to define the fascination of music, the Narrator is spurred on by the belief that Vinteuil's work marks a high point in artistic attainment. As a result, he sets music above literature. The reasons that he offers in support of this help explain his own view of art:

Cette musique me semblait quelque chose de plus vrai que tous les livres connus. Par instants je pensais que cela tenait à ce que ce qui est senti par nous de la vie, ne l'étant pas sous forme d'idées, sa traduction littéraire, c'est-à-dire intellectuelle, en rend compte, l'explique, l'analyse, mais ne le recompose pas comme la musique où les sons semblent prendre l'inflexion de l'être, reproduire cette pointe intérieure et extrême des sensations qui est la partie qui nous donne cette ivresse spécifique que nous retrouvons de temps en temps. (III, 374).

The whole drift of his argument is that much of our intimate feeling cannot be captured in a conceptual framework. And it is rather the pliant, supple qualities of music that lend themselves to the otherwise elusive 'inflexion de l'être'. To that extent, one might liken the Narrator's view of the septet to what a contemporary critic defines as the function of music generally, 'a total analogue of emotive life'.[3] For the Narrator, then, music becomes the ideal expressive medium. If the translation of feeling into words can only be effected with a certain wastage, so to speak, nothing of the inner experience is lost when conveyed through music. As for the form his own work of art is to take, the Narrator feels that it should be as near as possible to the elusive condition of music, to Vinteuil's reproduction of 'cette pointe intérieure et extrême des sensations qui est la partie qui nous donne cette ivresse spécifique que nous retrouvons de temps en temps' (III, 374). For Proust's Narrator, any dry conceptualisation of the distinctive accent of individual sensitivity would seem a mere appendage, and therefore artistically superfluous.

In the light of the Narrator's artistic awakening, the experience with the 'jeunes filles' becomes retrospectively more significant. Obviously, what the Narrator most admires is their spontaneity of emotion. But of course they give themselves to physical, bodily impulses in the main; Vinteuil's work is clearly an invitation to more spiritual activity. Indeed, in the context of that music, he speaks of 'une certaine réalité spirituelle où la vie n'aurait aucun sens' (III, 374). Yet common to both is the Narrator's enthusiasm for a naturalness of expression. Referring to his adolescent love for those girls, he speaks of 'le génie de cet âge qui emporte tout' (I, 893; see above, Chapter 4e). Like the musical experience, this contact with a youthful vivaciousness guards against any sterile intellectualising of life.

Just why the adolescent Narrator should have a total faith in these girls can be explained by his boundless and slightly blind enthusiasm at that time. As a mature observer, however, he tries to introduce a clearly spiritual dimension to experience. In doing this, he comes to a gradual realisation of what might be termed the absolute vitality and suppleness, not of female youth, but of music. Certainly, the more sensitive he becomes to the artistic merit of the septet, the more limited in scope his juvenile infatuation would appear. Yet curiously enough, the description of a series of musical phrases may throw the reader back momentarily into the world of *A l'ombre des jeunes filles en fleurs*:

Puis elles [i.e., les phrases] s'éloignèrent, sauf une que je vis repasser jusqu'à cinq et six fois, sans que je pusse apercevoir son visage, mais si caressante, si différente – comme sans doute la petite phrase de la Sonate pour Swann – de ce qu'aucune femme n'avait jamais fait désirer, que cette phrase-là, qui m'offrait d'une voix si douce un bonheur qu'il eût vraiment valu la peine d'obtenir, c'est peut-être – cette créature invisible dont je ne connaissais pas le langage et que je comprenais si bien – la seule Inconnue qu'il m'ait jamais été donné de rencontrer. (III, 260.)

The tone of the language used is so reminiscent of *A l'ombre* and the descriptions there of tantalising female beauty.

The suggestion that the Narrator has the girls of Balbec in mind here is far from being fanciful. For he now compares the two experiences and more importantly contrasts them, seeing the litttle phrase as offering an altogether greater pleasure than that promised by any of thee 'jeunes filles'. He thereby distances his experience of Vinteuil from that of Balbec. Nevertheless, he is revealing indirectly what it is that he had hoped to find with the young girls. And if he fails to secure the elusive promise of the unknown in the latter relationship, he can now boast a more lasting achievement in knowing the phrase of Vinteuil, 'la seule Inconnue qu'il m'ait jamais été donné de rencontrer'. Moreover the telling use of capitalisation marks the important position, almost conceded to the 'jeunes filles', but finally reserved for Vinteuil (see above, note 2). With the girls of the Balbec beach, his impression of their mystery finally gives way to a sense of their dull, predictable existence. Only with music does an enchanting beauty survive.

It is nevertheless important not to lose sight of how the Narrator's thinking has developed. The urge to avoid excessive intellectualising can account for his curiosity about varying degrees of mindlessness: he becomes interested in characters like Françoise and his grand-mother, and is quick to follow the young girls at Balbec. Nearer the end of the *Recherche*, he discovers, in the permanence of music, the escape into 'l'inanalysé [...] si enivrant' (III, 258). There, his desire may be said to be unconditionally satisfied.

(b)   The Narrator realises the subject of his own work of art

The joy produced by the music of Vinteuil is consolidated for the Narrator when he links its effect to that of other experiences that he has enjoyed. He describes the profound impact of the septet as being analogous to that made on him by different perceptions, among them the sight of the Martinville spires and the taste of the 'madeleine' (III, 374). For the Narrator, this interconnection between the world of Vinteuil and that of the 'moments bienheureux' is of far-reaching significance; it is to provide the linch-pin for his own work of art. The importance of this realisation for the Narrator is nowhere better illustrated than in a preparatory sketch in *Cahier 57*:

Capitalissime issime, issime, peut-être le plus de toute l'oeuvre: quand je parle du plaisir éternel de la cuiller, tasse de thé etc. = art. Etait-ce cela ce bonheur proposé par la petite phrase de la Sonate à Swann qui s'était trompé en l'assimilant au plaisir de l'amour et n'avait pas su où le trouver (dans l'art) [?]. (*Cahier 57*, fo 19v.)[4]

The reader of Proust's manuscripts will be aware that virtually everything in certain *Cahiers* is classified as 'Capital', while a fair number of pages are headed 'Capitalissime'! But even if Proust is extravagant in his use of such superlatives, the triple '-issime' points undeniably to the singular importance of this finding. Indeed the spirit of these manuscript words is present with a vengeance in the *Recherche* itself. If music reflects the depth of Vinteuil's artistic vision, then for the Narrator, his comparable privileged moments are to be prominent in his planned work of art.

His slow awareness of this parallel is often frustrated by uncertainty as to the merit of what he considers fortuitous sense-impressions. In a moment of self-doubt, he concedes that the effect of the septet and the 'madeleine' episode are related only in so far as they are vague and difficult to analyse:

> En tout cas, me disait l'esprit du doute, même si ces états sont dans la vie plus profonds que d'autres, et sont inanalysables à cause de cela même [...], la beauté d'une phrase de musique pure paraît facilement l'image ou du moins la parente d'une impression inintellectuelle que nous avons eue, mais simplement parce qu'elle est inintellectuelle. (III, 381.)

In this way, the Narrator is unsure as to whether or not such feeling should have a place in the work of art.

This hesitation is of course essentially the same as that confronting the adolescent Narrator. We have seen in Chapter 3 the latter's inability to evaluate fully certain sense-perceptions. There, his difficulty is that he is hidebound by rigid preconceptions, among them the belief that the only valid experience is an intellectual one. He refers, on one occasion, to his urgent literary preoccupations, and finds but poor consolation in 'impressions [...] liées à un objet particulier dépourvu de valeur intellectuelle et ne se rapportant à aucune vérité abstraite' (I, 178–9; see above, Chapter 3b). Not suprisingly, he will be slow to shed this exaggerated respect for a work's intellectual value. Indeed those haunting adolescent doubts reappear nearer the end of the novel to thwart his artistic self-realisation. Yet once the awe of things intellectual declines – and this is helped immeasurably by his appreciation of Vinteuil – he begins to enjoy a more lucid view of what his own art is to involve. No longer believing in narrowly cerebral criteria, he can apply his whole self, his sensibility as well as his intelligence, to an understanding of his experience:

> La recréation par la mémoire d'impressions qu'il fallait ensuite approfondir, éclairer, transformer en équivalents d'intelligence, n'était-elle pas une des

conditions, presque l'essence même de l'oeuvre d'art telle que je l'avais conçue tout à l'heure dans la bibliothèque? (III, 1044.)

By upgrading his own sentient experience, the mature Narrator moves an important step nearer to formulating a coherent artistic plan. He may concentrate his undivided creative effort now that he is convinced of the intrinsic merit of his own feelings: the result is a rapid blossoming of ideas for the work of art.

(c) The projected novel: questions of medium and message

The process of self-disabusement to which I have just referred has the effect of freeing the Narrator from the strictures of many literary conventions. In this respect, he is particularly happy to throw off the shackles of what he refers to as the so-called Realist school. He condemns those writers 'qui tendaient à "faire sortir l'artiste de sa tour d'ivoire", et à traiter des sujets non frivoles ni sentimentaux, mais peignant de grands mouvements ouvriers' (III, 881). For the Narrator, this constant theorising is spurious, failing to get at all close to the greater reality of intimate impressions. Indeed this is a none too subtle attack on authors such as Barrès; the first of Proust's four *Carnets* already contained several disparaging references to Barrès' work.[5] It is also worth noting how Proust views endless intellectualising in art. He refers to

la grossière tentation pour l'écrivain d'écrire des oeuvres intellectuelles. Grande indélicatesse. Une oeuvre où il y a des théories est comme un objet sur lequel on laisse la marque du prix. On raisonne, c'est-à-dire on vagabonde, chaque fois qu'on n'a pas la force de s'astreindre à faire passer une impression par tous les états successifs qui aboutiront à sa fixation, à l'expression. (III, 882.)

His rejection of certain writing is sufficiently clear to show by implication what the subject of his own work is to be. Indeed he is touching the nerve-centre of his art when he speaks of the difficult transition between felt impression and verbal expression. The principal obstacle in this respect is the opaque quality of words themselves. Hence when referring to Vinteuil, his enthusiasm is tinged with a hint of envy that musical sounds can

reproduire cette pointe intérieure et extrême des sensations qui est la partie qui nous donne cette ivresse spécifique que nous retrouvons de temps en temps et que, quand nous disons: 'Quel beau temps! quel beau soleil!', nous ne faisons nullement connaître au prochain, en qui le même soleil et le même temps éveillent des vibrations toutes différentes. (III, 374.)

Ideally, the Narrator's aim is to respect the qualitatively different mode of feeling in each individual, and to convey this multiplicity of response in his work. Language, however, may jeopardise his plan, for it inevitably tends to render uniform what is essentially individual. Accordingly, he will refuse to accept the reductionism imposed by verbal forms. He describes as 'cette espèce de déchet de l'expérience' the belief that everyone shares an identical mental picture when we speak of 'un mauvais temps, une guerre, une station de voitures, un restaurant éclairé, un jardin en fleurs' (III, 890).

The belief that language tends to give only a pale reflection of inner experience is not restricted to the *Recherche*. For looking back to the much earlier *Jean Santeuil*, we see that Proust is already concerned with the question of verbal communication, and how it gives an impoverished view of what one feels. What is more, he seems, even in this formative work, to have a very developed sense of its importance.

One particular episode involving M. Santeuil is especially revealing. Jean frequently points out that his father has a quite rigid, limited mind, not easily given to aesthetic appreciation. One evening, as M. Santeuil and his wife travel along in a pleasure boat, he indulges his old habit of naming to her the lit-up buildings that they can see on the river-bank. Yet Jean senses that there is something new about this ritual experience. And he pauses to reflect on the change that has almost imperceptibly come over his father in old age:

Mais si les formes de sa conversation étaient restées les mêmes, un sens nouveau s'y était insinué. Et ces paroles étaient moins comme autrefois l'étalage de sa science ou la satisfaction de sa découverte que la notation, au moyen des signes dont il s'était toujours servi mais qu'il employait alors pour eux-mêmes, des sensations douces et presque poétiques qu'il ne savait pas exprimer autrement qu'en appelant l'attention sur leur cause. Ces reflets dans l'eau, ces voix arrivant sur l'eau, ces mouvements dans l'obscurité: il s'attachait comme à des points de repère aux faits qui en étaient la raison d'être, mais qui n'expliquaient pas le plaisir qu'il y trouvait et à la recherche duquel il venait souvent maintenant le soir.... (*JS*, p. 870.)

Here, we have a clear example of verbal structures remaining the same, and failing to reflect an inner transformation, in this case M. Santeuil's. Jean is now ready to concede that his father is capable of 'des sensations douces et presque poétiques'. This in itself is a tribute to Jean's perspicacity, for he has penetrated behind and beyond the father's unchanging conversation, to unveil important nuances of feeling and note the shift in what is signified.

Even as early as *Jean Santeuil*, therefore, Proust shows himself to be sensitive to the question of language, and its frequent inability to register the complexity of individual thought. It is hardly surprising that when the Narrator of the *Recherche* forms his own artistic credo, he should be keenly aware of verbal forms and their tendency to homogenise. Vinteuil, he reflects enviously, may dispense with these. Not so the novelist. But that will not weaken the Narrator's resolve to articulate a language that will accommodate his most intimate experiences. He recalls some of his earlier failures to find a suitable medium for what he describes as 'la racine personnelle de notre propre impression' (III, 891). The 'Zut, zut, zut, zut' cries, he suggests, are the most notable illustration of that impotence of expression. In addition, he quotes other instances of this, among them his reaction to a sentence of Bergotte's: 'Tout ce que j'eusse vu de mon impression c'est ceci qui ne lui convient pas spécialement: "C'est admirable"' (III, 890). The lameness of these words throws down a challenge to the mature Narrator.

Forewarned of this problem of language, he is also forearmed. He realises that his goal is to find a suitable expressive medium for experience:

Je m'apercevais que ce livre essentiel, le seul livre vrai, un grand écrivain n'a pas, dans le sens courant, à l'inventer, puisqu'il existe déjà en chacun de nous, mais à le traduire. Le devoir et la tâche d'un écrivain sont ceux d'un traducteur. (III, 890.)

In the Narrator's own case, the 'moments bienheureux' are to be prominent in his work of art. He stresses that in spite of their apparent insignificance, they embody a real truth (III, 880). Hence his scorn for any literary activity that diverts attention away from this vital, intimate self-discovery. For him, the value of the moments of involuntary memory is that they are 'plus précieux pour mon renouvellement spirituel que tant de conversations humanitaires, patriotiques, internationalistes et métaphysiques' (III, 882). In addition to this, he regrets that irrelevant writing of this kind should be very much the order of the day at the time of the war.

There are some interesting comparisons here with Proust's own position around about the same time. In a letter to Jacques Rivière of September 1919, he points out to his publisher that in his novel, intelligence plays a secondary role: 'Je pose avant elle [i.e., l'intelligence] l'inconscient qu'elle est destinée à clarifier – mais qui fait la réalité, l'originalité d'une oeuvre.'[6] At the same time, he refers to Rivière's article on 'Le Parti de l'Intelligence', which had appeared in the *Nouvelle Revue Française*, and states how misguided he believes this group to be, in particular Daniel Halévy. An extract from their manifesto contrasts sharply with the point being made by Proust's Narrator about what he sees as an alien kind of intellectualising. The manifesto reads:

Si nous sentons la nécessité d'une pensée philosophique, morale, politique, qui organise nos expériences, si nous prétendons opposer au désordre libéral et anarchique, au soulèvement de l'instinct, une méthode intellectuelle qui hiérarchise et qui classe, si en un mot nous savons *ce que nous voulons et ce que nous ne voulons pas* [...].[7]

The suppression of inner reality that this implies differs radically from the almost infinite self-exploration being advocated by the hero of the *Recherche*.

But of course it was precisely this kind of restriction that the 'Parti de l'Intelligence' so energetically promoted. From the outset, the policies that it pursued were more politically than intellectually inspired, and tended to be ultra-Catholic and strongly right-wing. In fact, in another article on the group, which he entitles 'Catholicisme et Nationalisme', Rivière states categorically that it was nothing other than a front for the 'Action Française' (*NRF*, 13 (1919), 965–8). Prominent in their ranks were Henri Ghéon and Charles Maurras, who gained publicity for their ideas in contributions to the *NRF* in the years immediately after the war. Jean Schlumberger was a close sympathiser and, in a public letter addressed to Rivière, he declared that had he been a Catholic, he too would have been a signatory to the manifesto (*NRF*, 13 (1919), 788–91).

Generally, the group pursued a crudely anti-intellectual line – contrary to what its pretentious name suggested! As such, it was extremely critical of individual expression in art, and went on to attribute national decay to what its members dubbed the hair-splitting of intellectuals. To quote from Schlumberger's own analysis of the situation: 'Il s'agit de ramener un peu d'ordre, de discipline, de discrétion, dans la république bruyante et brouillonne des lettres' (*NRF*, 13 (1919), 790).

It is clear from Proust's letter to Rivière (see above, note 6) how much he disapproved of the group's utterances. By the same token, it would seem reasonable to assume that the group itself was unimpressed by Proust's own work. Even as early as 1914, Ghéon had given *Du côté de chez Swann* a cool (if also muddled) reception in the *NRF*.[8] Strangely enough, a general observation made by Ghéon has an immediate and striking relevance to the comments I have been making on the *Recherche*. Ghéon warns: 'La pensée n'a pas de pire ennemi qu'elle-même. L'habitude de l'analyse et de la discrimination la rend dangereusement accessible au scrupule et c'est parfois à ses dépens.'[9] In many ways the course of Proust's novel offers an ideal illustration of this. But whereas Ghéon's aim is of course to restrict thought, Proust's position is radically different. His Narrator's soul-searching and introspection form the very core of the *Recherche*; however problematical such an existence is, Proust is set on presenting it in all its depth and complexity. In the final analysis, the 'Parti de l'Intelligence' is too closed both intellectually and imaginatively ever to attract Proust.

It is for largely similar reasons that the Narrator castigates abstraction for its own sake. His argument is that to choose to ignore intimate feelings is merely self-deception. Real artistic achievement, he insists, comes with plumbing the depths of the most fleeting and intangible experiences. He therefore decries 'cette fuite loin de notre propre vie que nous n'avons pas le courage de regarder, et qui s'appelle l'érudition' (III, 891). The unhesitating tone of the mature Narrator's observation reflects a newfound assurance and conviction. Yet earlier, in adolescence, he anguishes over the import of certain sense-impressions. This is because he is handicapped at that stage by his insistence on 'un sujet où je pusse faire tenir une signification philosophique infinie' (I, 172–3). For in nurturing this ideal, he allows the daunting character of his goal to convince him that any sentient joy is a spurious one. In *Le Temps retrouvé*, however, the reverential fear of quasi-philosophical truths gives way to a joyful awareness of the spiritual potential in the 'moments bienheureux' themselves. We might now examine how it is that he conveys the nature of that happiness.

(d) The role of intelligence in the writing of the novel

We have already seen how Roger Shattuck is unwilling to accept the moments of involuntary memory as the high point of Proust's novel. He comments on their excessive passivity, and sees them as encouraging the 'substitution of pleasure for effort'.[10] His criticism is stimulating and valid. But this is not to say that the Narrator is incapable of applying himself mentally. He is aware of the constant gap separating the original lived impression and a viable expression: 'L'impression est pour l'écrivain ce qu'est l'expérimentation pour le savant, avec cette différence que chez le savant le travail de l'intelligence précède et chez l'écrivain vient après' (III, 880). The question now to be asked is how intelligence may serve the Narrator, and whether or not it can be harmonised with the greater spontaneity of inner feeling and sensation. This is not a problem that critics have superimposed on Proust's work, for he himself was visibly concerned with it. The evidence of some preparatory sketches in *Cahier 57* would suggest that he has gone to considerable lengths to define the role of intelligence in art.

If some of our earlier references to this theme have shown the Narrator to be averse from intellectualising, then *Cahier 57* does much to counter this. For that reason, his probing on sensitivity and intelligence is worth recording.[11] It becomes immediately clear that intelligence in itself can yield nothing in the way of artistic creation:

L'intelligence seule ne peut rien trouver car tous les chemins qui ne mènent à rien sont aussi bien ouverts pour elle que le seul qui mène au vrai. Elle n'est pas plus capable de découvrir ce dernier, qu'un homme qui cherchera toutes les combinaisons d'accords possibles ne fera tel morceau de Beethoven. Aussi pour quelqu'un qui sent en lui les réalités profondes, qui ne les perd jamais de vue, l'homme intelligent qui ne les verra jamais et qui court dans tous les sentiers avec vitesse en voyant le vrai partout où il n'est pas, vous donnera la sensation d'une agilité inutile et dangereuse. (*Cahier 57*, fo 30v.)

The striking referennce to Beethoven gives some indication of the impossibility of an art based solely on the intelligence. Nevertheless, if the pre-condition of a fine sensitivity has been satisfied, the Narrator concedes that thee intelligence may then come into play. In fact, its contribution may be vital:

L'élan profond qui est comme le battement, l'acte même de la vie, n'est pas intellectuel, il faut qu'en nous la sensibilité l'imite, nous le joue, le répète, se fasse élan et vie. Mais l'intelligence peut servir. Elle sait que cet élan si particulier qu'il soit est comparable à d'autres, a quelque chose de général, peut être défini. Cela la sensibilité ne pourrait le faire car si l'intelligence n'est pas capable de la vie, la sensibilité ne connaît pas du général. (*Cahier 57*, fo 32v.)

This idea of a levelling-out of artistic sensibility and intelligence does, I suggest, reflect the more general equilibrium that is a notable feature of the end of the *Recherche*. With the balancing of 'la vie' and 'le général', the Narrator can stress the spontaneous impact of a privileged moment, while simultaneously reflecting on it. And once on the path of generalising, he finds a whole series of convenient stepping-stones for his thought. Involuntary memory links two identical but separate moments in time, and the resulting sense of joyous coincidence is enough to project the experience into the realm of extratemporality. The ability of the 'moments bienheureux' to span time is then given a more general applicability. From there the Narrator moves on to consider less instantaneous experiences that also become detached from the temporal niche in which they have been lodged. When they are thus gathered up again, they provide an exhilarating over-view of life itself. This is what the Narrator senses on meeting the young Mlle de Saint-Loup. For him, she is a living image of the marvellous synthesis that his total life now becomes. Indeed, it is almost with a sense of intoxication that he reflects on the multiplicity of experience involved:

Sans doute tous ces plans différents suivant lesquels le Temps, depuis que je venais de le ressaisir dans cette fête, disposait ma vie, en me faisant songer que, dans un livre qui voudrait en raconter une, il faudrait user, par opposition à la psychologie plane dont on use d'ordinaire, d'une sorte de psychologie dans l'espace, ajoutaient une beauté nouvelle à ces résurrections que ma mémoire opérait tant que je songeais seul dans la bibliothèque. (III, 1031.)

Before ending this section, we might consider another way in which the Narrator sees intelligence as contributing to his art. Looking back on his different experiences of love, he reflects on the important role that those liaisons would play in the projected novel. It is obvious that the Narrator's immediate response to love is often one of anxiety and perplexity; one has only to look at the Albertine crisis to see this. Nevertheless, as he now reassesses that experience with some detachment, he succeeds in escaping its more damaging impact. It is informative that it is his ability to generalise about suffering that effectively distances him from it. In this way, intelligence rises, perhaps unexpectedly, in the Narrator's estimation:

Certes, nous sommes obligé de revivre notre souffrance particulière avec le courage du médecin qui recommence sur lui-même la dangereuse piqûre. Mais en même temps il nous faut la penser sous une forme générale qui nous fait dans une certaine mesure échapper à son étreinte, qui fait de tous les copartageants de notre peine, et qui n'est même pas exempte d'une certaine joie. Là où la vie emmure, l'intelligence perce une issue, car s'il n'est pas de remède à un amour non partagé, on sort de la constatation d'une souffrance, ne fût-ce qu'en tirant les conséquences qu'elle comporte. L'intelligence ne connaît pas ces situations fermées de la vie sans issue. (III, 905.)

In the light of the present study, this assertion has important consequences. The younger Narrator knows what can only be described as a dread of intellectual truths. These seem totally inaccessible to him, with the result that he often immerses himself in an opposite, non-reflective living. But when, in Le Temps retrouvé, he overcomes his fear of the general and the conceptual, he actually finds that the workings of the intelligence may serve as a delightful palliative to the bitterness of lived experience itself. This reversal is interesting, for the Narrator may now look candidly at his former relationship without sensing emotional involvement. The evidence of Chapter 5 is that in *La Prisonnière*, he is incapable of any such detachment. Rather, he must content himself with prettifying his affair with Albertine, even to the point of limiting his own as well as Albertine's reflection on their love: 'Il vaut mieux ne pas savoir, penser le moins possible, ne pas fournir à la jalousie le moindre détail concret' (III, 24–5; see above p. 151). One can see, in this desire to euphemise, the Narrator's fear of acknowledging a mutual incompatibility.

With the growth of a temporal and emotional distance from the liaison, he finds a great release from the intensity of that experience:

Les idées sont des succédanés des chagrins; au moment où ceux-ci se changent en idées, ils perdent une partie de leur action nocive sur notre coeur, et même, au premier instant, la transformation elle-même dégage subitement de la joie. (III, 906.)

In aiming to combat this 'action nocive', the Narrator is echoing his adolescent concern to insulate the affective self against harsh, unpalatable reality. Yet if the emotional imperative remains largely unchanged, the means of achievement now seem markedly different. As a youth, he saw the frivolous company of the 'jeunes filles' as distracting him from intellectual doubt. Or again, with Albertine, the delight of watching her sleep was that it allayed his fear of her as a conscious being as well as stimulating an abundance of furtive sensual and emotional pleasures. In *Le Temps retrouvé*, we see the formulation of a new axiom: 'Là où la vie emmure, l'intelligence perce une issue' (III, 905).

(e) Final echoes of the 'jeunes filles' for the Artist–Narrator

With intelligence assuming a positive role, the Narrator is clearly redressing the balance between intuitive feeling and one's capacity to reason. Far from his earlier leanings towards a life of non-reflection, we now find the mature Narrator reacting differently to awareness. But the more balanced view that he comes to adopt is something that Proust has intimated earlier:

La pensée et la vie nous sont comme administrées par Dieu, comme antidotes l'une de l'autre. Les plaisirs de la pensée nous adoucissent les chagrins de la vie, et les plaisirs de la vie corrigent ce qu'il y a de trop vide dans les chagrins de la pensée.[12]

Nevertheless, one should guard against accepting totally the neat schematisation offered by this aphorism. In *Le Temps retrouvé*, as indeed in other parts of the *Recherche*, it is not a matter of 'la vie' or 'la pensée' being dominant to the point of excluding the other. Rather, we have a complex fusion of reflective forces and spontaneous, vital ones. And in fact it is on their interplay that the Narrator will base much of his own planned work of art. But on his admission, the chief prerequisite for that work is that it should be based on intimate human experience. So he sees any excessively intellectual emphasis as moving into some secondary, less vital area of consciousness. For this reason, he insists on a spontaneity of feeling as holding the key to artistic self-realisation. A passing comment illustrates how fundamental this is to his thought: 'Je ressentis devant tous les gens qui ne sont qu'intelligents une extrême fatigue' (*Cahier* 57, fo 30v; see above, note 4). What he wishes to avoid, then, is an over-reliance on narrowly abstract criteria. Hence his impatience with people who are intelligent and yet arguably lacking in impulse and feeling. But how does he define these latter qualities?

The preference that the Narrator is voicing recalls his earlier liking for the 'jeunes filles' in *A l'ombre*. It was evident there that he saw himself as the archetypal intellectual in the presence of radically different beings. They appear oblivious to the reality of mental activity. And it is this novel quality of awareness that excites his eager curiosity. Bearing these details in mind, it is perhaps not coincidental that the motif of the 'jeunes filles en fleurs' should recur in the final volume of the novel. On this occasion, they enjoy the privilege of being intimately linked to the Narrator's artistic creation, not unlike Françoise, who re-emerges with fresh prominence. Admittedly, he insists on solitude as being indispensable to the writing of his novel:

Mais enfin, quand des intervalles de repos et de société me seraient nécessaires, je sentais que, plutôt que les conversations intellectuelles que les gens du monde croient utiles aux écrivains, de légères amours avec des jeunes filles en fleurs seraient un aliment choisi que je pourrais à la rigueur permettre à mon imagination semblable au cheval fameux qu'on ne nourrissait que de roses. (III, 987.)[13]

The Narrator allows himself a moment of reverie in which he recalls the girls of Balbec as they had first appeared to him. Very clearly, their charm lay in their totally sentient mode of being. And if the Narrator's novel aims at presenting his own spontaneous living, one can argue that he finds something of this reflected in the girls of Balbec. This is not to say that they experience the heightened aesthetic awareness that he associates with the 'moments bienheureux'. These girls are frankly incapable of the intellectual effort still required of the artist. Nevertheless, they stand for the kind of instantaneous, automatic feeling that is so dear to him. To that extent, they have a contribution to make to the Narrator. His reference to this contact as an 'aliment choisi' is an obvious indication of its value. However unlike the Narrator they may be, they offer a precious viaticum to the pilgrim writer.

We have seen in *Jean Santeuil* how a vague bond unites the artist-figure with some ordinary, uncomplicated people. The lighthouse keepers of the preface, for example, were closely associated with C.'s literary pursuits. Although ignorant of the intricacy of his art, they enjoy a quality of living that in some obscure way inspires him. What is more, he deems it a happier and more beneficial experience to be with them than with the leading figures of Paris. The mature Narrator of *Le Temps retrouvé* is making a comparable judgement, albeit in a more pointed way, when he complains that his work is to be assessed by established literary critics:

Un écrivain devrait presque préférer être jugé par le grand public (si celui-ci n'était incapable de se rendre compte même de ce qu'un artiste a tenté dans un ordre de recherches qui lui est inconnu). Car il y a plus d'analogie entre la vie instinctive du public et le talent d'un grand écrivain, qui n'est qu'un instinct religieusement écouté au milieu du silence imposé à tout le reste, un instinct perfectionné et compris, qu'avec le verbiage superficiel et les critères changeants des juges attitrés. (III, 893.)

The ambivalence of the Narrator's stance is immediately evident. Granted, he is shunning the interpretation of literary pundits and leaning more towards the anonymous 'grand public'. Still, he has to concede that the latter is not in a position to appreciate the genesis and subtlety of creative writing. But even then a link persists, however tenuously, between the instinctive living of ordinary folk and the artist's own inner experience.

Essentially, his work is 'un instinct perfectionné et compris'. This implies both the intimacy of instinctual feeling and a strong measure of self-awareness and perceptiveness. Ironically, then, he comes very near to the 'jeunes filles en fleurs' and yet moves inexorably away: the force of 'instinct' brings them together, the need for it to be 'perfectionné et compris' drives them apart. Clearly the Narrator must make the break with purely sentient living. For, while instinctualism is bound up with his artistic projections, it is not enough simply to relate this in a passive, supine way. This is as true of the adventure with the Balbec girls as it is of the chance impressions that spark off the 'moments bienheureux'. But while the Narrator believes that everyone is capable of such experience, he also emphasises that if he is to be a writer, or as he prefers to say, a 'translator', then he cannot content himself with the limited awareness of others. The move towards a fuller understanding of the self will clearly stretch the Narrator's powers of comprehension to the limit. In doing this, he makes the greatest intellectual effort to relay what is largely unintellectual being.

With the young girls, then, he shares but also transcends their sentience. In that sense, he is not a prisoner of non-reflection itself. The effects of this dual role are varied. At Balbec, one has the impression that he longs to feel at one with the barbaric young women. In the case of a young milkmaid, he even wishes that he could only lose sight of their unlikeness. Nevertheless, he recognises that to be conscious of the essential difference between himself and others may actually stimulate the creative mind. In fact, a constant feature of the present study has been the Narrator's willingness to lay himself open to new experience.

In view of the Narrator's fascination in *A l'ombre des jeunes filles en fleurs*, it is interesting that the final peripeteia of the *Recherche* should be his meeting with the young Mlle de Saint-Loup. While not revealing any of the specifically unintellectual characteristics of the Balbec girls, she does reactivate the Narrator's sensitivity to the freshness of youth. For him, she is the almost miraculous incarnation of the two great influences in the Narrator's life, the 'côté de Guermantes' and the 'côté de chez Swann' (III, 1029). Curiously enough, his belief in the supremacy of a direct, non-rational perception of reality is illustrated here in a quite dramatic manner. He dwells on the graphic way in which he is made aware of the two formerly divergent roads – now a marvellously tangible reality:

Je fus étonné de voir à côté de [Gilberte] une jeune fille d'environ seize ans, dont la taille élevée mesurait cette distance que je n'avais pas voulu voir. Le temps incolore et insaisissable s'était, pour que pour ainsi dire je puisse le voir et le toucher, matérialisé en elle, il l'avait pétrie comme un chef-d'oeuvre, tandis que parallèlement sur moi, hélas! il n'avait fait que son oeuvre. (III, 1031.)

What is for the Narrator the conceptually difficult notion of time has been made accessible by the presence of the young girl. Transmitted in this concrete, visual way, the sense of time's remorseless advance now has an immediate and overwhelming impact on him. And if his reaction is tinged with nostalgia for his own lost youth, he appears reassured by the likeness between the child and her father, Saint-Loup. But more importantly, she is the incarnation of eternal youth for the Narrator: 'Je la trouvais bien belle: pleine encore d'espérances, riante, formée des années mêmes que j'avais perdues, elle ressemblait à ma Jeunesse' (III, 1032). Mitigating his sense of lost time is the belief that those same years have been redeployed, as it were, and somehow converted into a new creation, the youth of Mlle de Saint-Loup. Naturally, the immortality that this represents for the Narrator is an attenuated one. Yet the organic link-up between the young girl and himself makes his recall of youth all the more intense and gratifying. Significantly too, the encounter has important repercussions on the proposed work of art. If the little band of Balbec starts the Narrator off on the long road to self-discovery, it is fitting and not altogether fortuitous that the mature Narrator should see his plans to write crystallising around the young daughter of Gilberte and Saint-Loup.

For the Narrator, hearing the Vinteuil septet is one of his most intense aesthetic experiences. As a young man, he knew a feverish exhilaration with certain girls at Balbec. Or again alcohol produced in him a state of wild euphoria. But however all-engaging love or bodily intoxication might prove, their instantaneity is no guarantee of their permanence. In contrast, the beauty of music for the mature Narrator is that it is unconditional, beyond the contingent. It will not be ephemeral as was the relationship with the 'jeunes filles'. Yet that earlier playground of Balbec and the adventure world of music draw curiously close to one another. For when the Narrator refers to a musical phrase as 'la seule Inconnue qu'il m'ait jamais été donné de rencontrer' (III, 260), he is commenting not merely on what he has found in Vinteuil, but also on what he sought in earlier meetings with the unknown women of the seaside town. But at Balbec, the enigma surrounding these girls dissolved as the Narrator approached. More excitingly, Vinteuil now offers the prospect of real encounter with the 'Inconnue'; in music, the Narrator can touch the web of mystery and still preserve it.

Admittedly he makes errors of judgement, overestimating certain experiences and playing down others. But what these instances of misplaced enthusiasm and lack of foresight point to is something essential to the whole idea of the *Recherche*. The Narrator's development will not be linear and unhindered, precisely because he is unsure of what his goal actually is. His progress is made difficult by what Shattuck aptly terms 'false scents'.[14] We have seen much of that disorientation in this study. There was, for example, Jean Santeuil's belief that were one to penetrate the world of animal living, one might end the problem of reflective crisis. In the *Recherche* itself, there is the idolatry of things conceptual, which plagues the young Narrator and leads him far from the path of self-realisation. Similarly, his faith in the 'jeunes filles' seems misguided in retrospect, and one sees the naivety and recklessness of his assertion that they might 'cure' him emotionally and spiritually.

The pattern of successive aberrations is ended, however, with the work of Vinteuil. The Narrator senses that in this more than in anything else, one achieves the vital 'retour à l'inanalysé'. As for Proust, the vision of this final goal does not prevent him from faithfully recording the Narrator's voyage of self-discovery. To reiterate his words to Rivière, 'Cette évolution d'une pensée, je n'ai pas voulu l'analyser abstraitement, mais la recréer, la faire vivre.'[15]

A further development in the Narrator's thought comes with his reappraisal of intelligence in *Le Temps retrouvé*. There he is less impatient with reason's inability to feel the pulse of lived experience. This comes with an awareness of the role to be played by intelligence in the writing of the novel. Earlier he cited Elstir and Vinteuil as being intellectually gifted men whose art was essentially irrational. For the Narrator, there is no incompatibility in this; but that is always conditional on the intellect playing a secondary part. What is true of painting and music will also hold for the Narrator's proposed novel. At the heart of each of these art-forms lies the 'instinct religieusement écouté'. In this way, the supremacy of inner feeling, of deep intuition and of primary perception is never challenged. The Narrator takes this as a fundamental aesthetic principle, in the hope that his work will assume something of the ideal of music, that totally pliant medium which can register 'l'inflexion de l'être' (III, 374).

As for the reappearance of the girls of Balbec and Françoise near the end of the novel, it is in a sense the Narrator's way of paying tribute to them. Given their ignorance of art, one might ask what their contribution really is. The answer is that they release the Narrator from a rarefied intellectual atmosphere, thereby enriching his experience. Freed from isolatory introspection, he becomes curious about life-styles foreign to his own. He sees that a primitive feel of consciousness is the lot of many: Françoise and to a lesser extent the 'jeunes filles' are among the principal exponents of this. The Narrator's imagination is stimulated as a result. Indirectly, this same contact with others also enhances his awareness of self, convincing him of the importance of his own primordial feeling in the planned novel.

Conclusion

Writing about the strange lands that feature so prominently in his poetic world, Henri Michaux explains: 'Mes pays imaginaires: pour moi des sortes d'Etats-tampons, afin de ne pas souffrir de la réalité'.[1] It is a curious but revealing confession. At the same time, he speaks of other bulwarks such as the 'Mages' who feature in his voyage to the 'Pays de la Magie'. These he describes as 'des personnages-tampons suscités par le voyage'. With them, the poet sees himself as being cushioned from the harshness of reality. Yet almost inevitably, this presupposes his own vulnerability and uncertainty.

The situation is not unlike that of Proust's Narrator. He too is insecure, unable to overcome a sense of intellectual and artistic inadequacy. And while long convinced that his self-fulfilment lies in art, his progress in that direction is constantly obstructed, largely because of the exaggerated respect that he has for what is conceptual. Like Michaux, he has ways of fighting off tortured thinking, of making his position more tolerable. Not that his 'personnages-tampons' are surreal like the 'Mages', nor his imaginative worlds as exotic as those created by Michaux. Nevertheless, the notion of buffer states and characters seems especially applicable to the novelist's work. Buffers, of course, are sometimes symptomatic of a precarious peace, their existence presupposing a fear of what lies beyond their frontiers. It is a similar kind of delicate balance sought after by Proust's main characters, Jean Santeuil and the Narrator of the *Recherche*. But for them the war is with themselves and their inner sensibility.

In Chapter 1, we saw the different ways in which Jean Santeuil's hypersensitivity was relieved. The company of the level-headed Henri de Réveillon and that of uncomplicated minds such as the fisherman or the faithful maid allow him to postpone the inevitable encounter with his own self. Among his other defences is the possibility of absorption into an all-embracing Nature in which individual reflective doubt is put to rest. Yet the most forthright assertion of the desire to be freed from self-analysis is the nostalgic depiction of animal life. This is executed with a naivety of vision that can only be explained by Proust's immaturity as a writer. Still, it awakens the reader's mind to the possibility of a more subtly disguised escape from selfhood in Proust's later work. In fact, we see movement in a similar direction in the period immediately prior to the *Recherche*, although there the buffer zone is more accessible than that of the animal kingdom. In critical studies and in sketches for the novel, we find Proust toying with the delightful abdication of self that comes with entry into the world of objects and sleep. In the novel itself, the Narrator's satisfaction is enhanced by the fact that he is no more conscious than the objects in his room. This coincidence with the inanimate provokes a shadowy pleasure that barely reaches consciousness.

Yet even in the sphere of interpersonal relationships, as seen in Chapter 3, the Narrator finds an alternative to the constant inner dialogue that he finds so taxing. There is Françoise for example. Strangely enough, the Narrator feels superior to her and yet simultaneously envies her unshakeable faith, faith in the sureness of what she says, of what she thinks and of what she is. Thus outweighing even the ridiculousness of her malapropisms is the young Narrator's genuine curiosity and admiration for her cast-iron self-assurance: 'Si Françoise avait la brûlante certitude des grands créateurs, mon lot était la cruelle inquiétude du chercheur' (I, 446). The mature Narrator is clearly exploiting this childhood experience, giving it the mock seriousness that colours much of the depiction of the Françoise/child-Narrator relationship. But Proust's portrayal of Françoise reveals more than the author's confident intellectual flirtation. Significant among his post-1914 additions are further developments on characters like Françoise, in which their powers of discernment are likened to those of primitive men. In their grasp of situations, they are often infinitely superior to intellectuals, the Narrator speculates. The reaction comes, predictably, from an extremely delicate mind, bound to the rock of constant self-investigation. For him, the mystery remains that while escaping the burden of analysis, their knowledge is unimpaired. Indeed it may even be heightened in this automatic, unreflecting form.

Perhaps the nearest we come to Michaux's fantastic 'personnages-tampons' in the *Recherche* is with the young girls of Balbec. Like the soldiers of Doncières, they help to right the distortion resulting from the Narrator's introspection. But as well as this, the 'jeunes filles' are semi-mythological creatures who fire the

Narrator's imagination with the prospect of 'l'inconscience', 'l'inin-tellectualité' and 'la joie' (I, 830). For him it is the dream of escape from self come true. It promises the end of mental torment and the advent of a new, rejuvenating awareness. But this initial fascination and hope of self-realisation give way to a weariness and frustration, with the Narrator's close involvement with Albertine. Chapter 5 is an attempt to show how their liaison is fraught with difficulties, almost all of which arise from the Narrator's emotional and mental intensity – the hypersensitivity of old returned to haunt him, this time under the guise of the lover's suspicion. To allay this doubting, he practises a partial atrophy of the mind, limiting his consciousness of Albertine to that of her as an endearingly subservient partner. This is sustained by tranquil images of her asleep and so unable to think and to imagine. For the Narrator, then, mind is the enemy in the relationship with Albertine; peace lies in the suppression of her consciousness, of her affectivity.

There are other interesting adjuncts to the Narrator's intellectual and emotional self-protection. Among these are the Brueghel-like merry-making that the Narrator associates with Doncières, the graceful, soothing contours of Grecian beauty that he sees in the 'jeunes filles en fleurs', and the gentle, anaesthetising effect of bed-time reading in his childhood – each of these helps make reality all the more palatable for the Narrator. We also see the grand-mother's conscious campaign to restore him to a soundness of mind and body. As part of this, she advocates a reading of writers such as Mme de Sévigné and Joubert, and condemns contemporary Sym-bolist poets in the strongest possible way. Ironically, the Narrator ends up nurturing a keen interest in one of the very writers condemned by her, namely Baudelaire. This development is impor-tant in many respects. For it represents a maturing of the Narrator's mind, showing his willingness to explore the complex imaginative world of the poet. Perhaps most significantly of all, it marks the inefficacy of a plan to restrict him to a cautious and unimaginative view of existence.

By meeting inner chaos head-on, the Narrator takes an important step nearer self-realisation. This will only come when he has taken the intricacy of his own being into account. He does this indirectly when laying himself open to the influence of Baudelaire. But the admission of a complex inner self becomes finally and totally livable with the journey into the world of Vinteuil, which I considered in Chapter 6. The beauty of music is that it can capture directly 'l'inflexion de l'être', the gamut of intimate feeling. For the Narrator, it is an automatic register of consciousness and thus the ideal expressive medium. Dogged by an excessive preoccupation with self-analysis, he now sees that concern swept aside by music.

With the removal of intellectual anxiety, bulwarks and defences then become superfluous. Music is not an 'état-tampon', for that would imply a much greater concern for something outside it. Rather, it exists in itself and represents a final goal in which he may know self-fulfilment. In that sense, it is totally positive, representing not the abnegation of mind with which the Narrator flirts on occasions but a total integration of the conscious self. As such, it offers a faithful reflection of individual awareness. For so long the Narrator speaks of our innermost being as 'ce résidu réel que nous sommes obligés de garder pour nous-mêmes' (III, 257) – opaqueness of expression being the Achilles' heel of the artist. He is as it were condemned to silence, since communicating this core of experience is not to be achieved by its conceptualisation. Yet against this,

L'art, l'art d'un Vinteuil comme celui d'un Elstir, le fait apparaître, extériorisant dans les couleurs du spectre la composition intime de ces mondes que nous appelons les individus, et que sans l'art nous ne connaîtrions jamais. (III, 258.)

In this way, the world of Vinteuil opens up exciting possibilities for the Narrator. And if his discovery of its beauty is as exhilarating as his initial contact with the 'jeunes filles', the two experiences differ in their nature and degree of permanence. While the youthfulness of the girls at Balbec is relatively short-lived, music represents a lasting source of self-renewal:

Le seul véritable voyage, le seul bain de Jouvence, ce ne serait pas d'aller vers de nouveaux paysages, mais d'avoir d'autres yeux, de voir l'univers avec les yeux d'un autre, de cent autres, de voir les cent univers que chacun d'eux voit, que chacun d'eux est; et cela nous le pouvons avec un Elstir, avec un Vinteuil, avec leurs pareils, nous volons vraiment d'étoiles en étoiles. (III, 258.)

Art thus becomes synonymous with Youth itself. It is not a bodily youth, such as that of the 'jeunes filles', but rather a spiritual suppleness, a vigorous inner sensitivity that enables us to experience the infinite possibility offered by art.

This rejuvenation through music now encourages the Narrator to accept and indeed to promote the complexity of his own self. To that extent, Vinteuil's work has an emboldening effect on him, allowing him to face with confidence the spiritual contradiction that had formerly perplexed him. Perhaps Ortega y Gasset's pronouncement on modern art generally has a particular relevance to the *Recherche*: 'All modern art begins to appear comprehensible and in a way great when it is interpreted as an attempt to instil youthfulness into an ancient world' (*The Dehumanisation of Art*, p. 47). In the case of Proust's Narrator, the old order was one in which he practised the cult of a sterile intellectualising. Replacing this is a regeneration in art that offers a wide and varied self-expression. Gone is his conceptual schematisation of life; in its place there comes a more authentic awareness, through art, of individual human consciousness.

In the introduction, I referred to some of Proust's comments on the power of the novelist (*CSB*, pp. 413–14). What pervades those observations of the *Jean Santeuil* years is a great belief in the writer. He is, the young Proust enthuses, capable of transforming the reader, making him sensitive to the condition of a Napoleon, a Savonarola, a weaver or a lover. The list seems endless. Yet perhaps his most perceptive remark is that through the novelist, 'nous sommes nous-même'. The reference is as brief as that. But if it is not expanded here, we see just how great its implications are for Proust's later novel. Hence the imperative of self-knowledge that dominates the *Recherche*. Interestingly enough, this awareness of self is deepened by contact with others, even the most superficial and impoverished of minds. The character-studies in Chapters 3 and 4 are aimed at showing how true this is for the Narrator. Still, the process only reaches its apotheosis in the findings of *Le Temps retrouvé*. There the Narrator asserts that the ever-changing quality of human perceptions may be faithfully conveyed in painting and music. It may be a feigned modesty or genuine self-effacement that prevents Proust from adding that in his own novel he might emulate Vinteuil or Elstir. But that is not the important point. What does matter is that the *Recherche* itself achieves in the field of individual consciousness what the Narrator so extolled in other artists – the success of being able to 'voir l'univers avec les yeux d'un autre, de cent autres, de voir les cent univers que chacun d'eux voit, que chacun d'eux est' (III, 258). And it is on this note of high optimism that the spiritual search of the *Recherche* ends. For Proust, art, although always seeking to capture the non-conceptual quality of life, rises above any belligerent anti-intellectualising. In this way, the multiplicity of moods, the interplay of emotional and intellectual states is no longer problematical, but rather becomes liberating and ennobling.

Notes

Introduction

1 This appears in *Adam*, 349–51 (1971), 10–20. I have given just a few random examples here. Others can be easily found in a perusal of general bibliographies of Proust criticism.

2 This reference is to the Pléiade edition of the so-called *Contre Sainte-Beuve* (see Abbreviations). Only part of this volume (pp. 209–312) actually deals with Proust's views on Sainte-Beuve, the rest being a collection of notes, essays and articles scattered over Proust's entire career. What we have here is one such note which the editors attribute to the *Jean Santeuil* years and which they entitled 'Le Pouvoir du romancier' (*CSB*, p. 897, note 1 to p. 413).

3 *Cahier 25* dates from *c.* 1910–11. I shall be referring to the value of Proust's *Cahiers*, with their preliminary sketches for *A la recherche* and *Contre Sainte-Beuve*, later in the introduction.

4 Walter A. Strauss, *Proust and Literature* (Cambridge, Mass.: Harvard U.P., 1957), p. 175.

5 This has been published as *Le Carnet de 1908* (Paris: Gallimard, 1976), ed. Philip Kolb.

6 Kolb refers us to the Conard edition of Flaubert's *Oeuvres complètes* (Paris, 1910); vol. 5 of his *Correspondance* contains exclusively the letters to Caroline (576 pages).

7 Philip Kolb has published the text of the notes on Senancour in *Textes retrouvés*, Cahiers Marcel Proust, n.s. 3 (Paris: Gallimard, 1971), pp. 82–6. He speaks of the importance of the pre-Romantic's work as a possible influence on Proust (*Textes retrouvés*, pp. 14–15), mentioning the pioneering work of Giorgetto Giorgi, 'Senancour e Proust', *Studi Francesi*, 9 (May–August 1965), 290–6.

8 Etienne de Senancour, *Rêveries sur la nature primitive de l'homme* (2 vols., Paris: Cornély, 1910), vol. 1, p. 75.

9 Susan Sontag, 'The Pornographic Imagination', in *Styles of Radical Will* (London: Secker and Warburg, 1969), p. 72; Sontag's italics.

10 Where I, II and III are used in this study, they refer exclusively to *A la recherche du temps perdu* (see Abbreviations).

11 J. Ortega y Gasset, *The Dehumanisation of Art*, trans. Willard R. Trask *et al.* (New York: Doubleday, 1956), p. 20.

12 This appears among a series of scattered jottings that Philip Kolb has gathered together in the *Textes retrouvés*, Cahiers Marcel Proust, n.s. 3,

pp. 362–3. The date of composition is uncertain, although the endearingly simple reference to God might suggest it was early, probably before the *Recherche*.

13 'Les Egoïsmes de l'amour chez Proust', *RHLF*, 71 (1971), 887–908.

14 A good example of this is Michael Finn's article '*Jean Santeuil* and *A la recherche du temps perdu*: Instinct and Intellect', *Forum for Modern Language Studies*, 11 (1975), 122–32.

15 This is the eye-catching note on which Proust opens his study of Sainte-Beuve (*CSB*, p. 211).

16 Henri Bonnet, '*Le Temps retrouvé* dans les Cahiers', *Etudes proustiennes*, 1, Cahiers Marcel Proust, n.s. 6 (Paris: Gallimard, 1973), pp. 111–62 (p. 144).

17 Maurice Bardèche, *Marcel Proust romancier* (2 vols., Paris: Les Sept Couleurs, 1971), vol. 1, pp. 11–12.

18 *Correspondance Marcel Proust – Jacques Rivière 1914–1922*, 2nd enlarged ed. (Paris: Gallimard, 1976), p. 28.

1 Proust's Early Work

1 See notes on the preface of *Jean Santeuil* (*JS*, p. 987).

2 The study is given the title '[Chardin et Rembrandt]' by the *CSB* editors; see *CSB*, pp. 372–82 and the introductory note on *CSB*, p. 885. In the light of Proust's letter to Pierre Mainguet on the subject, in November 1895 (see *Corr.* vol. 1, p. 466), it can be dated 1895, and is therefore contemporaneous with *Jean Santeuil* (1895–9).

3 *JS*, p. 988: note 1 to p. 191. Proust intended part of the preface as we now have it for the section on Jean's stay at Beg-Meil. The extract that I am discussing here actually features in the Beg-Meil section.

4 This title, like several others in *Jean Santeuil*, is Clarac's. Titles of sections that are not Proust's are written in square brackets.

5 This is part of a more general contentment in *Jean Santeuil* with what John M. Cocking refers to as 'sensation in the raw state' (*Proust* (London: Bowes and Bowes, 1956), p. 16).

6 'La Chevelure', for example, reveals a similar tone of longing with its reference to 'La langoureuse Asie et la brûlante Afrique, / Tout un monde lointain, absent, presque défunt' (*Oeuvres complètes* (Paris: NRF (Pléiade), 1961), p. 25). In the *Recherche*, the Narrator makes direct reference to Baudelaire in a description of a visit to the sea: 'Je m'efforçais de regarder plus loin, de ne voir que la mer, d'y chercher des effets décrits par Baudelaire' (1, 694).

7 Jean-Pierre Richard, *Proust et le monde sensible* (Paris: Editions du Seuil, 1974).

8 R.C. Zaehner, *Mysticism, Sacred and Profane* (London: Oxford U.P., 1961), pp. 50–83.

9 *Ibid.* p. 40. The author stresses this reciprocal movement to underline the excessive reductionism of the psychoanalytical school in its treatment of this experience. For Zaehner, Jung is a primary example of this. 'According to this school of psychology [...] the commonest symbols of mysticism – the sea, the air, trees, water – are nothing more than symbols

of the eternal feminine both in mythology and psychology' (*ibid.*). Zaehner rightly notes that it is oversimplifying to see nature mysticism as a 'back to the womb' theory.

10 The image reappears in *Le Carnet de 1908*: 'Dans les moments où on a besoin de se verser dans l'âme du potage chaud, visite Parent – Montargis qu'on ne savait pas à Paris comme gaie lampe' (p. 99). Montargis, later to become Saint-Loup in the *Recherche*, radiates an affection like Henri's. I shall be returning to the reference from the *Carnet* in the next chapter.

11 The reference to 'une église italienne qui n'est ni mesquine ni excessive' (*JS*, p. 411) offers a useful pointer to Jean's liking in architecture. We shall be seeing in the *Recherche* a rather similar 'happy medium' in aesthetic taste, with preference being voiced by the Narrator's grandmother for the 'pondération' of such writers as Mme de Sévigné and Joubert (Chapter 3). Even the Narrator himself expresses an interest in certain schools of painting and sculpture that offer a very balanced, tranquil view of existence (see Chapter 4). Nevertheless, he often leans towards an involved, problematical art based on more extreme human situations.

12 Arthur Schopenhauer, *Parerga and Paralipomena* (2 vols., Oxford: Clarendon Press, 1974), vol. 1, p. 415.

13 *Textes retrouvés*, Cahiers Marcel Proust, n.s. 3, p. 328. I shall be considering other implications of this informative insight in Chapter 3.

14 For a thorough examination of the Buddhist influence in Proust, see Barbara Bucknall, *The Religion of Art in Proust* (Urbana: University of Illinois Press, 1969), pp. 193–200, and cross-references to Zaehner, *Mysticism*; cf. also Milton Hindus, *The Proustian Vision* (London and Amsterdam: Southern Illinois U.P., 1967), p. 100, where reference is made to Proust's goal of Nirvana. An interesting account of Proust's schooling is contained in Henri Bonnet, *Alphonse Darlu: le maître de philosophie de Marcel Proust* (Paris: Nizet, 1961).

15 Kolb sees the prisoner idea in the *Carnet de 1908*, where Proust notes: 'Dans la seconde partie jeune fille ruinée, entretenue sans jouir d'elle [...] par impuissance d'être aimé' (p. 50).

16 In the preface that he wrote in 1920 to Paul Morand's *Tendres Stocks*, Proust explains how many images just fail to hit the mark, as it were: 'Or, tous les à-peu-près d'images ne comptent pas. L'eau (dans des conditions données) bout à 100 degrés. A 98, a 99, le phénomène ne se produit pas' (*CSB*, p. 616). There are several such 'close seconds' in *Jean Santeuil*.

17 For a sound study of the genesis and format of *Jean Santeuil*, see Philip Kolb, 'Historique du premier roman de Proust', *Saggi e ricerche di letteratura francese*, 4 (1963), 215–77.

18 André Gide, 'En relisant *Les Plaisirs et les jours*', *NRF*, 20 (1923), 123–6. Gide notes with some regret 'un ordre de préoccupations que Proust, hélas, abandonnera complètement par la suite et qu'indique suffisamment cette phrase de *L'Imitation de Jésus-Christ* qu'il y épingle en épigraphe: "Les désirs des sens nous entraînent çà et là, mais l'heure passée, que rapportez-vous? des remords de conscience et de la dissipation d'esprit"' (p. 125). The critical focus that Gide adopts would seem to tally with some of his own early works, e.g., *Les Cahiers d'André Walter*,

La Porte étroite and *La Symphonie pastorale*, where moral and specifically religious preoccupations are very prominent.

2 Between *Jean Santeuil* and *A la recherche*

1 In his preface to *Le Carnet de 1908*, Kolb elaborates on this idea, showing how, in his work of 1909, Proust began to see his 'Sainte-Beuve' as combining critical and artistic writing (pp. 20–5).

2 This was published in *Le Figaro littéraire* (27 March 1954), 5. The title is taken from the text of the article itself (*CSB*, p. 382).

3 The question of friendship is an involved one in Proust. In *A la recherche*, for example, there are times when the Narrator expresses a belief in friendship (e.g. II, 104). Yet more often than not, he rejects it in principle, attributing this to the inconstancy of others and the superficiality of the emotions involved. In the Chardin study, however, a deeper communion with the material world seems more feasible. For an informed essay on the friendship question, see L.A. Bisson, 'Marcel Proust: Friends and Friendship', in *Essays presented to C. M. Girdlestone* (Newcastle-upon-Tyne: King's College, 1960), pp. 29–48.

4 For an enthusiastic treatment of this aspect of the *Recherche*, see Claude Vallée's *La Féerie de Marcel Proust* (Paris: Fasquelle, 1958).

5 This is the *Cahier* with Proust's own title 'Le Peintre' (*c.* 1911).

6 These differences are noted by Clarac (*CSB*, pp. 793–6) but they have little bearing on our present considerations.

7 In some ways, critics' efforts to find a definitive date of commencement for *A la recherche* have been misdirected. Bardèche's insistence that 1908 marks the beginning of Proust's preparation, and his rejection of 'la légende de 1905', is not of primary importance (Bardèche, *Marcel Proust romancier*, vol. 1, pp. 152–6). Clearly the Ruskin preface of 1905 brings out preoccupations that are largely similar to those expressed in the 1908 drafts for the *Recherche*.

8 The *Cahiers* in question are numbers 1–7. Certain of these have particularly lengthy developments, e.g. *Cahier 1*, fos 65–71; *Cahier 3*, fos 1–33 *passim*; *Cahier 5*, fos 109–14. These are all early volumes, *c.* 1908–9.

9 *Cahier 1*, fo 64v and twice in *Cahier 5*, fo 113v.

10 D.H. Lawrence, *Women in Love* (London: Penguin, 1960), p. 361.

11 Elizabeth Brady Tenenbaum, *The Problematic Self: approaches to identity in Stendhal, D.H. Lawrence and Malraux* (Cambridge, Mass.: Harvard U.P., 1977), p. 79.

12 The date of *Cahier 50* is *c.* 1911–12.

13 Chapter 5 will deal more fully with the Albertine crisis for the Narrator. I am also leaving reference to Albertine's sleep to the same chapter. The thematic implications of this are in some ways different from the Narrator's own experience of sleep.

3 The Narrator's Childhood and Adolescence: Formative Influences

1 *Cahier 32*, fo 21v. The *premier jet* of this volume, from which the present quote is taken, dates from *c.* 1910.

2 *Cahier 44*, with early proper names such as Montargis and Monfort, can

be no later than the summer of 1913. It was then that Proust decided on the name Saint-Loup, not long before the publication of *Du côté de chez Swann*, where the name appears early on in the text. The same theorising is reproduced almost verbatim in an assessment of Mme de Villeparisis' literary abilities (II, 185–6).

3 See *CSB*, pp. 557–9. This is actually based on some of Proust's notes on *Swann* contained in a letter to Antoine Bibesco of November 1912. For a very lucid account of Proust's public relations exercises in these creative years, see Douglas W. Alden, *Marcel Proust and his French Critics* (New York: Russell and Russell, 1973), Chapter 2.

4 Cocking, *Proust*, p. 23.

5 See III, 866–80. In Chapter 6, we shall be seeing how much of the Narrator's doubting is finally dispelled in *Le Temps retrouvé*; there, the divorce between inner feeling and intellectualising gives way to a new harmony.

6 *Textes retrouvés*, Cahiers Marcel Proust, n.s. 3, p. 238. It is interesting that Proust should instance Sully Prudhomme as an example of a philosophical poet. In 1882, Ollendorff of Paris published a small volume by Constant Coquelin, the title of which suggests a view of the poet similar to Proust's, *Un Poète philosophe: Sully Prudhomme*. One might point out here one or two curious similarities between the poet's work and Proust's own ideas: see 'L'Habitude', *Oeuvres*, vol. 1, pp. 13–14; 'Pensée perdue' (*ibid.* vol. 1, pp. 33–4); 'Le Temps perdu' (*ibid.* vol. 3, p. 96). All references are to the Lemerre edition (5 vols., Paris, 1900–1). Remembering the Narrator's own dilemma about the inter-relationship of concepts and poetry, we might note how Sully Prudhomme sees ideas as forming the hard core of his poems: 'Comme autour des fleurs obsédées / Palpitent les papillons blancs / Autour de mes chères idées / Se pressent de beaux vers tremblants' ('Au Lecteur', *ibid.* vol. 1, p. 3).

7 This *Cahier* is early, probably not later than 1910. Immediate evidence of this can be found on fos 5–7, where Proust has a development headed 'A ajouter sur la sonate de Saint-Saëns'. Later, of course, this will be transformed into Vinteuil's Sonata.

8 See Alison Winton, *Proust's Additions* (2 vols., Cambridge University Press, 1977), vol. 2, p. 27. The limits of the later addition on I, 450 are: 'ce qui est du reste [...] ne s'accroît plus. N'importe.'

9 When the Narrator refers to the reaction of the parterre, his distinction seems to be more an intellectual than a social one. Evidently, theatre audiences would have been largely aristocratic and bourgeois in social composition around that period. But the Narrator's main aim is to contrast his own developed intellectual response to Berma with the more current, untechnical appraisal of most of the audience. In this way, the highest social classes may show very unrefined aesthetic taste in Proust's work. This is nowhere better exemplified than in the *arriviste* Mme Verdurin who, in her desire to give an appearance of great artistic insight, goes through all sorts of facial contortions during performances of music by Vinteuil and others. As the Narrator observes ironically: 'Ses traits ne prenaient plus la peine de formuler successivement des impressions

esthétiques trop fortes, car ils étaient eux-mêmes comme leur expression permanente dans un visage ravagé et superbe' (II, 906). In a more serious vein, the Narrator sees the aristocratic Duchesse de Guermantes as being not far removed in mind from the 'jeunes filles en fleurs' (see Chapter 4*f*). Proust would therefore seem less interested in social class than in the quality of mind of individuals.

10 See Richard Bales, *Proust and the Middle Ages* (Geneva: Droz, 1975), p. 80, where the uniformity of her presentation in the novel is also referred to. In a section on Françoise (*ibid.* pp. 80–7) the author deals with the medieval dimension to her character. As we shall see, the question of Françoise's primitivism can be taken in tandem with a study of her medievalism.

11 See Arthur Schopenhauer, 'The Metaphysics of the Love of the Sexes' in *The World as Will and Idea*, trans. R.B. Haldane and J. Kemp (3 vols., London: Trübner, 1883–6), vol. 3, p. 347. The parallel is confirmed by both Barbara Bucknall, *The Religion of Art in Proust*, p. 195, and Hindus, *The Proustian Vision*, pp. 94–5.

12 Quotations from Baudelaire are many, among them III, 379, 759 and 920. We have a further, albeit oblique, reference to the Narrator's predilection for Baudelaire and Verlaine in the ridiculous posing of Brichot, who hurls abuse at the 'éthéromanes' of the Symbolist school (II, 956). I referred to this at the start of this chapter. When, in *Le Temps retrouvé*, the Narrator is on the point of making a breakthrough in his planned work of art, he is strengthened by the knowledge that he is carrying on the tradition of his predecessor: 'J'allais chercher à me rappeler les pièces de Baudelaire à la base desquelles se trouve ainsi une sensation transposée, pour achever de me replacer dans une filiation aussi noble' (III, 920).

13 Proust replaced 'mes parents' with 'ma grand'mère', without adjusting 'des complices'. The main text of *Cahier 41*, written on the recto pages, can be dated pre-1913 (reference is made to Montargis). Our present quotation is from that base text, later additions occurring in the margins and on verso pages.

14 There is one case in the *Recherche* where the Narrator remarks: 'J'attendais un nouveau dîner où je pusse devenir moi-même une sorte de prince de X' (II, 551–2). The stories he has heard at the home of Mme de Guermantes were 'entrées un instant en moi, qui n'en étais que physiquement possédé; on aurait dit que (de nature sociale et non individuelle) elles étaient impatientes d'en sortir' (II, 551). The Narrator is evidently engrossed in the superficiality of the experience.

15 We might remember how doctors are frequently verbose, self-important, and even occasionally ridiculed in Proust: see G. Cattaui's paper: 'Proust et les sciences', *Proceedings of the Congress of the International Federation of Modern Languages and Literatures* (Oxford: Blackwell, 1956), pp. 287–92; Winton, vol. 1 pp. 83–4; Serge Béhar, *L'Univers médical de Proust*, Cahiers Marcel Proust, n.s. 1 (Paris: Gallimard, 1970) and especially the section 'Portraits de médecins', pp. 135–64.

16 The Narrator explains other points of similarity between himself and his grandmother. Both feel compassion for the sufferings of relative

strangers, he concedes (I, 852), while another of his admissions is that he has inherited something of her self-effacement: 'Je tenais de ma grand'mère d'être dénué d'amour-propre à un degré qui ferait aisément manquer de dignité' (III, 290).

17 It would however be incorrect to say that the grandmother's artistic sense is very developed. In references that she makes to the spire of the Combray church, we see the non-specialist character of her judgement – which is not to deny that her praise can be engaging and persuasive:

'Ignorante en architecture, elle disait: "Mes enfants, moquez-vous de moi si vous voulez, [le clocher] n'est peut-être pas beau dans les règles, mais sa vieille figure bizarre me plaît. Je suis sûre que s'il jouait du piano, il ne jouerait pas *sec*."' (I, 64.)

We might even go as far as to say that in her aesthetic taste there is a faint echo of the simplicity and chattiness of Françoise's diction.

18 *Proust et le monde sensible*, p. 210. Richard's work is valuable for its detailed analysis and categorisation of felt experience in Proust's works.

19 Although the reference to Noah is only an oblique one, Proust, in his dedication of *Les Plaisirs et les jours*, refers directly to the biblical father. Only in illness, Proust claims, was he able to appreciate Noah's enforced confinement: 'Je compris alors que jamais Noé ne put si bein voir le monde que de l'arche, malgré qu'elle fût close et qu'il fît nuit sur la terre' (*JS*, p. 6). While Proust is suggesting that withdrawal from the world can be a source of visionary advantage, the present indirect allusion to a Noah figure in the *Recherche* points to an overshadowing of the reflective self.

20 Looking back briefly to *Jean Santeuil*, one sees a like case of instinctual exhilaration, as a slightly intoxicated Jean travels along in a coach:

'Il ne pouvait s'empêcher de faire aller son corps, de tenir la portière, et quand il avait commencé un mouvement ne pouvait l'arrêter, comme s'il eût interrompu et violé quelque musique intérieure frémissant en lui, et il éprouvait une incroyable douceur à laisser aller son épaule jusqu'à choquer la paroi du fiacre, à laisser échapper tout haut et à entendre résonner trop fort les paroles de reconnaissance qui lui venaient aux lèvres pour le cheval rapide.' (*JS*, p. 777.)

In particular, the anaphora in 'ne pouvait s'empêcher', 'ne pouvait l'arrêter', 'laisser aller' and 'laisser échapper' has the effect of heightening the sense of a pleasant but also ineluctable immersion in sensation itself.

21 *Cahier 8* contains some 'Sainte-Beuve' material (fos 1–6), which Fallois inserts in his first and second chapters (see *CSB/NM*), although some early drafts for *Du côté de chez Swann* form the bulk of its contents (fos 9–95). Given the presence of the *CSB* material, the *Cahier* can be dated c. 1908–9.

22 In his article, '*Jean Santeuil* and *A la recherche*', Michael Finn refers to the 'Zut, zut, zut, zut' episode, arguing that it in no way satisfies the Narrator, who is 'filled with conscience pangs' because of his inability to express himself. Such a view seems to ignore the sense of overwhelming emotion the Narrator does in fact experience. But perhaps this is a consequence of Finn's desire to establish a clear watershed between *Jean Santeuil* and the *Recherche*. He remarks that in parts of the earlier novel, 'the fullness of life

is in sensation itself' (p. 124), the implication being that this is not the case in the *Recherche*. The evidence of my present analysis would tend to underline the oversimplification of his view. Furthermore, he points to areas of *Jean Santeuil* that 'might be considered unProustian in fashion' since they rely totally on pleasurable sensations. Yet they are surely as Proustian as any other part of his work!

23 One might note in passing the Narrator's mention of the humble folk who work daily on the trains: 'Je songeai avec nostalgie à la vie des cheminots, lesquels, passant tout leur temps en chemin de fer, ne devaient guère manquer un seul jour de voir ce vieil employé' (I, 653). The nostalgia here is very close to that which the Narrator feels for Françoise and those like her (see above, section *c*.) Walter Benjamin, in a chapter of his book *Illuminations*, trans. Harry Zohn (London: Fontana, 1973), refers to Proust's interest in the poorer classes. He speaks of how this aspect of Proust 'has been preserved by Maurice Barrès in the most apposite words that have ever been written about Proust: "un poète persan dans une loge de portière"' (*ibid.* p. 211).

4 Characterisation: the Functioning of a Law of Opposites

1 *Sésame et les lys* (Paris: Mercure de France, 1906), pp. 45–6. The preface is reproduced in *Contre Sainte-Beuve*, pp. 160–94, with the Schopenhauer reference at pp. 185–6.

2 C. 1910.

3 The references include II, 694, 696, 723, 752–4, 841, 856; III, 86, 307, 474, 513, 989.

4 The initial draft of *Cahier 50* was written *c.* 1911–12. This is partly evident from the use of early proper names: Borniche later becomes Jupien (see Bardèche, *Marcel Proust romancier*, vol. 2, p. 160n.) and Saint-Jean-des-Bois goes to Saint André-des-Champs.

5 Perhaps the Narrator's observation on these playful girls could be likened to that made by Johan Huizinga on the play element in culture: 'The *fun* of playing resists all analysis, all logical interpretation. As a concept, it cannot be reduced to any other mental category' (*Homo Ludens* (London: Routledge and Kegan Paul, 1949), p. 3). The freedom from intellectual self-examination won by the 'jeunes filles' is an exciting prospect for the Narrator.

6 One might compare this to the contrasting of Joubert, Mme de Sévigné and others with the later, more problematical Baudelaire, Poe, Rimbaud and Verlaine (I, 727). The literary opposition is similar in its thematic implications to the sculptural polarities that I am at present discussing. In both of them, what is being driven at is the possibility of the Narrator's contentment and stability (see above, Chapter 3*e*).

7 *Cahier 25* dates from *c.* 1910–11.

8 The fairylore element becomes all-pervasive in another evocation where some girls appear as fleeting mythological creatures: 'Les rues, les avenues, sont pleines de Déesses. Mais les Déesses ne se laissent pas approcher. Çà et là, entre les arbres, à l'entrée de quelque café, une servante veillait comme une nymphe à l'orée d'un bois sacré, tandis qu'au

fond trois jeunes filles étaient assises à côté de l'arc immense de leurs bicyclettes posées à côté d'elles, comme trois immortelles accoudées au nuage ou au coursier fabuleux sur lesquels elles accomplissent leurs voyages mythologiques.' (III, 169–70.)

9 The *Recherche* contains no direct reference to Emily Brontë, and perhaps this explains why P.-E. Robert fails to mention her in his study, *Marcel Proust lecteur des Anglo-Saxons* (Paris: Nizet, 1976). On the other hand, D'Annunzio is mentioned in the *Recherche*, being described as a great admirer of the Princesse de Guermantes (II, 666–7). In the main novel, however, there is no specific allusion to the writer's work. As for this manuscript passage, Proust is clearly referring to the Italian author's second novel, *Le Vergini delle rocce* (publ. 1894), trans. G. Hérelle, as *Les Vierges aux rochers* (Paris: Calmann-Lévy, 1897). In the same *Cahier 25*, he makes a further comparison between the impact of new writers and that made by simple peasants: 'Et comme Annunzio à notre satiété de la vie ajoutait le goût des fontaines et Stevenson le goût de l'Ecosse, la blanchisseuse et la jeune fille que j'ai recontrées un soir m'ont donné le goût de leurs vies si différentes.' (*Cahier 25*, fo 18v.) Proust's admiration for R.L. Stevenson is well known (see Robert, *Marcel Proust lecteur des Anglo-Saxons*, pp. 79–102).

10 *Mensonge romantique et vérité romanesque* (Paris: Grasset, 1961), p. 181.

11 The next chapter will deal with the way in which Albertine's being is affected by her captivity; there too, the question of levels of consciousness plays an important part. We have already seen parallels between marine or animal life and human existence in *Jean Santeuil* (see Chapter 1).

12 Perhaps an even greater reversal is seen in the golf-player, Octave, a young man who, the Narrator believes, enjoys an intimate understanding with the group. Originally, he is the object of the Narrator's condescension and scorn. Yet although the latter speaks initially of 'la constante nullité intellectuelle qui habitait sous le front songeur d'Octave', we end up with an unexpected view of Octave as an accomplished artist and choreographer. Coincidentally, he marries another artistic 'convert', Andrée (III, 605–6). Proust's character transformations are well known, but in the context of the present study, the nature of these reversals would seem particularly striking.

13 Cf. Mme de Villeparisis' insensitivity at Hudimesnil (I, 717), or that of the farmer who witnesses the Narrator's 'Zut, zut, zut, zut' experience at Montjouvain (I, 155).

14 The reference to Albertine is much more explicit in an earlier draft of the text quoted by the Pléiade editors: 'Si Albertine depuis la scène du lit me semblait vide comme une créature sans réalité, Andrée ...' (I, 989, note to p. 943).

15 In the original manuscript (n.a.fr. 16706), there was simply a reference to her drowning cats. This seems almost innocuous in comparison with what we now have. The latter appears in a margin development in the 1919 Gallimard galleys for *Le Côté de Guermantes* (n.a.fr. 16763:39iii; see Winton, vol. 2, p. 89). Evidently Proust's concern in revising his drafts

was to intensify the Duchesse's unfeeling temperament; her growing insensitivity broadens the gap between herself and the Narrator.

16 One might note in passing how Paul Valéry, while slightly more guarded in his praise of military life, still writes to his wife during a period of military service in 1906: 'Quelle curiosité, plaisir parfois, de n'agir qu'avec le dixième de son cerveau, et, pendant des jours et des jours demeurer sans problèmes, sans profondeur, sans étendue' (*Oeuvres*, vol. 1 (Paris: NRF (Pléiade), 1957), p. 31).

17 We have seen some of the Narrator's early philosophical dilemmas in Chapter 3*b*. As for Albertine's captivity, I shall be discussing this in some detail in the next chapter.

18 The text of II, 845–50, forming a self-contained description of the two peasant women, was inserted in Proust's handwriting into the typescript of *SG* (n.a.fr. 16739: 104–11; see Winton, vol. 2, p. 115). The typescripts of *Sodome et Gomorrhe* were being drawn up between January and April 1921; cf. Winton, vol. 1, p. 18, and George D. Painter, *Marcel Proust* (2 vols., London: Penguin, 1977), vol. 2, pp. 311–12, 324. Hence, Proust inserted this 'block' on the two 'courrières' into the already fully-developed story of the difficult love for Albertine. Presumably he saw such an evocation as an effective palliative to the Narrator's doubting.

19 A good illustration of what I have in mind would be Rousseau's description of a mountain community in his *Lettre à M. d'Alembert* (Geneva and Lille: Droz, 1948), pp. 79–83. One might also look at Senancour, where the description of an Helvetian mountain tribe reveals interesting similarities with Proust's text (see *Rêveries*, vol. 1, p. 237).

20 This is the third of the 'Vingt *Cahiers*' that form a continuous base text for the second half of the *Recherche*. They belong to the years of the First World War. As to why this was not included in the 'final' version of the *Recherche*, it has to be said that so many other, no less interesting, ideas and insights are also absent from the published work. Ultimately, Proust may have seen the present passage as containing too frank and blunt a statement of a propensity that is nevertheless latent in the novel itself.

21 Roger Shattuck, *Proust* (London: Fontana, 1974), p. 99.

22 Michel de Montaigne, *Essais* (2 vols., Paris: Garnier, 1962), Book 2, Chapter 17 (vol. 2, pp. 33–4). Shattuck quotes a part of this in English translation (*Proust*, p. 99).

23 This *Cahier* dates from *c.*1910. The text in question has some similarities with a passage in the main novel (I, 656–7).

24 This is the penultimate in the series of 'Vingt *Cahiers*' (n.a.fr. 16726:35).

5 Albertine as Captive of the Narrator

1 *Pensées*, Edition Intégrale (Paris: Delmas, 1960), p. 136; 'pensée' 103, (111 in Brunschvicg's numbering).

2 In her important article, 'Les Egoïsmes de l'amour chez Proust', Claudine Quémar lays great stress on 'la particularité de la psychologie amoureuse' in Proust (p. 907). Her article is of general relevance to the discussion in Chapter 5 as a whole.

3 A good illustration of this is *La Jalousie*, where the tortured mental activity of the central figure assumes the proportions of an intense and elaborate obsession.

4 This text was only crossed out at the third typescript of *La Prisonnière*, on which Proust was working in 1922. It seems quite possible that he had intended working it in at another point in the novel. On the question of horticultural imagery, Stephen Ullman refers to its various functions in the *Recherche* in his *The Image in the Modern French Novel* (Cambridge University Press, 1960), pp. 185–91. See also V.E. Graham, *The Imagery of Proust* (Oxford: Blackwell, 1966), esp. pp. 110–12.

5 Writing is however occasionally mentioned in this part of the novel (see III, 84–7). But it is true nevertheless that here, the Narrator's over-riding concern is the relationship with Albertine.

6 Albertine is quoting from Racine's *Esther*; some of the other allusions to Ahasuerus in the *Recherche* also derive from Racine's dramatisation of the biblical story (see I, 61, 687; II, 378; III, 126).

7 This appears in the second typescript (1922). All the typescripts for *La Prisonnière* date from the same year (see Painter, *Marcel Proust*, vol. 2, p. 236).

8 It may be stretching things somewhat to call a pianola a musical instrument. For the Narrator, nevertheless, it serves an essentially similar function, providing a pleasant musical accompaniment to Albertine's imprisonment.

9 Sartre devotes a great deal of attention to the general question of 'autrui', and in particular to 'le regard d'autrui'. His view of the other person's gaze as challenging our own individual consciousness of the world is consonant with much of what Proust had already said on his Narrator's reaction to Albertine (see *L'Etre et le Néant* (Paris: NRF, 1950), Part 3, Chapter I, iv, 'Le Regard', pp. 310–67). In fact Sartre spends some time analysing the love conflict in *La Prisonnière*, observing that 'il est donc certain que l'amour veut captiver la "conscience"' (*L'Etre et le Néant*, p. 434). One might also mention a brief article on Proust's treatment of the human gaze in which specific reference is made to the Albertine crisis, M.A. Simons, 'Les Regards dans *A la recherche du temps perdu*', *French Review*, 41 (1968), 498–504.

10 Proust was working on this area of the novel in 1922. In August of that year, he agreed to give his publisher Jacques Rivière an extract on Albertine's sleep. This appeared in the *NRF* of 1922, under the title 'La regarder dormir' (pp. 513–19). Although the sleeping girl was there named Gisèle, the text of the extract and that of the *Recherche* (III, 69–75) are otherwise substantially the same (see Painter, *Marcel Proust*, vol. 2, pp. 347–8).

11 Reading the Narrator's confession, one thinks instinctively of how Françoise kills the poultry in the Combray kitchen. The inference there is that she finds a perverse pleasure in this bloody encounter (I, 121–2). Concerning his planned killing of Albertine, the Narrator protests that his action would be less self-gratifying than preventive in its nature. In spite of this, the passage still imparts a hint of delectation in this contemplated killing.

12 See Pope's first version of 'The Character of Atticus', line 19, in *The Works of Alexander Pope* (London: Murray, 1881), vol. 3, Appendix VI, p. 536.

13 *Pensées*, p. 136, 'pensée' 103 (ed. Brunschvicg, 111).

14 *Cahier 53*, fo 22r; this notebook contains drafts for *La Prisonnière*, probably all dating from 1916 or later. In the *Recherche*, one detects a similar reliance on unchanging cosmic activity in a description of sunlight re-entering the young Narrator's hotel room at Balbec. To end his period of daytime rest, Françoise would come and open the curtains, letting in 'le jour d'été [qui . . .] semblait aussi mort, aussi immémorial qu'une somptueuse et millénaire momie' (I, 955).

15 *Cahier 60* is very late, with its large handwriting of the period 1916 and later. One might compare this passage with the description of the Narrator's grandmother. There, sculptural images contribute to the Narrator's belief in her immortality. Death the sculptor fixes an image of her beauty in his mind: 'Un sourire semblait posé sur les lèvres de ma grand'mère. Sur ce lit funèbre, la mort, comme le sculpteur du Moyen Age, l'avait couchée sous l'apparence d'une jeune fille' (II, 345). Another specifically medieval reference occurs when the Narrator sees Albertine asleep in bed as someone laid out in the tomb. The scene reminds him of sculptural representations of the Last Judgement dating from the Middle Ages (III, 359–60).

16 The opening pages of this first *Cahier* are totally different from the present beginning of that volume. They have been published in *BSAMP*, 6 (1956), 165–70; see Winton, vol. 1, p. 37.

17 Much of the discussion in this chapter has led us to conclude that Albertine's being is seriously impoverished in captivity. In his stimulating inaugural lecture, Malcolm Bowie refers to this question. He points to how rigidly the Narrator judges Albertine:

'He is now intellectually incapable of granting in Albertine's case what he so readily grants in his own [. . .], that feeling may be muddled, that intentions may be precarious or half-formed or contradictory [. . .]. Against the need for simple and elegant solutions in the analysis of human conduct, the full complexity of the individual person has to be restored.' (*Proust, Jealousy, Knowledge* (University of London, Queen Mary College, 1978), p. 10.)

I shall be examining the re-emergence of that complexity in Albertine in the following section.

18 The addition 'J'ai dit [. . .] rendez-vous' (III, 94) appears in a margin of the first typescript (n.a.fr. 16742:94). This can be dated 1922 (cf. Painter, *Marcel Proust*, vol. 2, p. 3, and Winton, vol. 1, p. 113).

19 The addition 'Et je comprenais [. . .] à côté du vrai' (III, 100) is inserted in a margin to the manuscript of *La Prisonnière* (n.a.fr. 16716:1).

6 The Realisation of an Artistic Vocation

1 R. Shattuck, *Proust's Binoculars* (London: Chatto and Windus, 1964), pp. 36–7.

2 On the writing of 'la Musique' with a capital *M*, it should be said that Proust uses such capitals sparingly, and generally for certain key themes,

concepts and forces that he sees as being of over-riding importance in life. The most celebrated of these are the references to 'le Temps'. The device is first used in the early description of the Combray church, which the Narrator sees as having a fourth dimension, namely that of Time (I, 61); most instances of this are to be found in *Le Temps retrouvé*, where the notion is uppermost in the Narrator's mind. Again, in presenting Charlus' spiritual decline, the Narrator also uses capitalisation to help convey the impression that forces much greater than the individual are in play: 'Dans cette pure Matière [i.e., Charlus], il est possible qu'un peu d'Esprit surnageât encore' (III, 838). We shall be seeing presently how the mature Narrator reflects on past experience and in particular on the importance of '[sa] Jeunesse' (see below, p. 183). Generally speaking, Proust is using these special capitals more frequently towards the end of the *Recherche*, where what are almost monolithic truths become increasingly prominent.

3 Susanne K. Langer, *Feeling and Form* (London: Routledge and Kegan Paul, 1953), p. 27.

4 Henri Bonnet has spoken at length on *Cahier 57* in his important study, '*Le Temps retrouvé* dans les Cahiers', *Cahiers Marcel Proust*, n.s. 6, pp. 111–62. As he explains, although the *premier jet* of this volume can be dated *c.* 1910–11, the *Cahier* has been reworked at a later date (1915, 1916 and perhaps later), and contains several additions, mostly on verso pages and in the margins of the rectos. The passage quoted is one such addition.

5 Among Proust's notes in *Le Carnet de 1908*, we find the following judgement: 'Ecrivain sacrifiant à l'instinct intime devient pompier (Barrès)' (p. 67). Proust also criticises Barrès' novel *Colette Baudoche*, which he sees as being too concerned with superficial social portrayal to be an artistic success. As Philip Kolb points out, Proust classifies Barrès with other 'gens intelligents' – far behind true 'artistes' such as Gérard de Nerval (note 408, p. 187).

6 *Correspondance Proust – Rivière*, p. 64. In an interesting note, Philip Kolb suggests that Proust is directing his comments against Julien Benda, whose *Belphégor* was reviewed by Rivière in the *NRF*, 13 (1919), 146–53. Benda's insistence on the primacy of the intellect could only have met with Proust's opposition (see *Correspondance Proust – Riviere*, p. 273, note 1 to p. 64).

7 This is quoted by Rivière in 'Le Parti de l'Intelligence', *NRF*, 13 (1919), 612–18 (p. 617). Rivière stresses that the italics are not his and that they appear in the text of the manifesto itself.

8 *NRF*, 11 (1914), 139–43. This is reproduced in *Les Critiques de notre temps et Proust*, ed. Jacques Bersani (Paris: Garnier, 1971), pp. 20–5.

9 'Réflexions sur le rôle actuel de l'Intelligence française', *NRF*, 13 (1919), 953–64 (p. 964).

10 *Proust's Binoculars*, p. 37

11 The ideas quoted here are generally from the verso pages of the *Cahier*, and belong to the 1915–16 additions (see above, note 4).

12 From 'Quelques pensées', *Textes retrouvés*, Cahiers Marcel Proust, n.s. 3, pp. 362–3.

13 In spite of Proust's claim that the horse is a celebrated one, the reference proves quite elusive. One can only speculate as to his possible source in this case. From classical times, one has Apuleius' novel *The Transformations of Lucius Apuleius of Madaura*, more popularly known as *The Golden Ass*. In this story, Lucius' curiosity about the black art leads to his being turned into an ass. Disguised in this way, he lives through many strange experiences before being restored to human shape by the goddess Isis; he succeeds in effecting this retransformation by eating roses. One of his adventures that is perhaps reminiscent of the Narrator's contact with the 'jeunes filles' is his meeting with the delectable young Fotis, who is present when he is transformed (*The Golden Ass*, trans. Robert Graves (London: Penguin, 1964), Chapter 4, 'The Festival of Laughter'). Later, still in the form of an ass, he sees Venus with a whole assembly of beautiful girls, 'the most graceful Graces, the loveliest Seasons' (p. 265). One might tentatively compare this with the glorifying of beautiful young girls in *A l'ombre des jeunes filles en fleurs*. Likewise, in view of Lucius' references to sorcery and magic, one could recall how the Narrator himself likens the appearance of the 'petite bande' at Balbec to that of Mephistopheles (I, 855; see above p. 110). Another possible source for Proust was the story that St Denis was turned into an animal; he too regained his human form by eating a rose (see *Standard Dictionary of Folklore, Mythology and Legend*, ed. Maria Leach (2 vols., New York: Funk and Wagnall, 1949, 1950), vol. 2, p. 957).

14 Shattuck, *Proust*, pp. 84–92.

15 *Correspondance Proust – Rivière*, p. 28 (see above, Introduction).

Conclusion

1 This extract from an essay in *Passages* (Paris: Gallimard, 1963) is quoted in Michaux's *Au Pays de la Magie*, ed. Peter Broome (London: Athlone Press, 1977), p. 5.

Bibliography

I Proust

A Manuscripts

Bibliothèque Nationale, fonds Proust. Sixty-two *Cahiers* (n.a.fr. 16641–702): notebooks containing sketches and drafts principally for *A la recherche*. For details of contents of individual volumes, see J. Theodore Johnson, Jr, 'Notes towards a physical description of the Proust notebooks at the Bibliothèque Nationale' (see below), and also the *Inventaire matériel des Cahiers Marcel Proust conservés à la Bibliothèque Nationale* (see below).

Four *Carnets* (n.a.fr. 16637–40): notes for *A la recherche*. The first of these has been published as *Le Carnet de 1908*, ed. Philip Kolb (see below).

Twenty *Cahiers* (n.a.fr. 16708–27): these 'Vingt *Cahiers*' contain what is the near-definitive version of *A la recherche* from *Sodome et Gomorrhe* to the end of *Le Temps retrouvé*.

Other manuscripts, typescripts and proofs of Proust's works (n.a.fr. 16611–36, 16730–75). For a breakdown of these press-marks and the corresponding numbers under the old cataloguing, see Henri Bonnet, *Marcel Proust de 1907 à 1914* (see below).

B Works

Proust, Marcel. *A la recherche du temps perdu*, ed. P. Clarac and A. Ferré. 3 vols., Paris: NRF (Pléiade), 1954.

Contre Sainte-Beuve, suivi de Nouveaux Mélanges, ed. B. de Fallois. Paris: Gallimard, 1954.

Contre Sainte-Beuve, précédé de Pastiches et mélanges, et suivi de Essais et articles, ed. P. Clarac and Y. Sandre. Paris: NRF (Pléiade), 1971.

Jean Santeuil, précédé de Les Plaisirs et les jours, ed. P. Clarac and Y. Sandre. Paris: NRF (Pléiade), 1971.

Textes retrouvés, Cahiers Marcel Proust, n.s. 3, ed. Philip Kolb. Paris: Gallimard, 1971.

Textes retrouvés, ed. P. Kolb and L.B. Price. Urbana: University of Illinois Press, 1968.

Le Carnet de 1908, ed. Philip Kolb. Paris: Gallimard, 1976.

L'Indifférent. Paris: Gallimard, 1978.

Bibliography

'La regarder dormir', *NRF*, 19 (1922), 513–19 (prepublication, with slight variations, of III, 69–75).

Ruskin, John. *La Bible d'Amiens*, trans. Marcel Proust. Paris: Mercure de France, 1904.

Sésame et les lys, trans. Marcel Proust. Paris: Mercure de France, 1906.

C Correspondence

Proust, Marcel. *Correspondance*, ed. P. Kolb. 7 vols. to date, Paris: Plon, 1970–81.

Proust, Marcel. *Correspondance Marcel Proust – Jacques Rivière 1914–1922*, 2nd enlarged ed. Paris: Gallimard, 1976. (1st ed., Paris: Plon, 1955).

II Other writers

Adam, 349–51 (1971).

Alden, Douglas W. *Marcel Proust and his French Critics*. New York: Russell and Russell, 1973 (1940).

'Proust and Ribot', *Modern Language Notes*, 58 (1943), 501–7.

Apuleius, Lucius. *The Golden Ass*, trans. Robert Graves. London: Penguin, 1964.

Bales, Richard. *Proust and the Middle Ages*. Geneva: Droz, 1975.

'Des inédits de *Combray*', *Studi Francesi*, 64 (January–April 1978), 84–9.

'Proust, Maeterlinck et la philosophie populaire', *Jaarboek van de Nederlandse Vereniging van Vrienden van Marcel Proust*, 3 (1976), 217–31.

Banquet, Le, 1892–3. Reprinted Geneva: Slatkine Reprints, 1971.

Bardèche, Maurice. *Marcel Proust romancier*. 2 vols., Paris: Les Sept Couleurs, 1971.

Baudelaire, Charles. *Oeuvres complètes*. Paris: NRF (Pléiade), 1961.

Beckett, Samuel. *Proust*. New York: Grove Press, 1957.

Béhar, Serge. *L'Univers médical de Proust*, Cahiers Marcel Proust, n.s. 1. Paris: Gallimard, 1970.

Benda, Julien. *La France byzantine*. Paris: Union Générale d'Editions (Collection 10/18), 1970.

Benjamin, Walter. *Illuminations*, trans. Harry Zohn. London: Fontana, 1973.

Bersani, Jacques (ed.). *Les Critiques de notre temps et Proust*. Paris: Garnier, 1971.

Bisson, L.A. 'Marcel Proust: Friends and Friendship', in *Essays presented to C.M. Girdlestone* (Newcastle-upon-Tyne: King's College, 1960), pp. 29–48.

Bloemgarten-Barends, J.C.H. 'Albertine et Charlus', *Jaarboek van de Nederlandse Vereniging van Vrienden van Marcel Proust*, 3 (1976), 285–323.

Bonnet, Henri. *Alphonse Darlu: le maître de philosophie de Marcel Proust*. Paris: Nizet, 1961.

Marcel Proust de 1907 à 1914. 2nd ed. 2 vols., Paris: Nizet, 1971, 1976.

Le Progrès spirituel dans l'oeuvre de Marcel Proust. 2 vols., Paris: Vrin, 1946, 1949.

Bibliography

'*Le Temps retrouvé* dans les Cahiers', *Cahiers Marcel Proust*, n.s. 6 (Paris: Gallimard, 1973), pp. 111–62.

Bowie, Malcolm. *Proust, Jealousy, Knowledge*. University of London: Queen Mary College, 1978 (inaugural lecture).

Bucknall, Barbara. *The Religion of Art in Proust*. Urbana: University of Illinois Press, 1969.

Bulletin de la Société des amis de Marcel Proust et des amis de Combray, 1–29 (1950–79).

Bussom, T.W. 'Marcel Proust and Painting', *Romanic Review*, 34 (1943), 54–70.

Butor, Michel. *Essais sur les Modernes*. Paris: Gallimard, 1971.

Cattaui, Georges. *Proust perdu et retrouvé*. Paris: Plon, 1963.

'Du côté de chez Bloch', *Adam*, 349–51 (1971), 10–20.

'Proust et les sciences', in *Proceedings of the Congress of the International Federation of Modern Languages and Literatures*. Oxford: Blackwell, 1956.

Cattaui, Georges and Kolb, Philip. *Entretiens sur Marcel Proust*. The Hague and Paris: Mouton, 1966.

Cervantes, Miguel de. *Don Quixote*, trans. J.M. Cohen. London: Penguin, 1973.

Chantal, René de. *Marcel Proust, critique littéraire*. 2 vols., Montréal: Presses universitaires, 1967.

Cocking, John M. *Proust*. London: Bowes and Bowes, 1956.

'*Jean Santeuil* et *A la recherche du temps perdu*', BSAMP, 6 (1956), 181–97.

Coquelin, Constant. *Un Poète philosophe: Sully Prudhomme*. Paris: Ollendorff, 1882.

Couffignal, Robert. *La Paraphrase poétique de la Genèse de Hugo à Supervielle*. Paris: Minard, 1970.

Cruickshank, John. 'The Novel of Self-disclosure', in *idem* (ed.), *French Literature and its Background*, vol. 4 (London: Oxford U.P., 1969), pp. 170–88.

Curtius, Ernst Robert. *European Literature and the Latin Middle Ages*, trans. Willard R. Trask. New York and Evanston: Harper and Row, 1963.

D'Annunzio, Gabriele. *Les Vierges aux rochers*, trans. G. Hérelle. Paris: Calmann-Lévy, 1897.

Deleuze, Gilles. *Proust et les signes*. Paris: PUF, 1976.

Didier, Béatrice. 'Sur un inédit de Proust', *Revue de Paris* (May 1968), 108–13.

Esprit Créateur, L', 11, 1 (spring 1971).

Europe (August–September 1970; February–March 1971).

Evers, Meindert. 'Het Probleem der Schoonheid: een studie over Marcel Proust'. Doctoral Thesis, Amsterdam, 1974.

Feuillerat, Albert. *Comment Marcel Proust a composé son roman*. New Haven: Yale U.P., 1934.

Finn, Michael. '*Jean Santeuil* and *A la recherche du temps perdu*: Instinct and Intellect', *Forum for Modern Language Studies*, 11 (1975), 122–32.

Flaubert, Gustave. *Correspondance*, vol. 5, 'Lettres a sa nièce Caroline'. Paris: Conard, 1910.

Bibliography

France, Anatole. 'Bouddhisme', in *La Vie littéraire*, vol. 3 (Paris: Calmann-Lévy, 1919), 379–87.

Fromentin, Eugène. *Dominique*. Paris: Garnier-Flammarion, 1967.

Ghéon, Henri. 'Réflexions sur le rôle actuel de l'Intelligence française', *NRF*, 13 (1919), 953–64.

Review of *Du côté de chez Swann, NRF*, 11 (1914), 139–43; reproduced in Jacques Bersani (ed.), *Les Critiques de notre temps et Proust* (see above).

Gide, André. *Romans*. Paris: NRF (Pléiade), 1958.
'En relisant *Les Plaisirs et les jours*', *NRF*, 20 (1923), 123–6.

Giorgi, Giorgetto. 'Senancour e Proust', *Studi Francesi*, 9 (May–August 1965), 290–6.

Girard, René. *Mensonge romantique et vérité romanesque*. Paris: Grasset, 1961.

Graham, V. E. *The Imagery of Proust*. Oxford: Blackwell, 1966.

Hindus, Milton. *The Proustian Vision*. London and Amsterdam: Southern Illinois U.P., 1967.

Hommage à Marcel Proust, NRF, 20 (1 January 1923).

Hoog, Armand. *Le Temps du lecteur*. Paris: PUF, 1975.

Huizinga, Johan. *Homo Ludens*. London: Routledge and Kegan Paul, 1949.

Inventaire matériel des Cahiers Marcel Proust conservés à la Bibliothèque Nationale. Paris, CNRS, [1974].

Jackson, Elizabeth R. 'The Genesis of the Involuntary Memory in Proust's early works', *PMLA*, 76 (1961), 586–94.

Johnson, J. Theodore, Jr. '*Débâcle sur la Seine* de Claude Monet: source du *Dégel à Briseville* d'Elstir', *Cahiers Marcel Proust*, n.s. 6, pp. 163–76. Paris: Gallimard, 1973.

'Notes towards a physical description of the Proust notebooks at the Bibliothèque Nationale', *Proust Research Association Newsletter*, 2 (Summer 1969), 13–28.

Jones, Peter. *Philosophy and the Novel*. Oxford: Clarendon Press, 1975.

Joubert, Joseph. *Pensées et lettres*. Paris: Grasset, 1954.

Kolb, Philip. 'Historique du premier roman de Proust', *Saggi e ricerche di letteratura francese*, 4 (1963), 215–77.

Langer, Susanne K. *Feeling and Form*. London: Routledge and Kegan Paul, 1953.
Problems of Art. London: Routledge and Kegan Paul, 1957.

La Sizeranne, Robert de. *Ruskin et la religion de la beauté*. Paris: Hachette, 1897.

Lawrence, D. H. *Women in Love*. London: Penguin, 1960.

Leach, Maria (ed.). *Standard Dictionary of Folklore, Mythology and Legend*. 2 vols., New York: Funk and Wagnall, 1949, 1950.

Ley, A. S. 'The Influence of R. W. Emerson on Proust'. M.A. Thesis, University of London, 1956.

Luppé, R. de. 'Marcel Proust disciple de Schopenhauer', *Revue d'Esthétique* (1949), 395–415.

Macquarrie, John. *God Talk*. London: SCM Press, 1967.

Maurois, André. *A la recherche de Marcel Proust*. Paris: Hachette, 1949.

May, Gita. 'Chardin vu par Diderot et par Proust', *PMLA*, 72 (1957), 403–18.

Bibliography

Megay, Joyce. *Bergson et Proust*. Paris: Vrin, 1976.

Mein, Margaret. 'Le Général et le Particulier dans l'oeuvre de Marcel Proust', *BSAMP*, 20 (1970), 976–93.

Michaux, Henri. *Au Pays de la Magie*, ed. Peter Broome. London: Athlone Press, 1977.

Monnin-Hornung, Juliette. *Proust et la peinture*. Geneva and Lille: Droz, 1951.

Montaigne, Michel de. *Essais*. 2 vols., Paris: Garnier, 1962.

Newman-Gordon, Pauline. *Dictionnaire des idées dans l'oeuvre de Marcel Proust*. The Hague and Paris: Mouton, 1968.

O'Brien, Justin. 'Marcel Proust as a *Moraliste*', *Romanic Review*, 39 (1948), 50–69.

'La Mémoire involontaire avant Marcel Proust', *RLC*, 19 (1939), 19–36.

'The Wisdom of the young Proust', *Romanic Review*, 45 (1954), 121–34.

Ortega y Gasset, José. *The Dehumanisation of Art*, trans. Willard R. Trask *et al.* New York: Doubleday, 1956.

Painter, George D. *Marcel Proust*. 2 vols., London: Penguin, 1977.

Pascal, Blaise. *Pensées*, Edition Intégrale. Paris: Delmas, 1960.

Pensées, ed. Léon Brunschvicg. Paris: Nelson, [1910].

Pasco, A. H. 'Marcel, Albertine and Balbec in Proust's Allusive Complex', *Romanic Review*, 62 (1971), 113–26.

Picon, Gaëtan. *Lecture de Proust*. Paris: Mercure de France, 1966.

Pluchart-Simon, Bernard. *Proust: l'amour comme vérité humaine et romanesque*. Paris: Librairie Larousse, 1975.

Pope, Alexander. 'Versions of the Character of Atticus', in *The Works of Alexander Pope*, London: Murray, 1881, vol. 3, pp. 536–9.

Poulet, Georges. *L'Espace proustien*. Paris: Gallimard, 1963.

Etudes sur le temps humain. Paris: Plon, 1950.

Price, Larkin B., (ed.). *Marcel Proust: a Critical Panorama*. Urbana: University of Illinois Press, 1972.

Proust Research Association Newsletter (Lawrence, Kansas), 1–18 (March 1969–fall 1977).

Quémar, Claudine. 'Les Egoïsmes de l'amour chez Proust', *RHLF*, 71 (1971), 887–908.

Racine, Jean. *Théâtre complet*. Paris: Garnier, 1960.

Richard, Jean-Pierre. *Proust et le monde sensible*. Paris: Editions du Seuil, 1974.

Rivière, Jacques. 'Catholicisme et Nationalisme', *NRF*, 13 (1919), 965–8.

'Le Parti de l'Intelligence', *NRF*, 13 (1919), 612–18.

Review of Julien Benda's *Belphégor*, *NRF*, 13 (1919), 146–53.

Robbe-Grillet, Alain. *La Jalousie*. Paris: Editions de Minuit, 1957.

Robert, P.-E. *Marcel Proust lecteur des Anglo-Saxons*. Paris: Nizet, 1976.

Rousseau, Jean-Jacques. *Lettre à M. d'Alembert*. Geneva and Lille: Droz, 1948.

Sainte-Beuve, C.-A. *Chateaubriand et son groupe littéraire*, vol. 1, 14ᵉ leçon (on Senancour), Paris: Garnier, 1861, pp. 329–63.

Sartre, Jean-Paul. *L'Etre et le Néant*. Paris: NRF, 1950.

Schlumberger, Jean. 'Sur le Parti de l'Intelligence', *NRF*, 13 (1919), 788–91.

Bibliography

Schopenhauer, Arthur. *Parerga and Paralipomena*. 2 vols., Oxford: Clarendon Press, 1974.

The World as Will and Idea, trans. R. B. Haldane and J. Kemp. 3 vols., London: Trübner, 1883–6.

Senancour, Etienne de. *Rêveries sur la nature primitive de l'homme*. 2 vols., Paris: Cornély, 1910.

Shattuck, Roger. *Proust*. London: Fontana, 1974.

Proust's Binoculars. London: Chatto and Windus, 1964.

Simon, Pierre-Henri. *Témoins de l'homme*. Paris: Payot, 1967.

Simons, M. A. 'Les Regards dans *A la recherche du temps perdu*', *French Review*, 41 (1968), 498–504.

Sontag, Susan. *Against Interpretation, and other essays*. New York: Dell Publishing Co., 1966.

Styles of Radical Will. London: Secker and Warburg, 1969.

Soupault, Robert. *Marcel Proust du côté de la médecine*. Paris: Plon, 1967.

Souza, Sybil de. *La Philosophie de Marcel Proust*. Paris: Rieder, 1939.

Strauss, Walter A. *Proust and Literature*. Cambridge, Mass.: Harvard U.P., 1957.

Sully Prudhomme, René-François-Armand. *Oeuvres*. 5 vols., Paris: Lemerre, 1900–1.

Tadié, Jean-Yves. *Proust et le roman*. Paris: Gallimard, 1971.

Tenenbaum, Elizabeth Brady. *The Problematic Self: approaches to identity in Stendhal, D. H. Lawrence and Malraux*. Cambridge, Mass.: Harvard U.P., 1977.

Thibaudet, Albert. 'Réflexions sur la littérature: le centenaire de George Eliot', *NRF*, 14 (1920), 265–79.

'Sur la démobilisation de l'intelligence', *NRF*, 14 (1920), 129–40.

Ullman, Stephen. *The Image in the Modern French Novel*. Cambridge University Press, 1960.

Valéry, Paul. *Oeuvres*, vol. 1. Paris: NRF (Pléiade), 1957.

Vallée, Claude. *La Féerie de Marcel Proust*. Paris: Fasquelle, 1958.

Virtanen, Reino. 'Proust's metaphors from the natural and the exact sciences', *PMLA*, 69 (1954), 1038–59.

Walsh, Dorothy. *Literature and Knowledge*. Middletown (Conn.): Wesleyan U.P., 1969.

Warnock, Helen Mary. *The Philosophy of Sartre*. London: Hutchinson, 1965.

Weitz, Morris. *Philosophy in Literature: Shakespeare, Voltaire, Tolstoy and Proust*. Detroit: Wayne U.P., 1963.

Wilson, Edmund. *Axel's Castle*. [London]: Collins/Fontana, 1976.

Winton, Alison. *Proust's Additions*. 2 vols., Cambridge University Press, 1977.

Zaehner, R. C. *Mysticism, Sacred and Profane*. London: Oxford U.P., 1961.

Index

Index